# The Great Dissent

# The Great Dissent

*John Henry Newman
and the Liberal Heresy*

ROBERT PATTISON

New York   Oxford
OXFORD UNIVERSITY PRESS
1991

Oxford University Press

Oxford  New York  Toronto
Delhi  Bombay  Calcutta  Madras  Karachi
Petaling Jaya  Singapore  Hong Kong  Tokyo
Nairobi  Dar es Salaam  Cape Town
Melbourne  Auckland

and associated companies in
Berlin  Ibadan

Copyright © 1991 by Oxford University Press, Inc.

Published by Oxford University Press, Inc.,
200 Madison Avenue, New York, New York 10016

Oxford is a registered trademark of Oxford University Press

Library of Congress Cataloging-in-Publication Data
Pattison, Robert.
The great dissent : John Henry Newman and the liberal heresy / Robert Pattison.
p.  cm.  Includes bibliographical references and index.
ISBN 0-19-506730-4
1. Newman, John Henry, 1801-1890—Contributions in criticism of liberalism in religion.
2. Newman, John Henry, 1801-1890—Contributions in criticism of modern civilization.
3. Liberalism (Religion)—History of doctrines—19th century.
4. Civilization, Modern—19th century.
5. Christianity and culture—History of doctrines—19th century.
6. Hampden, Renn Dickson, 1793-1868.
7. Arius, d. ca. 336. 8. England-Intellectual life—19th century.
I. Title.  BR1615.P37  1991
230'.2'092—dc20  90-44104

9 8 7 6 5 4 3 2 1

Printed in the United States of America
on acid-free paper

# Preface

Is Newman still a great Victorian? More and more, Newman's work seems like a parenthesis in Victorian studies. In the 1969 edition of the *Cambridge Bibliography of English Literature,* Newman commanded twenty-nine columns—more than Ruskin, Carlyle, or Tennyson. In the Modern Language Association's annual bibliography for 1987 Newman rated only two citations—the same number as Bulwer-Lytton, half as many as Mrs. Gaskell, and a mere fraction of George Eliot's seventy-eight. The remnant of Newman scholarship is largely the work of partisans. Practicing Catholics and genteel Anglicans still find something to say for and about Newman. It may be as much because of their attention as in spite of it that Newman is now an object of sublime neglect in mainstream criticism.

This is a *quo warranto* action challenging Newman's work to justify its place in intellectual history. Victorian studies would benefit if similar proceedings were instituted against all its major figures, but Newman is especially liable to prosecution. Of course, Newman will always be worthy of study—in the same way that Harriet Martineau or Herbert Spencer is. But does Newman deserve that high place among the worthies of nineteenth-century literature that has heretofore been accorded him in the anthologies and commentaries as a matter of right? Why bother with a man whose career was a succession of reversals and whose thought seems moribund when compared with the still-lively intellectual traditions of Darwin or Ruskin or Mill?

The first chapter of this book explains why the customary arguments for Newman's greatness will no longer suffice. An examination of

Newman's lack of success in influencing the modern world has the secondary advantage of providing a survey of the religious milieu in which his ideas have had to compete, but its primary purpose is to establish Newman's impeccable credentials as a failure. This harsh judgment seems to me not to cancel Newman's importance but to validate it. He is the uncontaminated antagonist of everything modern, and appropriately, his reputation is unsullied by any tribute that contemporary civilization can bestow. The totality of his failure is the measure of his grandeur as a critic of our culture.

What Newman despised in modern culture was the anti-dogmatic principle of its liberalism. I have tried to let the facts of Newman's life and the sense of his words define what he meant by the term liberalism, and in the second and third chapters I have chosen two exponents of the antidogmatic principle to illustrate what Newman meant by this expression.

During his Oxford years Newman had constantly before him the bad example of Renn Dickson Hampden, a living oracle of liberalism who rose—not without unrelenting opposition from Newman and his followers—to be the university's regius professor of divinity. Chapter 2 tells the story of why Newman came to hate him. Newman's violent reaction to liberals like Hampden coincided with his researches into fourth-century heresy. In the pages of the neglected Fathers of the Church he discovered that the intellectual depravity he saw around him had a pedigree extending further back than Locke and the empiricists, further back than Luther and Calvin, further back even than Wycliffe and the Lollards. It was Arius, the fourth-century heresiarch, who had first defiled Christian civilization with liberal apostasy, and Chapter 3 explains how Newman reached this conclusion.

Other heretics than Arius and Hampden might have been selected to illustrate the anti-dogmatic principle against which Newman rebelled. Among his contemporaries, Blanco White and John Stuart Mill provoked his indignation as much as Hampden did, and the ancient errors of Nestorius and Sabellius were, he thought, tainted with the same proto-liberalism that infected the theology of Arius. But Arius and Hampden are at least representative of the humanistic tradition against which Newman hardened his heart, and in addition each can claim to be important in his own right.

Arius is a familiar name in intellectual history. He has been controversial for sixteen hundred years, and if Newman was right, he is one of the pivotal figures of Western thought. Renn Dickson Hampden hardly seems to belong in such illustrious company; he was truculent in person and turgid on paper. But the effort of deciphering his lugubrious prose is more than repaid by the discovery of his bold and original mind. Hampden deserves a distinguished place in the history of English philosophy, and his uncouth spirit may without apology be summoned from obscurity to join the company of Locke, Hume, Mill, and Russell.

From his confrontations with the contemporary liberalism of Hampden and with the ancient error of Arius, Newman emerged with his own dogmatic philosophy fully developed. Heresy had led him to truth. Chapter 4 describes this truth as Newman saw it. Newman's prose has always induced in his followers a belief that his thought is too subtle or too profound to admit of succinct exposition. This reverence is misplaced. While Newman's style is ironic and elusive, his major ideas are clear and straightforward, and they did not change over the course of a lifetime. In a world inclined to specialist studies of Newman's views on justification or doctrinal development, it may be helpful to have a summary of the first principles from which these derivative theories were deduced.

Few moderns will agree with Newman's philosophy, and many will find it repellent, but Newman's opinions are neither false because they are obnoxious nor useless because they failed to have an impact. Chapter 5 offers some suggestions for evaluating the importance of Newman's Christian vision.

Under the guise of discussing Catholic dogmatics, Newman addressed a central modern question: is the world we make a product of our beliefs, or are our beliefs a product of the world we make? His unyielding adherence to the perverse proposition that belief precedes action, coupled with his devotion to the antique vocabulary of Catholic disputation, made him unfashionable in his own day and makes him almost unintelligible in ours. But if Newman spoke of dogma and heresy instead of superstructure and base, his concerns are nonetheless the same as those of modern ideologists, and if he came to conclusions contrary to what any contemporary would consider orthodox, he saw as far into the problem of belief as anyone has. Armed with this insight, he produced the most uncompromising condemnation of modern civilization yet attempted.

Those true believers who busy themselves in establishing Newman's credentials for beatification may consider the portrait of the cardinal offered here uncomplimentary.[1] Their efforts to sanctify Newman's memory have succeeded only in relegating him to the company of distinguished but forgotten nineteenth-century theologians like Father Perrone and F. D. Maurice. In my appraisal, Newman was a zealot whose true intellectual counterparts were Marx and Nietzsche. Disinterested readers will have to judge which estimate of Newman is more flattering to his reputation.

Newman believed that in Scripture study there is "some one definite and sufficient sense . . . which it is the business of the expositor to unfold." I have treated his works as if they were Scripture. I have tried to resist the urge to give Newman's words any psychological, sociological, or paradoxical reading that would subvert what I take to be his own "definite and sufficient sense." This procedure works very well to establish Newman's philosophy, but it is less reliable as a means of ascertaining the facts of his life. The *Apologia,* for instance, is an invaluable statement of his views but misleading as a guide to the events it describes. Wherever possible, I have relied on the monumental thirty-one-volume edition of Newman's letters and diaries to establish the record of what actually happened.

A fellowship from the John Simon Guggenheim Foundation and support from Long Island University facilitated the completion of this book. I want to thank both institutions.

*Southampton, New York*                                                   R. P.
*March 1991*

---

[1] The lobby for Newman's canonization is nothing if not industrious. In 1989 Pope John Paul II was presented with a thousand-page résumé of Newman's "reputation for holiness"; this document was only an abstract of the six thousand-page report prepared for the diocese of Birmingham. See *The Tablet* (London), July 15, 1989, p. 827, and Joyce Sugg, *A Saint for Birmingham* (London, 1978).

# Contents

# Footnote Abbreviations

With some minor alterations, the footnotes use the abbreviations for Newman's works employed throughout the Oxford English Text editions and by Ian Ker in his *John Henry Newman* (Oxford, 1988). Except where better modern editions are available, references are to the uniform thirty-six-volume edition of Newman's work published by Longmans, Green of London between 1868 and 1881. Several other frequently mentioned sources, including the major works of R. D. Hampden, are also noted in the abbreviated forms supplied below. References to Locke's *Essay on Human Understanding* are given by book, chapter, and section.

## Works by Newman

| | |
|---|---|
| *Apo.* | *Apologia pro Vita Sua*, ed. Martin J. Svaglic (Oxford, 1967) |
| *Ari.* | *Arians of the Fourth Century* |
| *Ath.* 1, 2 | *Select Treatises of St. Athanasius in Controversy with the Arians*, 2 vols. |
| *A.W.* | *John Henry Newman: Autobiographical Writings*, ed. Henry Tristram (London, 1956) |
| *Call.* | *Callista. A Tale of the Third Century* |
| *Cons.* | *On Consulting the Faithful in Matters of Doctrine*, ed. John Coulson (London, 1961) |

*D.A.*  *Discussions and Arguments on Various Subjects*

*Dev.*  *An Essay on the Development of Christian Doctrine,* ed.
Charles Frederick Harrold (New York, 1949)

*Diff.* 1, 2  *Certain Difficulties Felt by Anglicans in Catholic Teaching,*
2 vols.

*Ess.* 1, 2  *Essays Critical and Historical,* 2 vols.

*G.A.*  *An Essay in Aid of a Grammar of Assent,* ed. I. T. Ker
(Oxford, 1985)

*H.S.* 1, 2, 3  *Historical Sketches,* 3 vols.

*Idea*  *The Idea of a University,* ed. I. T. Ker (Oxford, 1976)

*Jfc.*  *Lectures on the Doctrine of Justification*

*K.C.*  *Correspondence of John Henry Newman with John Keble
and Others. 1839–1845,* ed. at the Birmingham Oratory
(London, 1917)

*L.D.*  *The Letters and Diaries of John Henry Newman,* ed. Charles
Stephen Dessain, vols. 1–6 (Oxford, 1978–84), 11–22 (London, 1961–72), 23–31 (Oxford, 1973–77)

*L.G.*  *Loss and Gain: The Story of a Convert*

*Mir.*  *Two Essays on Biblical and Ecclesiastical Miracles*

*Mix.*  *Discourses Addressed to Mixed Congregations*

*Moz.* 1, 2  *Letters and Correspondence of John Henry Newman During
His Life in the English Church,* ed. Anne Mozley, 2 vols.
(London, 1891)

*O.S.*  *Sermons Preached on Various Occasions*

*P.S.* 1–8  *Parochial and Plain Sermons,* 8 vols.

*Phil. N.* 1, 2  *The Philosophical Notebook of John Henry Newman,* ed.
Edward Sillem, 2 vols. (Louvain, 1969–70)

*Prepos.*  *Present Position of Catholics in England*

*S.D.*  *Sermons Bearing on Subjects of the Day*

*T.P.* 1  *The Theological Papers of John Henry Newman on Faith and
Certainty,* ed. Hugo M. de Achaval and J. Derek Holmes
(Oxford, 1976)

*T.P.* 2  *The Theological Papers of John Henry Newman on Biblical
Inspiration and on Infallibility,* ed. J. Derek Holmes (Oxford, 1979)

*T.T.*  *Tracts Theological and Ecclesiastical*

*U.S.*  *Fifteen Sermons Preached Before the University of Oxford*

V.M. 1, 2   *The Via Media*, 2 vols.
 V.V.   *Verses on Various Occasions*

## Works by Renn Dickson Hampden

M.P.    *A Course of Lectures Introductory to the Study of Moral Philosophy* (London, 1835)

*Dissent*   *Observations on Religious Dissent*, 2d ed. (Oxford, 1834)

P.E.    *Philosophical Evidence of Christianity* (London, 1827)

S.P.    *The Scholastic Philosophy Considered in Its Relation to Christian Theology. The Bampton Lectures of 1832* (Oxford, 1833)

*Sermons*   *Parochial Sermons Illustrative of the Importance of the Revelation of God in Jesus Christ*, 2d ed. (London, 1836)


## Other Works

DNB    *Dictionary of National Biography*

Ker    I. T. Ker, *John Henry Newman* (Oxford, 1988)

*Tracts* 1–6   *Tracts for the Times* (London, 1840–41), 6 vols.

*Ward* 1, 2   Wilfred Ward, *The Life of John Henry, Cardinal Newman* (London, 1912), 2 vols.

The Great Dissent

"Who is like unto the beast? Who is able to make war with him?"

REVELATION 13:4 (KJV)

# 1

## Failure: Newman's Vanquished Reputation

### Conversions

He converted in the fall of 1845 after five years of study and reflection. Opponents at his own university of Oxford had long since denounced him as a supporter of Catholicism, and now his sympathy with arguments usually heard only in the mouths of the Irish made him still more suspect to his enemies and perplexed even his most devoted English admirers. But nothing he did was impulsive, and his change of allegiance, which struck contemporaries as a duplicitous break with his former doctrine, seemed to him the logical conclusion of beliefs long held. By embracing a position he had formerly assailed, he shattered a party which until then had seemed united by a conservative tradition of which he was the living oracle. Many of his colleagues joined him in his conversion, but others, the majority of those with whom his name had been associated, remained true to the old principles he seemed to be forsaking, principles comfortable to their class and outlook. With his defection, the great movement he had led died a spiritual death. It never regained its vigor in his lifetime.

And so Prime Minister Robert Peel broke the Tory party late in 1845 by his determination to repeal the corn laws in the face of the Irish potato famine. Free trade in corn seemed to be Ireland's last hope. Peel had flirted with free trade for several years, but in abandoning the protection of grain, he alienated the Tory landowners and forced the realignment of interests that after his death in 1850 issued in the formation of the two great Victorian parties.

Oxford had detected Sir Robert's unorthodoxy sixteen years earlier when he had abandoned his opposition to Catholic Emancipation, and the university had punished the heretic by ejecting him as its parliamentary representative. The 1829 campaign at Oxford that ousted Peel had marked the debut of twenty-eight-year-old John Henry Newman as a controversialist. He had denounced Peel's policies as the manifestation of "a systematic hatred of our Church borne by Romanists, Sectarians, Liberals and Infidels." Peel's defeat was "a glorious Victory."[1] In 1841, Newman continued his dissection of Peel's crypto-liberalism in seven letters to the *Times* on Sir Robert's immoral political philosophy. When in 1845 Peel espoused free trade and allied himself with the likes of Richard Cobden and Lord John Russell, Newman might well have said, "I told you so."

But Newman was busy in the fall of 1845 with the details of his own conversion. Like Peel, he was by then the leader of a notable conservative party. In the sixteen years since he had challenged Sir Robert over Catholic Emancipation, he had emerged from the shadow of his more illustrious Oriel colleagues Richard Whately and Edward Hawkins and established himself as a formidable intellect. He was by 1845 the author of the recondite *Arians of the Fourth Century,* the daunting *Prophetical Office of the Church,* and the still more obscure *Lectures on Justification.* No rank or office distinguished him from the common herd of Oxford dons and clerics, but by charm, diligence, and theological profundity, he had made himself the spokesman for a growing religious movement based in equal parts on the style of eighteenth-century Anglican thought and the substance of fourth-century Catholic dogma.

He had come to embody the reverential and dogmatic spirit of what was variously called Newmanism, Puseyism, Tractism, Tractarianism, and the Oxford Movement. The quintessential academic politician, he

---

[1]*L.D.*, 2: 119, 125.

had fought in the common rooms and councils of Oxford for the appointment of churchmen and scholars who honored the moral and intellectual legacies of Anglo-Catholicism. As vicar of Saint Mary's, the intense sobriety of his *University Sermons* had enraptured a new and increasingly pious generation of undergraduates. Under his guidance, the ninety *Tracts for the Times* had between 1833 and 1841 spread the Oxford principles of dogmatic rigor and Catholic piety through the ranks of the English clergy and beyond.

Now, in 1845, just as Tractarianism began to find its voice among secular disciples like James Hope-Scott, Frederic Rogers, and William Gladstone, and so to extend its influence to law, diplomacy, and government, Newman defected from the movement whose leading spirit he had been. His *Essay on the Development of Christian Doctrine,* published in 1845, the year of his conversion, distinguished absolutely between orthodox Roman and heretical Anglican doctrine. And since it was the essence of Newman's thought that for every intellectual distinction there is a corresponding moral obligation, he now took the action to which his theological insights compelled him. On October 8, 1845, he summoned the Passionist Father Dominic to his cottage at Littlemore outside Oxford, and there on a stormy autumn night he was received into the Catholic Church.

The conjunction of Peel's and Newman's defections serves as a reminder that the Oxford Movement did not exist in the sacred vacuum its historians usually portray. Newman's conversion belongs to an era of broken allegiances. In 1845, Newman went over to Rome, Peel embraced free trade, and Gladstone laid aside his Anglican scruples to vote for the Maynooth grant. Each change of heart startled contemporaries and roused erstwhile supporters to cries of treason. But in retrospect, each accords perfectly with the temper of the time. Liberalism was the force behind the conversions of 1845. Peel and Gladstone acceded to the liberal current and were swept on to worldly fame. Newman resisted and found his calling in the prosecution of a movement that carried him and his beliefs to what those outside Catholicism would now regard as the margins of intellectual history. But looked at one way, Newman was the creature of the liberalism he despised.

Peel's and Newman's conversions seem to have taken them in opposite directions, the one to laissez-faire doctrines propounding competition, the other to patristic dogmas claiming a monopoly on truth. Both were in fact affirmations of the open market. Newman's defection to Rome would have been unthinkable in an earlier century, almost in an earlier year. But by 1845 the established church, like corn, had lost the rationale for the protection it enjoyed and had to compete with other religious groups, many of them more attractive in the conviction with which they proclaimed themselves the one true way. For centuries the state had protected the position of the Church of England and erected a barrier of legislation and practice that amounted to an exclusionary tariff on dissent. But by 1845, the laws and customs that supported this religious monopoly had eroded sufficiently to permit something like free trade in belief as well as in grain. Gladstone implicitly acknowledged the free trade in religion when he supported a state grant to the Irish Catholic seminary at Maynooth, and the Oxford Movement is only the fullest expression of the religious freedom it anathematized, a living witness that even the most conservative members of the established church were now at liberty to barter in the deregulated market of religious belief. Newman's conversion was evidence that the centuries-old tariff on Romanism had been repealed.

Newman himself would have been the first to acknowlege the link between the free-market forces of liberalism and his conversion to Roman Catholicism. For him the liberalism of modern culture was pervasive, ubiquitous, and comprehensive. To know what Newman meant by liberal is to know the substance of the thirty-six volumes that contain his collected works, and the bulk of this study is a meditation on Newman's struggle with this single word. But here it must be noted that the contest was unequal. By his resistance to the spirit of the age, Newman assured that he would be judged a failure according to its liberal standards.

From the comfortable distance of another century, the conversions of 1845 appear to have a single cause—capitalism, the invisible hand that shaped the ideological as well as the economic marketplace of the nineteenth century. But if Peel, Gladstone, and Newman were driven by one irresistible impulse, its effects seemed to them, as well as to us, random and incongruous. A single historical impulse turned the efforts of Peel and Gladstone to success, while those of Newman were destined to failure.

Peel's embrace of free trade ushered in the great age of English prosperity. Thirty years later John Bright was still regaling working-class audiences with the virtues of a doctrine which had put bread in their mouths, newspapers on their tables, and sugar in their tea.[2] To this day, Peel's formula for prosperity through open markets is the orthodoxy of Western economics. Every Mazda driven in Cleveland, every banana consumed in Leeds, is a memorial to Peel's change of mind.

In 1845 Gladstone gave up the rigid idealism he had espoused seven years earlier in *The State in Its Relation with the Church*. There he had argued that the government, as the guardian of established churches of England and Ireland, should have refused support to any institution so abhorrent to the truth as the papistical seminary at Maynooth, dedicated to training a Roman priesthood for a country whose official religion was austerely Protestant. Instead, with incomprehensible rhetoric but sure political instinct, Gladstone voted for the grant to Maynooth.[3] By this vote he won the respect of those outside the established churches and built the base of the Liberal party. His principled toleration remains a central tenet of the parties which today dominate Western politics. This at least in the eyes of the world is success: to have touched myriad lives, to have risen to leadership, to have left behind a policy honored in the common practice of civilized societies.

By these standards, Newman's conversion led to failure. The Oxford Movement, which he gave up, faltered and declined into ritualism. Its principles, which he had largely formulated, had found only the most ineffectual constituency even when he remained at Oxford to give them voice. As a Catholic he was always misunderstood and finally isolated in the Roman communion. His Tractarian principles, in either their Anglican or Roman incarnations, were never translated into practice by any but the most precarious and isolated community of disciples. His failure, so pristine and comprehensive, has a unity and grandeur unmatched by the checkered careers of Peel and Gladstone, whose successes were marred

[2] Bright on free trade sounds like Portia on divine mercy: "It blesses him who gives and him who takes. It has blessed all our manufacturing districts with a steadiness of employment and an abundance they never knew before, and it has blessed not less the very class who in their dark error and blindness thought that they could have profited by that which was so unjust, so cruel to the bulk of their countrymen" ("Free Trade," an 1877 address to the Working Man's Club of his home town, Rochdale, in *Select Speeches* [London, 1907; Everyman ed.], p. 237).

[3] "I really have great difficulty sometimes in comprehending what Gladstone means," Peel remarked of Gladstone's attempt to explain his position on the Maynooth grant. When his constituents at Newark asked him to appear and explain his vote, Gladstone begged off by reminding them that "the day named was the Vigil of St. Simon and St. Jude" (Philip Magnus, *Gladstone* [New York, 1954], p. 69).

by doubts and reversals. It has the momentum and weight of a great if absurd drama.

Success and failure are subjective terms. Newman would have said that his conversion saved his soul and impelled others toward redemption. What could be a greater success to a man who held it "better for the sun and moon to drop from heaven, for the earth to fail, and for all the many millions on it to die of starvation in extremest agony, as far as temporal affliction goes, than that one soul, I will not say, should be lost, but should commit one single venial sin, should tell one wilful untruth, or should steal one poor farthing without excuse"?[4] In Newman's calculus of salvation, only God knows the merit of the converts of 1845. But it was a basic point of Newman's philosophy that the world cannot renounce its obligation to judge. Its verdict in the case of Newman is clear. By its incomprehension and indifference, the world has declared Newman not only wrong but trivial. "Securus iudicat orbis terrarum, bonos non esse qui se dividunt ab orbe terrarum in quacumque parte terrarum"[5] (The world judges surely: those are not good men who separate themselves from the world in any part of the world) had been Augustine's judgment on the Donatists, and in the *Apologia,* Newman made it his judgment on the Anglicans. It has become the modern world's judgment on Newman himself. From our perspective, few figures of the last two hundred years so thoroughly separated themselves from the world. By Augustine's standard, Newman was a failure.

The easiest way to appreciate the magnitude of Newman's failure is candidly to inspect the reasons usually alleged for his success. Newman's reputation is supported by five pillars of conventional wisdom. He was important (1) because he embodied the Tractarian spirit; (2) because he led the revival of English Catholicism; (3) because he gave Romanticism a sublime religious expression; (4) because he was a great theologian; and (5) because he was the prophet of a new order that will follow the inevitable collapse of liberalism. Each of these claims is false in fact or in logic, or in both.

---

[4]*Apo.,* p. 221.

[5]Newman quotes only the phrase, "Securus iudicat orbis terrarum" in the *Apologia*. Perhaps the full sentence struck too close to home. See *Apo.,* p. 110, and Augustine, *Contra epistolam Parmeniani* 3.24.

## Newman the Tractarian Hero

Newman, says one venerable tradition, is significant because he led the Tractarian party.

This claim makes Newman's reputation rise or fall with the significance of the Oxford Movement. Dean R. W. Church and his celebrated history of the Tractarians have much to answer for here. Church's dignified prose imparted to the movement the considerable solemnity at the command of a high-church divine who rises to become dean of Saint Paul's. What were the roots of Tractarianism? "There was room, and there was a call, for new effort; but to find the resources for it, it seemed necessary to cut down deep below the level of what even good men accepted as the adequate expression of Christianity, and its fit application to the conditions of the nineteenth century. It came to pass that there were men who had the heart to make this attempt."[6] Dean Church's Tractarians are brave but deliberate. Their movement had none of the unseemly antecedents of modern political parties. Like the providential events of Scripture, "it came to pass." The righteous gravity of the passage illustrates the procedure by which the Oxford Movement attained its reputation. But on sober examination the Oxford Movement itself was a failure, and Newman's reputation only suffers from his association with it.

Newman dated the beginning of the Oxford Movement from John Keble's Assize Sermon of July 14, 1833, in which the author of *The Christian Year* denounced the national apostasy of a Whig government bent on the reformation of the established church. Later that month, the nucleus of the Tractarian party met at Hugh James Rose's vicarage at Hadleigh in Suffolk, and the movement was launched. What was the condition of the Church of England in 1833 when the Tractarians came to her rescue?

Five years earlier, Parliament had ended the charade of the Test and Corporation Acts—dissenters had long since held office by annual indemnity or by hypocritical compliance with the antique provisions of these laws. Oxford had ousted Peel four years earlier for his vote in favor of Catholic Emancipation. Lord Grey's Whig cabinet had been in office three years when Keble preached on national apostasy. The Reform Bill was a year old. Dissenters and Catholics sat in Parliament and legislated

[6]R. W. Church, *The Oxford Movement* (London, 1900), p. 20.

for the established church. In other words, as a protest against the liberal
spirit of the age, the Oxford Movement was fatally slow in formation.
The immediate object of Keble's sermon—the government's proposed
suppression of ten bishoprics or archbishoprics in the Church of Ireland—was tangential to the circle of reforms already in motion. By the
time the *Tracts for the Times* began to appear late in 1833, the damage
they were intended to forestall had either been done, or else the elements
were in place by which it would inevitably be accomplished.

Like Tories everywhere, Keble and the Oxford protestors had early on
deplored the reforms that encroached on the traditions of church and
state, but the Anglican propriety they struggled to preserve thwarted their
resistance. On January 30, 1831, the day on which high churchmen
commemorated the martyrdom of Charles I at the hands of an earlier
rogue Parliament, Keble had expounded "the good old principles, of
plain submission and cheerful obedience," and like the high-church
eighteenth-century divines he sought to emulate, he had advocated "the
Gospel rule of non-resistance." The Assize Sermon was outspoken only
by contrast with this supine Anglicanism, which was the heart of Keble's
more usual orthodoxy. While denouncing the national apostasy of the
Whig government, the Keble of 1833 still insisted that "no despiteful
usage, no persecution, could warrant her in ceasing to pray, as did her
first fathers and patterns, for the State, and all who are in authority."
"Candour, respectfulness, guarded language" are the churchman's
weapons.[7] To Newman the Assize Sermon sounded a call to battle; in
retrospect it was a belated grumble. Its deferential indignation was not
likely to inspire successful opposition to a political confederation of deist
aristocrats, nouveau-riche industrialists, rick-burning peasants, and
overworked proletarians. Even the date of Keble's sermon mocks the
political pretensions of the Oxford Movement. Keble preached before the
judges of the Oxford assizes on July 14, 1833, the forty-fourth anniversary of the fall of the Bastille. But Keble speaks as if Danton and
Robespierre had never existed, or if they had, as if their revolution could
hardly touch the Church of Butler and Law.

[7] *Sermons Academical and Occasional* (Oxford, 1847), pp. 123, 124–25, 143. As late as
1976 the Assize Sermon was still said to have "thundered forth" and probably will be said
to have done so as long as the history of the Oxford Movement is recorded by partisans. See
Stephen Prickett, *Romanticism and Religion* (Cambridge, 1976), p. 252. John R. Griffin
makes a less biased judgment of Keble's politics: "it is impossible to make any coherent
sense of Keble's theory" (*The Oxford Movement: A Revision* [Edinburgh, 1984], p. 15).

In later years, the Oxford Movement would demonstrate no more political sense than did Keble's sermon. The *Tracts for the Times* and the articles in the *British Critic,* once this high-church quarterly had fallen to Tractarian editorship, were relentlessly theological, indulging in occasional sallies against the dangerous liberalism of the day but always retreating to the safe bastion of abstract theology. The Oxford Movement, rich in political prejudices, never formulated a political program. The only Tractarian with any political instincts was Hurrell Froude, who contributed "The Position of the Church of Christ in England, Relatively to the State and the Nation" as the fifty-ninth of the Tracts and composed an allegory of church-and-state relations masquerading as a study of Thomas à Becket. But Froude's tuberculosis limited his contributions and ended his life in 1836, after which the Tracts and the *British Critic* confined themselves to the politics of the deanery or of the common room.

The Oxford Movement was no more successful in addressing the practical needs of the Church of England than it had been in challenging the political agenda of the nation. Once again, it came too late to the struggle and offered little concrete help. By 1833 churchmen in and out of orders had long since begun to understand and address the problems confronting the Church. These were massive. The literal and figurative dilapidation of the established religion in the age of Pitt was already legendary. In 1800, only six worshipers presented themselves for communion during the lone Easter eucharist at Saint Paul's. The Archbishop of Canterbury was an undistinguished nepotist.[8] Pluralism disgraced the Church as rotten boroughs did the state; a clergyman might hold two lucrative benefices and set foot in neither, just as a politician might win election from a constituency of three persons, all his tenants. The ecclesiastical organization of the realm was ludicrously inadequate to cope with the shifts in population under way since the middle ages and now accelerated by the dislocations of the industrial revolution. The physical condition of church property reflected the organizational decrepitude. Given these conditions, the congregations of the establishment dwindled while the dissenting chapels waxed fat in membership.

About these practical problems the Tractarians had little or nothing to

[8] See Horton Davies, *Worship and Theology in England* (Princeton, 1961–62), 3: 280. John Moore, Archbishop of Canterbury from 1783 to 1805, was memorialized with discreet malice by the Methodist J. M. Rigg in the *DNB:* "He appears to have dispensed his patronage with somewhat more than due regard to the interests of his own family."

say. Here as in much else other churchmen had already taken the initiative. From the beginning of the century, the leaders of both parties devoted themselves to the maintenance of the state religion. Perceval and Peel thought the state should be holy; Wellington and Russell thought it should be powerful. Either view countenanced a strong national Church. Some five hundred new Anglican churches went up in the thirty years after 1801, funded in part by parliamentary grants of £1.5 million and by even more generous public contributions. At Oxford in 1825, Newman himself had played a minor role in this restoration of Anglicanism. In his first curacy he presided over the fund-raising for a new Saint Clement's— he raised five thousand pounds, one hundred of them from the incipient heretic Peel.[9] The pattern was repeated across England.

Meanwhile Parliament began in 1831 to curb pluralities and establish equity in clerical salaries. And education had been a matter of concern for churchmen at least since 1811 when Archbishop Charles Manners-Sutton and Bishop William Howley of London founded the National Society for Promoting the Education of the Poor in the Principles of the Established Church, thereby inciting Bentham to produce a volume whose prolix indignation can be sampled in its title: *Church-of-Englandism and Its Catechism Examined, Preceded by Strictures on the Exclusionary System, as Pursued in the National Society's Schools: Interspersed with Parallel Views of the English and Scottish Established and Non-Established Churches: and Concluding with Remedies Proposed for Abuses Indicated: and an Examination of the Parliamentary System of Church Reform Lately Pursued and Still Pursuing: Including the Proposed New Churches.* As Bentham's title suggests, church reform was already an explosive topic fifteen years before the Oxford movement was conceived.

In these years groups such as the Society for the Propagation of the Gospel, the National Society for the education of the poor, and the Church Building Society sprang up and prospered. Despite Bentham's protestations, by 1817 Robert Southey had decided that "the state of religion in these kingdoms is better than at any time sine the first fervour

---

[9] The religious census of 1851 gives the details of church-building. See Horace Mann, *Religious Worship in England and Wales* (London, 1854; the religious census of 1851), p. 14. About two thousand more churches went up between 1831 and 1851, these funded primarily by private donations. For Peel's contribution to Saint Clement's, see *L.D.*, 1: 206.

of the Reformation.''[10] Even assuming the poet laureate's complacency, the legal and educational movements for the restoration of the Church were well under way when at Oxford the Tractarians discovered that it was under assault. Newman and his associates deserve little credit for discerning what other high churchmen had already sought to repair.

Not that the Oxford Movement took much interest in the practical needs of the nineteenth-century Church. When Tractarians diagnosed a crisis in the established religion, it was not to pluralities or crumbling roofs that they pointed but to less tangible symptoms of spiritual malaise. The ninety *Tracts for the Times* can be read from cover to cover without encountering any mention of the churchless populations of England's manufacturing centers, though frequent reference is made to the neglected mysteries of baptism and excommunication. In 1835 Newman did write a pamphlet to suggest the appointment of suffragans as a means of aiding overworked bishops whose sees had grown beyond the capacity of a single administrator. But this practical suggestion was made only to secure a theoretical point. The clergy are ''a standing army, insuring the obedience of the people to the Laws by the weapons of persuasion.'' Such an army must have leaders, and a creation of suffragans would fortify ''the Episcopal form, ever repressive of democratic tendencies.''[11] In the year of the People's Charter, Newman believed the creation of sixty auxiliary bishops would constrain the forces of republicanism. The same naiveté had been apparent five years earlier when Newman sacrificed his place as secretary to the Oxford branch of the Church Missionary Society because it proposed to convert the heathen in Senegal without first consulting Archbishop Howley.[12] Regarding practical issues of church reform as secondary, he and the Oxford Movement concentrated on the restoration of damaged ecclesiastical ideas.

But if the reputation of the Oxford Movement were made to depend on the success with which it revived the deliquescent notion of episcopal authority—and this is the issue which dominates the first Tracts and Newman's early polemics—in this too it would have to be called a failure. In print Newman addressed the clergy as ''but one of

[10] In J. H. Overton, *The English Church in the Nineteenth Century* (London, 1894), p. 8.
[11] *V.M.*, 2: 84, 86.
[12] ''By sending out missionaries for the propagation of the Gospel, this Society has taken on itself a function, which not less than that of ordination, is to be considered the prerogative of the supreme rulers of the Christian Church'' (*V.M.*, 2: 11).

yourselves—a presbyter,'' ambitious only to be the shieldbearer of bishops in their battle against infidelity.[13] Was the harried Bishop Richard Bagot of Oxford really to imagine his apostolic burdens lightened, however, when he received from Newman an eight-thousand-word letter beginning, ''It may seem strange that, on receipt of a message from your Lordship, I should proceed at once, instead of silently obeying it, to put on paper some remarks of my own on the subject of it''?[14]

The satire of Newman's dealings with the bench surpasses the genial style of Trollope's Slope and only finds its match in Dickens's Heep. An incident from the heyday of Newman's Tractarian activities illuminates his habitual condescension to episcopal office. In 1836 Keble married, and Newman with his curate, Isaac Williams, visited the newlyweds at Bisley in Gloucestershire. J. H. Monk, the diocesan bishop, was stopping there for a confirmation, and was feted with a lavish dinner. ''It would be better at such a time,'' Newman told Williams, ''that a bishop should only ask for a little dry bread and salt and water.'' In time Newman admitted he was not the person to have ''confidence in any superiors.''[15] The Oxford Movement—Newman's Oxford Movement, at any rate—might profitably be considered as a revolt against the very bishops whose authority it ostensibly sought to preserve, a revolt that completed itself when Newman denied the authority of the English Church altogether and began again in the Roman.

Latter-day disciples of the Oxford Movement have convinced themselves that the Tracts bore fruit among the neglected poor of England's cities or villages. Keble and E. B. Pusey are held up as saints with social purpose and Newman as the prophet of a restored ritual which alone could strike the religious note in laboring hearts hardened by industry and

[13]*Tracts* 1, Tract 1, p. 1. Newman could desire for his episcopal superiors ''no more blessed termination of their course, than the spoiling of their goods, and martyrdom.'' Even Bentham had not wished to see the bishops executed.

[14]*V.M.*, 2: 397. In this letter, written in 1841 during the crisis over Tract 90, one paragraph vies with another to see how many times the expression ''Your Lordship'' can be used in a single sentence. The repetition turns deference into abuse. Newman's episcopal insults were carefully studied. During his 1832 Mediterranean holiday he wrote home that should Blomfield of London offer him a Whitehall preachership, the bishop should be answered in exactly these words: ''Circumstances have arisen which have decided me in declining.'' *L.D.*, 3: 131. Blomfield had voted for the Reform Bill.

[15]Isaac Williams, *Autobiography* (London, 1892), p. 107; *A.W.*, p. 262.

neglect.[16] This is fantasy, and Newman's reputation can only suffer by association with the Oxford Movement's bungled attempts at social consciousness.

The record of the Oxford Movement's collisions with the social realities of nineteenth-century Britain constitutes a comedy of errors. Keble, for instance, who gave up his Oriel tutorship to practice the pastoral virtues of Law's *Serious Call,* wrote to his brother that "the travelling on Sundays on the railroad is disgusting; they quite disturb the people at Otterburn Church."[17] This is the remark of an eighteenth-century parson at sea in an age of industry.

Pusey, who is usually remembered for his metaphysics of sacramental reality—he defended the real grace of baptism, the real absolution of penance, and the real presence of the eucharist—has in fact a better claim than any other Tractarian to social consciousness. Pusey was wealthy, and after the death of his wife he anonymously founded the parish church of Saint Saviour's to serve one of the slums of Leeds. The church was to embody the Tractarian spirit. Pusey planned it to have a stained-glass window depicting the Virgin crowned in glory, a cross hanging over the chancel screen, a clergy offering up prayers while facing the altar, and most important of all, a regular system of confession. The bishop of the newly created see of Ripon, in which Saint Saviour's lay, was Charles Longley, a liberal exponent of Anglican moderation who forbade all Pusey's innovations. But Pusey held the advowson giving him the right to name the clergy of Saint Saviour's, and he used it to appoint vicars who, while maintaining an abstract doctrine of priestly obedience, worked to subvert the episcopal veto.[18] Five years of ecclesiastical warfare followed the dedication of the church in 1845. The Puseyites preached the intercession of the saints. They adopted the eastward position at the consecration of the host. They seemed to permit prayers for the dead.

[16] See, for instance, Geoffrey Rowell's chapter on "Pioneers in the Parish: Ritualism in the Slums," *The Vision Glorious* (Oxford, 1983), pp. 116–31, or R. W. Franklin, "Pusey and Worship in Industrial Society," *Worship* 57 (1983): 386–412.

[17] Brian Martin, *John Keble* (London, 1976), p. 178. Martin adduces this extract to refute the accusation that Keble was "unaware of the real conditions of society." If this refutes the charge, what evidence could prove it?

[18] The story of Saint Saviour's is told in two pamphlets, J. H. Pollen, "The Statement of the Clergy of St. Saviour's, Leeds, in Reference to the Recent Proceedings Against Them" (Leeds, 1851), and Longley's reply, "A Letter to the Parishioners of St. Saviour's, Leeds" (London, 1851).

And as a last straw they invited or commanded their parishioners to unburden their souls in auricular confession.

In 1849 a deacon of Saint Saviour's, Mr. Rooke, directed one of the married women of the parish who sought confirmation to confess herself to the curate, Mr. Beckett. Mr. Beckett, in an effort "to drag sin from its lurking-place," asked the woman leading questions of an indelicate character—other parishioners, he knew, were known to be "living in open adultery." Mr. Rooke may have instructed the penitent to keep the particulars of her confession from her husband. He learned too late that she was "notorious in the parish for garrulity."[19] Having told Mr. Rooke her secrets, she repented her confession and complained to higher ecclesiastical authority of indecent interrogation in the confessional.

The incident of the prurient confessor provided a happy occasion for Bishop Longley and his rural dean to intervene. An inquisition of ten hours was held in the vestry of the parish church, after which the bishop revoked the license of Mr. Beckett, preventing him and Mr. Rooke from ministering in the diocese. A vituperative correspondence ensued between the clergy and their bishop, including letters from the Puseyites breathing ill-concealed contempt for their apostolic superior, a petition from the parishioners of Saint Saviour's that was clearly suborned by the vicar, and pamphlets of self-justification on all sides. The incident was exacerbated by the national hysteria of 1850 surrounding the papal restoration of the Roman hierarchy in England. By 1851 most of the clergy that had served Saint Saviour's since its foundation had gone over in pique to Catholicism. Pusey's advowson seemed to be a passport to Rome. Bishop Longley was in due course rewarded for his diligence at Leeds by elevation to Canterbury. Pusey remained a simple presbyter.

One of the chief inquisitors of Saint Saviour's Puseyite clergy had been Walter Hook, a high-churchman of the old school, sometimes cited as a precursor of the Tractarians. In 1825 he had preached a sermon entitled "An Attempt to Demonstrate the Catholicism of the Church of England," and his 1838 sermon, "Hear the Church," went through twenty-eight editions and one hundred thousand copies. But as a senior clergyman in Longley's diocese he denounced the Puseyites as "wicked."[20] The odium evoked by the Oxford Movement crossed all lines separating

---

[19] Pollen, "Statement of the Clergy," pp. 8–10.

[20] "What do I complain of?" Hook wrote to Pusey, "I complain of your building a Church and getting a foot in my parish to propagate principles which I detest. . . . [I]t is wicked." H. P. Liddon, *Life of Pusey* (London, 1893–97), 3: 128.

Evangelical and High Church. If the low-church bishop John Bird Sumner of Chester had objected to the Anglo-Catholicism of Newman's Tract 90, so had the high-church bishop Henry Phillpotts of Exeter, the one occupant of the bench from whom the Tractarians might have expected cantankerous support. Not only the Rookes and Becketts, but the Newmans and Puseys were a splinter party in a Church itself increasingly isolated. Tractarian attempts to translate Oxford principles into social realities invariably ended in legal or theological wrangles that did nothing to benefit actual parishioners.

In the countryside, Thomas Allies tried the Tractarian experiment on the farmers of Launton, Oxfordshire, where he was rector from 1842 to 1850. Allies, a product of Oxford in its early Tractarian days, was a thorough disciple of Newman and Keble. He piously named his children after two of Newman's favorite fathers of the church, Saints Basil and Cyril. At Launton he instituted daily evensong, but no one came except his wife, who resented having to cut short her afternoon drives. He endeavored to interest a dying parishioner in the beauty of paradise. "It may be very well, Sir," said the rustic Gerontius, "but Old England for me!"[21] Meanwhile, elsewhere in Oxfordshire, the undogmatic and non-Tractarian Edward Elton, vicar of Wheatley, took a village of tenements where bull-baiting was still a favorite pastime and made the parish respectable by the practical expedient of infusing cash. He raised ten thousand pounds for building a school, a church, and parish houses and successfully lobbied to put the village on the railway line. The church prospered at Wheatley, while Allies gave up Launton in 1850 and joined the disillusioned clergy at Saint Saviour's in their trek to Rome. The established clergy were more conscientious pastors in 1860 than they had been in 1800; there were more services and fewer pluralists. But to attribute the Church's amelioration to the Oxford Movement is a species of post hoc, ergo propter hoc reasoning that credits idealists like Allies with the successes that properly belong to pragmatists like Elton.[22]

The Church of England did its best to quarantine the Oxford Movement, but the Tractarians made the job easy. Allies is a case in point. At twenty-nine he was examining chaplain to Charles James Blomfield,

[21] Mary H. Allies, *Thomas William Allies* (London, 1907), p. 45.

[22] Diane McClatchey, *Oxfordshire Clergy, 1777–1869* (Oxford, 1960), gives a detailed account of the established clergy in a county where the Tractarian influence ought to have been at its strongest, but "surprisingly few of the parish clergy stand out for their avowed sympathy with the Oxford Movement" (p. 89).

bishop of London, a promising position for a young Tractarian. When one day Blomfield mentioned that the King of Prussia was one of his godfathers, Allies was shocked "that a Prussian Protestant who was outside the Church should be admitted as godfather" and had the poor sense to say so to his patron. The bishop averred that while he liked Oxford principles, he preferred "moderate Oxford," and a few days later offered Allies the living at Launton. "I advise you to take it," the bishop added.[23] So Allies wound up in ecclesiastical Siberia. The Tractarians were ill-fitted for success in an establishment where tact was preferred to piety as a virtue.

Practical questions of church organization or politics were as incomprehensible to the Tractarians as the religious lives of the lower classes or the protocol of ecclesiastical politics. They excelled instead in litigation and spiritual volatility. Much time and effort was wasted appealing obscure matters of canon law through the Court of Arches and the Privy Council. The inevitable adverse judgments assured a certain number of Tractarian conversions to Rome, but the subtleties of tradition and church law annoyed men like Blomfield and mystified the citizens of Leeds or Launton.

Hurrell Froude, Newman's closest friend and Tractarian confidant, might have made some sense of the Oxford Movement as a revival of Catholicism for the masses. He recognized the French church reformer F. R. de Lamennais as a kindred spirit and had the requisite impertinence to sever the Gordian knot of Anglican propriety that prevented the likes of Pusey and Keble from descending to common politics and vulgar strategy. But Froude was alone among the Tractarians in possessing these gifts, and after 1836 he was gone. Newman was offended by the populism of Lamennais and squeamish about contact with anything vulgar.[24] Under his leadership the Oxford Movement addressed itself more and more *ad clerum*.

Regarded solely as an effort to elevate the religious tone of England by appealing to its spiritual establishment, the Oxford Movement has always seemed successful and, within these limits, important. Dean Church's history of the movement's influence hardly moves beyond an account of

[23] Allies, p. 42. Blomfield made a Catholic out of more than one chaplain. George Spencer, the future Father Ignatius, served him for two years before his conversion in 1830.

[24] Lamennais "seems to believe in the existence of certain indefeasible rights of man." According to Newman, this kind of thinking not only implied a denial of original sin but encouraged the Irish. *Ess.*, 1: 158, 160.

its purifying effect on the Anglican priesthood, and ninety years after Church, Archbishop Arthur Michael Ramsey could still speak of the Oxford Movement as "a powerful religious revival within the Church of England." If the movement had little impact on the masses, its devotees will say, at least it made itself felt in the lives of the clerisy, the elite class that really mattered in the formation of opinion and policy. In 1833, 7,000 of the 11,000 English clergy and 230,000 laymen signed a petition sponsored by the Association of the Friends of the Church, a tenuous alliance of high churchmen and Oxford protesters formed to preserve the traditions and prerogatives of Anglicanism, goals at least superficially like those of the Oxford Movement. In 1864 Pusey was able to gather 11,000 clerical signatures to protest the liberal heterodoxy of *Essays and Reviews*. The expensive Library of the Fathers, the Tractarians' great essay into scholarship, had 3,700 subscribers at one point.[25] The Tracts were widely disseminated first among the clergy, later among curious laymen. There is no denying the Oxford Movement a degree of importance in shaping the attitudes of the clerisy, but importance is not success. Julian the Apostate is an important figure in the formation of European religious thought, but no one now worships at the altars of Zeus. The influence of the Oxford Movement on the clerisy was insignificant.

Newman himself, preferring principled failure to popular success, dissociated himself from the Friends of the Church. "No great work was done by a system," he wrote in the *Apologia*.[26] And while the Tracts found their way into many a parsonage, much of their distribution was due to the missionary zeal of Tractarian disciples like Thomas Mozley,

[25] Michael Ramsey, "Newman the Anglican," in Terence Wright, ed., *John Henry Newman* (Newcastle, 1983), p. 3. Specifically, the petition of 1864 protested the Privy Council's judgment in the *Essays and Reviews* trial that a priest in the Church of England need not necessarily believe the doctrine of eternal punishment. But the language of the protest was so weak that one of the Oxford Movement's chief opponents, Bishop Thirwall, remarked he could sign it himself; see Frederick Maurice, *Life of F. D. Maurice* (New York, 1884), 2: 470. In his *Life of E. B. Pusey* (London, 1893), 1: 432, Canon Liddon may have invented some two thousand subscribers to the Library of the Fathers; see Richard W. Pfaff, "The Library of the Fathers: The Tractarians as Patristic Translators," *Studies in Philology* 70 (1973): 333. The last subscription list contained only 1215 names. Liddon's claims for the extent of Tractarian support represent the outside limit of what may actually have existed.

[26] *Apo.*, p. 48. In 1833, Newman wrote to J. W. Bowden that if there were to be a system, Oxford was to take the credit for it: "Whenever you talk of the Tracts, mind and persist they are not connected with the Association, but the production of 'Residents of Oxford'" (*L.D.*, 4: 100).

who on vacation from Oxford in 1834 rode about Northamptonshire dropping off copies at every rectory and vicarage. By this standard of success, *The Watchtower* would be the most influential religious publication in America. How many of the clerical recipients of the Tracts actually read them? On a single day of his vacation rounds, Mozley visited three county parsons, "the most distinguished churchmen in Northamptonshire"—Mr. Sikes of Guilsborough, Mr. Crawley of Stowe Nine Churches, and Mr. Crawley's son, Lloyd. All received their Tracts cordially—presumably they were given gratis—but Crawley the elder was "puzzled" by them, Lloyd Crawley "kept returning to the London world, and the work of the Societies, as the true scene of action," and Mr. Sikes was "against pushing Church principles too hard." Nothing suggests that any of them actually read the Tracts. How many clergy were enthusiastic about the Tractarian message? Any number might, like Crawley senior, acquiesce "in that eager thought of a better time coming," but such a vague sentiment was no commitment to the rigors of Oxford theology.[27] In their first three years the Tracts hardly circulated beyond this uncommitted clerical audience. Three thousand copies made a large first printing of the early numbers, so that even with reprints there was not one tract for each member of the established church's clergy.[28]

By 1836 the pamphlets had attracted a lay audience as well, and Newman was excited to learn that "Lord Melbourne has *sent for our Tracts.*"[29] If Newman was hopeful that this high-placed interest in Oxford principles would trigger a national debate, he was mistaken. The prime minister's curiosity in Puseyism never translated into an influence. "I have got one of their chief Newman's publications," he told Lord Holland, "with an appendix of four hundred and forty-four pages. I have read fifty-seven and cannot say I understand a sentence, or any idea whatever."[30] And Melbourne was well above the level of the likely

---

[27] Mozley, *Reminiscences, Chiefly of Oriel College and the Oxford Movement* (London, 1882), 1: 329, 330.

[28] *L.D.*, 4: 90. Newman was amazed when Tract 75 on the breviary sold out its first printing of 750 copies; *L.D.*, 6: 9. Five hundred copies made a second edition of Tract 29; *L.D.*, 5: 75. A Victorian religious tract might accomplish a good deal more. The evangelical tract, *The Sinner's Friend*, with a very different audience in mind, went through at least 140 editions and 800,000 copies in numerous languages. Owen Chadwick, *The Victorian Church* (Oxford, 1966), 1: 443.

[29] *L.D.*, 5: 244.

[30] David Cecil, *Lord M* (London, 1954), p. 140. What book can Melbourne have got hold of? He was talking to Holland, who died in 1840. *The Arians, Lectures on Justification,* and

reader of the Tracts in his breadth of reading and in his capacity for difficult speculation. Mockton Milnes read the Tracts with admiration and after their suspension imitated them in his pamphlet, "One Tract More," but when he tried to interest Peel in Oxford theology, Sir Robert politely changed the subject: "I am very much in arrear with the Tracts," he said. The Oxford Movement did little to shape the thought of the establishment, and in Peel's or Melbourne's case failed even to provoke an argument.[31]

Of the first twenty Tracts, fourteen dealt with apostolic succession. Of these fourteen, seven were written by Newman himself. Perhaps no better proof of the intellectual isolation of the movement could be offered than its obsession with the unbroken descent of spiritual power through the episcopal successors of the apostles. The doctrine was remote from the concerns of a Church under siege by the forces of industrialism and obscure to ordinary worshipers seeking a more immediate solace. Its only conceivable appeal was to the established clergy. Like the defeated Indians of the Plains who performed the Ghost Dance to make the conquering white man disappear, the Oxford Movement responded to the decline of its priestly influence by mystical incantations of cosmic power. "The Church of England stood long upon her tithes and her decencies," Carlyle wrote to John Sterling of the movement, "but now she takes to shouting in the marketplace, 'My tithes are nothing, my decencies are nothing; I am either miraculous celestial or else nothing.' It is to me the fatallest symptom of speedy change she ever exhibited."[32]

Nor can the Tractarians claim the success of originality. The gist of the Oxford Movement was its appeal to tradition, and the authors of the Tracts were at pains to prove that they had no ideas of their own. Theirs

---

*Prophetical Office* are therefore the only candidates. Of these, the *Lectures* is the most likely. Its first edition had much scholarly apparatus and was so obscure as to recommend itself to German theologians. Döllinger praised it.

[31] James Pope-Hennessy, *Monckton Milnes* (New York, 1955), 1: 142. Even Gladstone failed to keep up with the Tracts. In 1841, "he cannot profess to understand or to have studied the Tracts on Reserve"—Tracts 80 and 85 on reserve in communicating religious knowledge. Morley says that many were scandalized that these 1841 tracts bore the superscript "ad clerum"—a further proof the Tracts had not been much read outside Oxford (John Morley, *Gladstone* [New York, 1903], 1: 307). Some Tracts had been addreseed "ad clerum" since 1833.

[32] J. A. Froude, *Thomas Carlyle: A History of his Life in London* (New York, 1910), 1: 165.

were the doctrines of Saints Clement and Cyril, Bishops Wilson and Bull. The later Tracts often take the form of *catenae patrum,* collations of patristic passages on a single topic. "Don't be original," Keble warned his students.[33] But even in asserting the Catholic and apostolic traditions of the Church, the Oxford Movement had been anticipated. While Newman was still an undergraduate, Joshua Watson and Christopher Wordsworth were defending the idea of the apostolic succession, and in his *Ecclesiastical Sonnets* of 1822, Wordsworth's brother William had praised the liturgy as full of "stupendous mysteries," baptism as a "second birth," and Laud as a martyr. In the 1820s De Quincey, out walking with Wordsworth in the Lake District, had challenged the poet's assumption in the *Excursion* that the Church of England held the Catholic doctrine of baptismal regeneration. The poet appealed to his brother Christopher, Master of Trinity College and sometime chaplain to Archbishop Manners-Sutton, who decided, says De Quincey, " 'sans phrase,' that I, the original mover of the strife, was wrong; wrong as wrong could be; without an opening in fact to any possibility of being more wrong."[34] There were many for whom the tradition that the Oxford Movement rediscovered had never been lost.

Given that the Oxford Movement began from principles sanctioned by tradition and supported by a body of reputable Anglicans, its failure to gain any significant following is the more remarkable. Part of the answer is that many English of all classes did not want the Church renovated in body or in spirit. In the late eighteenth century, when the vicar of North Bradley tried to rebuild his decrepit church, the parishioners were "so barbarous that they opposed all improvements; and would pull down the

[33] In Prickett, *Romanticism and Religion,* p. 93.

[34] De Quincey accepted Wordsworth's dogmatic oracle and rightly prophesied that "this very question, now slumbering, will rouse a feud within the English Church" ("Protestantism" [1847], in *Collected Writings* [London, 1897], 8: 291–92). A. B. Webster records that "Bishop Blomfield once remarked to Joshua Watson that he could count on the fingers of one hand the number of those who still believed in Apostolic Succession. 'My Lord,' came Watson's firm reply, 'there are a good seven thousand' " (*Joshua Watson* [London, 1954], p. 19). This must have been in 1834 when the Association of the Friends of the Church had presented its petition with seven thousand clerical signatures. If churchmen were unsure what they believed, dissenters could have told them. Fifty years before the Oxford Movement, Priestley explained the doctrine of the established church: "In the Church of Rome, however, and also in that of England, *regeneration* and *baptism* are confounded, and the terms are used as expressing the same thing" (*An History of the Corruptions of Christianity* [Birmingham, 1782], 1: 303).

wall which we were building, and cut down and destroy the trees recently planted.'' In the 1850s Elton had a similar experience at Wheatley, where a hundred saplings meant to refurbish the vicarage garden were cut down in the night. Vandalism of church improvements was probably provoked by fear of higher church rates, but must also have reflected a visceral conservatism. ''The *people* do not care about Church Reform here—do not want any such thing,'' Greville noted in a diary entry for 1835.[35]

What the peasantry did to the Church's property the upper classes did to its intellectual patrimony. The Oxford Movement tried to revive an interest in the traditions of the Church, and the Library of the Fathers is a monument to this Tractarian ambition. A knowledge of the Fathers had not entirely died out even before the Oxford Movement—the venerable Martin Joseph Routh of Magdalen had published his *Reliquiae Sacrae* in 1814 and, before the Tractarian revival of ecclesiastical tradition began, Elizabeth Barrett improved her Greek by studying Gregory Nazianzen's *De Virginitate* with Hugh Boyd, editor of Chrysostom and Basil. The theology of the Fathers had been a recondite intellectual specialty before the Oxford Movement began. The Tractarians made it briefly an academic fashion, and Mozley records that old editions of the Fathers, ''almost on their way to the grocers,'' were suddenly bid up to five guineas a volume in the Tractarian era. But the movement resurrected the works of the fourth-century Athanasius of Alexandria and of the eighteenth-century English divine Daniel Waterland not to prove them important—a premise many educated people were willing to concede—but to prove them right, a conclusion hardly shared outside Tractarian or Catholic circles. The vogue for the Fathers made few converts to Tractarian principles. As dean of Christ Church, the classicist Thomas Gaisford voted with the Newmanites to examine the works of Oxford's liberal professor of moral philosophy, Renn Dickson Hampden, for heresy, but as regius professor of Greek he dismissed the Fathers as ''sad rubbish.''[36] Barrett commemorated her reading of Gregory in a wry tribute to Boyd:

[35] Overton, *The Church of England in the Nineteenth Century*, p. 6; McClatchey, *Oxfordshire Clergy*, p. 94; Charles Greville, *Diary*, ed. Philip Wilson (New York, 1927), 2: 300.

[36] Mozley, *Reminiscences*, 1: 356, 2: 38. ''These teachers of the classics had sided with the enemies of humanism,'' Mark Pattison writes in one of his frequent denunciations of Tractarian scholarship. ''Greek was useful as enabling you to read the Greek Testament and the Fathers. All knowledge was to be subservient to the interests of religion'' (*Memoirs*

Do you mind that deed of Ate
   Which you bound me to so fast,—
Reading "De Virginitate,"
   From the first line to the last?
How I said at ending solemn,
   As I turned and looked at you,
That St. Simeon on his column
   Had had somewhat less to do?

In an article for the *Athenaeum* on "The Greek Christian Poets" she instructed her readers how to honor the Fathers for their devotion even while we "refuse them the reverence of our souls, in the capacity of theological oracles." Her sentiments prevailed. When, at the end of the century Hardy's Jude was able to pick up a set of the Library of the Fathers in a thrift shop, he was surprised it went so cheap.[37]

Under the tutelage of Oxford, any number of educated Victorians learned to admire the apostolic heritage, but an appreciation of the antique charms of Gregory Nazianzen did not carry over into any love of Oxford theology, which Barrett cordially detested. The Victorians preferred their Catholicism as they did their monasteries—in admirable ruins. "The Oxford dream of an independent Church, the Oxford dream of an exclusive Church, are both in practice forgotten; their very terms are strange to our ears; they have no reference to real life," Walter Bagehot wrote for the *National Review* in 1860. The movement of 1833 was for him a failed delusion, and yet Bagehot was no enemy of Oxford principles. He quoted Newman with respect, appropriated his definition

---

[London, 1885], pp. 96–97). More recently Jaroslav Pelikan has turned Newman's subordination of history to religion into the virtue of "tradition"; see his *The Vindication of Tradition* (New Haven, 1984), pp. 38–40. In 1832 Newman opposed the appointment of Horace Wilson as Oxford's first Boden Professor of Sanskrit because "he has never taken an active part in religious objects." "We know nothing about him except that he is the best Sanscrit Scholar" (*L.D.*, 3: 15).

[37] "Wine of Cyprus," *Poetical Works* (New York, 1885), 3: 28; "The Greek Christian Poets" (1842), *Complete Works* (New York, 1900), 6: 173. Hardy, *Jude the Obscure*, pt. 3, ch. 3. Nineteenth-century readers needed little prompting to ignore the theology of the Fathers. William Allingham noted in his diary for 1865 that he had been reading the *Apologia:* "Does all this about Oxford and the Fathers, etc. etc., really matter?" (*A Diary* [New York, 1985], p. 111).

of liberalism, and adopted his sense of religious mystery: "Religion has its essence in awe," Bagehot says while disparaging the deism of the Edinburgh Reviewers, "its charm in infinity, its sanction in dread . . . its dominion is an inexplicable mystery . . . mystery is its power."[38] In other words, the Catholicism of the Oxford Movement was to be admired as Wordsworth had admired Tintern Abbey. It was a sublime monument to antiquity which would have been desecrated by any absurd attempt to restore it to worldly use. So Oxford ideas made an impression on the Victorian mind without ever having an impact. Hardy read the movement's failure into the Gothic piles of Christminster: "What at night had been perfect and ideal was by day the more or less defective real."[39]

If the movement of 1833 did no more than heighten a nebulous sentimentality about religious worship, its champions, such as Horton Davies, have been quick to convert this slender attainment into victory. "It is hardly too much to say that the restoration of reverence to English worship is the unpayable debt that the Church of England owes to the Oxford Movement."[40] But as Bagehot observed, to the extent that reverence took concrete forms, it seemed foolish to the English. The movement made converts in sentiment and enemies in practice.

Newman himself was the movement's greatest attraction for those like Matthew Arnold, who admired his "urbanity," or John Campbell Shairp, who recalled the "mysterious veneration" that surrounded him. "It was almost as if some Ambrose or Augustine of elder days had reappeared," Shairp wrote. "Surely," the eighteen-year-old Edward Benson exclaimed after he heard Newman preach in 1848, "if there be a man whom God has raised up in this generation with more than common powers to glorify His name, this man is he!"[41] Every one of these admirers went on to success as critic, academic, or archbishop; every one of them had been touched by the Oxford Movement in his youth; every one of them rejected Newman and his works. "The old, sterile, impossible assumption of their 'infallible church'" was Arnold's mature judgment on Newman and Lamennais. Shairp never forsook the Presby-

---

[38] "Mr. Gladstone" (1860), *Historical Essays* (New York, 1965), p. 258; "The First Edinburgh Reviewers" (1865), *Literary Studies* (London, 1911; Everyman ed.), 1: 34.

[39] *Jude the Obscure*, pt. 2, ch. 2.

[40] Davies, *Worship and Theology in England*, 3: 280.

[41] Arnold, "The Literary Influence of Academies," in *Lectures and Essays in Criticism*, ed. R. H. Super (Ann Arbor, MI, 1962), p. 244. Shairp is quoted in Randall Davidson, *Life*

terians. Benson thought the monstrosity of Newman's beliefs was written on his countenance: "It was awful—the terrible lines deeply ploughed over his face, and the craft that sat upon his retreating forehead and sunken eyes."[42] For every Oxford undergraduate convinced by the Tracts or converted by Newman's spiritual logic, somewhere else the same words made a dozen enemies for the movement. Edward Fitzgerald withheld publication of his *Euphranor* to avoid even the suspicion that the good-natured idealism of his Cambridge dialogue might conceal Puseyite sentiments: "I would not help even by a fart to fill their sails."[43]

As a brake on the Erastian reform of the state Church, the Oxford Movement was also unsuccessful. The proposed amalgamation of Irish bishoprics, the issue that in 1833 roused Keble to denounce the national apostasy of Lord Grey's government, went ahead in spite of Oxford, and Berkeley's see at Cloyne was swallowed up by the diocese of Cork. Howley, the only Victorian archbishop with any sympathy for the Tractarians, found himself sitting on the hateful Ecclesiastical Commission, designed by parliamentary reformers to recommend the very changes that Howley and Oxford conservatives opposed. In due course he presided over the restructuring of the traditional English dioceses. The state meddled with tithes from 1836 on. Church rates became voluntary after 1868. In 1880 the Church of England lost its monopoly on burials. Even within the established church the Puseyites made little headway. Howley at least had respected the Tractarians and made Benjamin Harrison, author of three Tracts, one of his chaplains. But the Tractarians themselves squandered these rare opportunities for advancement in mutual distrust and recrimination. Instead of using Harrison's position to advantage, Newman disdained his plodding Anglicanism and dismissed him as "puzzleheaded" and "but half a man."[44] When the Tractarian way became too hard even for Tractarians, it is not surprising that a larger public was bewildered by it.

---

of Archibald Tait (London, 1891), 1: 105; A. C. Benson, *Life of Edward White Benson* (London, 1899), 1: 63.

[42] Arnold, "DeMaistre's *Letters*" (1879), *Essays, Letters, and Reviews* (Cambridge, MA, 1960), p. 218; Benson, *Life of E. W. Benson,* p. 62.

[43] Fitzgerald, *Selected Works* (Cambridge, MA, 1963), p. 567.

[44] *L.D.,* 5: 201. Newman stigmatized Harrison with his favorite rhetorical anathema: "poor B.H.," he called him. The epithet "poor" was usually reserved for apostates, as in "poor Blanco White" or "poor Sibthorp."

After Howley no nineteenth-century Archbishop of Canterbury had the slightest partiality for the Tractarians or their ritualist descendants. John Bird Sumner was chosen by Russell in 1848 precisely because he had refused to join the Tractarian chorus that complained of Hampden's appointment to the see of Hereford. With his brother Charles, Sumner was an ancient object of Tractarian scorn. At Ripon, Longley had proved his worth by rooting out the confessors of Saint Saviour's. He was a moderate, and Palmerston appointed him to Canterbury in 1862. Longley's successors, Archibald Campbell Tait (1868–1882) and Edward White Benson (1883–1896), both studied and rejected the Tractarian creed in their youth. What sympathy they had for the Oxford Movement evaporated under the burden of church litigation spawned by the movement's ritualists. The vacillating Tait, who would have preferred to close out his tenure as archbishop by reading Dante, Wordsworth, and Thackeray, found himself threatened with resignations or secessions by Henry Parry Liddon, canon of Saint Paul's, and Pusey should the ancient anathemas of the Athanasian Creed be altered or abridged. The ailing Benson spent the last years of his life in the tedious compilation of canonical precedents to refute the Bishop of Lincoln's ritualist claims. Nor were vacancies at Canterbury always filled by apostate Whigs who might be expected to oppose the Tractarian spirit. Disraeli had reluctantly appointed Tait,[45] and Benson was Gladstone's choice. In 1896, Lord Salisbury, a pious high churchman who cherished Anglican tradition, nominated Frederick Temple to succeed Benson—Temple, who in his youth had contributed to *Essays and Reviews,* the collection of theological papers that on its publication in 1860 had been denounced by respectable opinion in all quarters of the Church of England as incompatible with Christian belief. And so the Tractarian century ended with one

---

[45] "My Church policy is this," Disraeli wrote Lord Derby at the time of Tait's nomination, "to induce, if possible, the two great legitimate parties to cease their internecine strife and to combine against the common enemies: Rits and Rats." W. F. Monypenny and G. E. Buckle, *Life of Benjamin Disraeli* (1929; reprinted, New York, 1968), 2: 408. High and low churchmen formed the legitimate parties. Ritualists were grouped with rationalists as fringe groups beyond the spiritual pale. Disraeli's view was widely shared everywhere but in the Church itself. Tait was objectionable to Disraeli not for his spiritual but for his secular failings; he was a Liberal and a mediocrity. But as Derby observed, "Your range of choice is limited, and your materials by no means first-rate" (*Disraeli,* 2: 409), an apt characterization of the problem facing all Victorian ministers in appointing bishops.

of the authors of *Essays and Reviews* enthroned at Canterbury, the
nominee of a Conservative prime minister and Tory lord.

Even assuming what is untrue—that the Oxford Movement wrought a
spiritual transformation in the established church—such a transformation
would have been a pyrrhic victory. By the end of the century the Church
of England had ceased to be a national Church in anything but name.
Mann's census of worship in England and Wales had established the
embarrassing fact that half the worshiping population was to be found in
dissenting chapels or Catholic churches. This was in 1851. The government and the bench found an efficient way of dealing with this statistic:
The census of church attendance was never repeated.[46] But the partial
information available for the last fifty years of the century and the witness
of the present day make clear that in spite of ecclesiastical reforms the
decline of the established church continued apace. Richard Mudie-
Smith's study of London's religious life, undertaken for the *Daily News*
over the year from November 1902 to November 1903, found that only
one in three potential worshipers went to church at all. Of this third, a
minority worshiped in the establishment's churches. While the percent-
age of worshipers in the total population seemed to have fallen as
measured against earlier surveys, dissent was holding its own at the
expense of the Church of England. Attendance was worst among the two
classes the Oxford Movement had tried to reach, the elite of the West End
and the poor of the East End.[47]

In 1903, Saint Peter's in the London Docks could still attract one
thousand or more worshipers on a Sunday. Charles Lowder had been
vicar there forty years earlier. Like the clergy of Saint Saviour's in Leeds,

---

[46] In 1835 Tocqueville had asked his English translator Henry Reeve if the number of
English dissenters was known. "No. One could only obtain this figure with the aid of the
Government, and it has been in its interest up to now to hide it" (*Journeys to England and
Ireland* [London, 1958], p. 79). The experiment of 1851 confirmed the government in its
caution.

[47] Mudie-Smith put the number of London Sunday worshipers at 832,000, including
those who attended two services. The population of London less those in institutions was
4,470,000. From this figure Smith subtracted 50 percent to account for those who because
of illness, work, or disability could not attend. This leaves 832,000 actual attenders out of a
possible 2,235,000, or about one in three. See Richard Mudie-Smith, *The Religious Life of
London* (London, 1904), pp. 15–16. Any census of this sort is sure to have its problems, but
Mudie-Smith and his census-takers were if anything biased in favor of religion in general
and the established church in particular. For the comparison of the 1903 results with those of
the *British Weekly* poll of 1886, see *The Religious Life of London*, pp. 280–323.

Lowder had hoped to save souls in the slums by "a Ritual and dignity of service—accompanied by the full teaching of the Catholic Faith." His Tractarian ministry had in 1859 provoked the parishioners of Stepney to riot. Lowder had said that through this enmity, "the very dregs of the people were taught to think about religion."[48] But in 1903 the majority of the congregation at Saint Peter's was not old enough seriously to think about religion—sixty percent of its worshipers were children, reflecting a trend throughout London churches. Children were brought to services either for their edification or their parent's relief, since the church might act as a baby sitter.[49] In fashionable Marylebone, the Church of England had lost six thousand worshippers between 1886 and 1903, all establishment churches sharing in the decline except for Holy Trinity, where an Evangelical clergyman had increased attendance. In middle-class Camberwell there were no Evangelicals to attract a crowd, and almost all Church of England congregations had lost members. At Saint Luke's, where the ritualists held sway, attendance was halved in seventeen years.[50] The depressing statistics continued from borough to borough. In the years when the first generation of Oxford apostles had grown respectable with age and a second generation professed Tractarian principles in Kensington and Stepney, the residents of London fell away from the Church of England in droves, a defection if anything more apparent in Ritualist or Tractarian churches than elsewhere.[51]

[48] Lowder, *Twenty-One Years in St. George's Mission* (London, 1877), p. 143.

[49] "Those who have studied the details will have seen how, at many places of worship, the children have saved the situation" (*The Religious Life of London,* p. 324). Children made up 37 percent of all London churchgoers. Put in the bleakest terms, the survey showed that in a city of 4.5 million people, only 525,000 adults attended church on Sundays—about 12 percent of the total population.

[50] *Religious Life of London,* pp. 283–86. The Tractarian influence scored one of its few successes in lower-class Poplar, where attendance at Saint Saviour's rose in seventeen years from 467 to 582 under the guidance of the ritualist Father Dolling, who died the year the census began. Dolling was remarkable among the movement's disciples for having a sense of humor. When the Protestant Archbishop Alexander of Armagh visited Dolling's slum parish, the congregation "rose up singing and pronouncing, 'We are marching to the *goal'* as though it were *gaol.* 'Only too true, poor fellows,' whispered Dolling, who was an Irishman, across the chancel to the Archbishop" (Shane Leslie, *The End of a Chapter* [New York, 1917], p. 105).

[51] J. E. B. Munson (in "The Oxford Movement by the End of the Nineteenth Century: The Anglo-Catholic Clergy," *Church History* 44 [1975]: 382–95), alleges that "by the end of the Victorian era the Oxford Movement had effected a revolution within the Church of England" (p. 393). This assertion is supported by data compiled by the English Church

Dozens of sects sprang up in these years to absorb the lost business of the established church, everything from the Salvation Army to the Theosophical Society. The example of Charles Voysey is instructive of how liberalism's free market in religion operated. A graduate of Saint Edmund's Hall, Oxford, he was for some years a Church of England curate, until in 1864 he published "Is Every Statement in the Bible about Our Heavenly Father Strictly True?" For his exercise in freethinking he was haled into the ecclesiastical courts and deprived of his curacy by the Privy Council in 1871. He then set up his own theistic chapel in Swallow Street, Piccadilly, where many of his former parishioners joined him in a worship without miracles or formularies. The followers of Voysey were lost to the Church of England. They were by and large respectable middle-class worshipers who ought to have formed its natural constituency and to whom the Oxford Movement was usually a mystery, often a monstrosity. If the Tractarians really had taken over the Church of England, they would have conquered a bankrupt establishment, one that at the present may be instilled with the movement's sense of ritual and tradition but is certainly devoid of communicants or influence. But even this meager success was denied the Oxford Movement, and it seems more just to say that the Church's tangential association with Tractarianism hastened its decline.

No one understood the failure of the Oxford Movement to influence the English Church better than Newman. How could "a thing without a soul" respond to living apostolic truths or one whose life "is an Act of

---

Union and other ritualist organizations. The figures suggest that in 1901, "three out of every ten of the parochial clergy could be considered 'high' " (p. 388), and that many parishes had adopted ritualist practices. But "high" was never synonymous with ritualist. The article does not examine Mudie-Smith's survey, which points to a different conclusion—that the clergy who believed themselves to be part of a Tractarian tradition gained ephemeral victories in establishing forms and rituals while sustaining permanent defeats in securing worshipers. For instance, from 1878 Canon Liddon and Dean Church labored to make Saint Paul's a national example of Oxford beliefs in practice. The full cathedral was restored to use for the first time in over a century, its interior refurbished, and daily services instituted. Liddon's sermons attracted as many as four thousand worshipers on a Sunday. Church and Liddon both died in 1890. Thirteen years later, *The Religious Life of London* noted "the decline at St. Paul's Cathedral from 4,705 in 1886"—Liddon's heyday—"to 2,337 in 1903." This may be partially accounted for by the fact that rain fell heavily on the Sunday in May, 1903, when the *Daily News* enumerators visited the cathedral. The bad weather did not, however, prevent the assembling of 7,000 persons at the City Temple, where the Rev. R. J. Campbell, a Congregationalist, was beginning his pastorate (p. 288).

Parliament'' adopt Catholic principles? "As a nation changes its political, so may it change its religious views; the causes which carried the Reform Bill and free trade may make short work with orthodoxy." This is not Mill or Bagehot, but Newman in the 1850 lectures, *Certain Difficulties Felt by Anglicans*.[52] Here is a cold-blooded appreciation of what Keble and Pusey, Liddon and Church could not grasp, that those Tractarians who remained in the established church were in the anomalous position of Peel's Tory followers who supported the anti–Corn Law legislation: They maintained their party only by betraying their principles. What sense was there in preaching the independence and indefectibility of Catholic truth within a church subordinate to the state and committed to toleration? To Newman, Catholicism offered clear-headed Tractarians the only refuge from the predicament in which English liberalism had placed them.

In the lectures of 1850 Newman accepted the challenge of liberalism and admitted the failure of the Oxford Movement as a brand of Anglicanism. What had it achieved? "It has hindered the promotion of high-minded liberals, like the late Dr. Arnold, at the price of the advancement of second-rate men who have shared their opinions." The long line of detractors who have lavished their irony on the Oxford Movement find their chief in Newman himself. The movement had failed just because the church it sought to reform was a government-protected community. In the free market of religious ideas, where it could assume its proper name of Catholicism, Tractarianism need have no fear. "Give us as much as this, an open field, and we ask no favour; every form of Protestantism turns to our advantage." In time, in the open market of belief, Catholicism must prevail, as God and truth must prevail, "And Israel, without a fight, will see their enemies dead upon the sea-shore."[53]

## Newman the Catholic Champion

The time so far elapsed since Newman made this prophecy has been insufficient to its fulfillment. If anything Newman the Catholic was more thorough in his failure than Newman the Anglican. The fortunes of

[52]*Diff.*, 1: 7, 1: 9, 1: 35.

[53]*Diff.*, 1: 11, 1:30, 32. The chief of the "second-rate men" who shared Dr. Arnold's opinions was the unspeakable R. D. Hampden.

nineteenth-century English Catholicism owed little to Newman or the Tracts.

Catholicism in England did not fare badly in the increasingly tolerant religious atmosphere of the nineteenth century. Before the Gordon Riots of 1780, there were perhaps seventy thousand English and Welsh Catholics in a total population of over seven million—less than 1 percent. By 1911 there were 1.8 million Catholics in a population of 36 million—about 5 percent.[54] Early in the nineteenth century Pope Gregory XVI had written off English Catholics as a fractious minority that gave him more trouble than the rest of the Church Universal, but by 1851 the Catholic population had increased sevenfold from its late eighteenth-century level, three times faster than the general population. Pope Pius IX had restored the hierarchy in 1850, and Cardinal Wiseman dreamed that he might follow Wolsey and Pole as papal legate to a Catholic England.[55] In the intervening years Tractarianism had revived the very notion of Catholicism, and the flower of the movement had seceded to Rome. It was only natural to connect the work of Newman and the Oxford Movement with the resurgence of Catholicism as cause and effect.

No reliable Catholic historian does so any longer. The increase in the Catholic population of England had three principal causes: Irish immigration, the success of Roman Catholicism among religiously uncom-

[54] Philip Hughes ("The Rise of English Catholics in 1850," in George Beck, ed., *The English Catholics, 1850–1950* [London, 1950], pp. 45–46) gives the number of English Catholics in 1780 as 60,000. Mann, in the census of 1851, put the number of English and Welsh Catholics for 1780 at 69, 376. These and all figures for Catholicism in England must always be suspect. For the historical population of England and Wales, see B. R. Mitchell and Phyllis Deane, *Abstract of British Historical Statistics* (Cambridge, 1962), p. 5. For the number of English Catholics in the early years of the twentieth century, see George Beck, "Today and Tomorrow," in *The English Catholics,* p. 587.

[55] Gregory XVI is quoted in Hughes, "The English Catholics in 1850," in *The English Catholics,* p. 72. The exact number of English Catholics in 1851 is a matter of dispute. Hughes makes it about 700,000. Wiseman meant to restore the hierarchy in all its dignity: "He had even insisted at first—until the conservativism of his friends persuaded him to moderate his zealous display—that whenever he went out in the evenings to a private function his carriage must be met, as for any Cardinal in Rome, by torch-bearers" (Denis Gwynn, *Cardinal Wiseman* [London, 1929], p. 215). Wiseman did not have to go to Rome to find his precedent. Archbishop Howley had torches light his noctural progresses, the last English primate to do so. Wiseman, an avid ecclesiastical historian, was very conscious that he was the first English cardinal resident in England since the unfortunate Reginald Pole, who died in 1558, twelve hours after his patron, Queen Mary. A few months before his death, Wiseman journeyed incognito to Pole's tomb at Canterbury, where he communed in melancholy silence with the spirit of his predecessor.

mitted members of the lower and middle classes, and its appeal to a well-educated but religiously unstable elite on the fringes of the establishment.

Of these three causes, Irish immigration is by far the most important. The Irish had been filling English cities since the late eighteenth century. In the year following Newman's conversion, 137,000 Irish refugees from the potato famine crowded into Liverpool alone.[56] Genteel English Roman Catholics, both old Catholics and new converts, were offended to find themselves coreligionists of the refuse of a "savage nation."[57] As superior of the newly founded English Oratory, Newman had to cope with the bigotry of his fellow converts Frederic William Faber and Bernard Dalgairns, who were disgusted by the presence of Irish brothers in the London house. "Never take another Irishman, padre mio," Faber pleaded in 1849, and Dalgairns whined that "the dirt and stink of the good Irelandesi are a really intolerable evil for all above the lowest."[58] Dalgairns had envisioned an Oratorian mission to "the moderately educated classes." Instead, the Oxford scenario began to repeat itself,

[56] "From the first day of November, 1846, to the twelfth day of May, 1847, the total number of Irish immigrants into Liverpool amounted to 196,338. Deducting the number actually recorded as sailing to America, no less than 137,519 persons had been added to the population of Liverpool. When the year ended, the total number of immigrants, excluding those who were bound for America, reached the immense total of 296,231" (Thomas Burke, *Catholic History of Liverpool* [Liverpool, 1910], p. 84). Of these masses, it is a fair guess that over three-quarters were Catholic. Estimating the number of Irish Catholics in the English population is made difficult because the British census only keeps track of English residents born in Ireland, not those of Irish extraction, and because no census except that of 1851 has taken account of religious affiliation.

[57] In 1860 Mrs. Charlton describes a typical house party at the Marquis of Westminster's, where some embarrassment was caused at dinner by disparaging references to Roman Catholics. When the Marquis attempted to spare further insult to her feelings by mentioning that she was a "Roman Catholic lady," she retorted at once, "Yes, but an English Catholic, not an Irish one, which is all the difference in the world. English Catholics are responsible beings who are taught right from wrong, whereas Irish Catholics belong to a yet savage nation, know no better and are perhaps excusable on that account." (Denis Gwynn, "The Irish Immigration," in *The English Catholics,* p. 270)

[58] *L.D.*, 13: 104, 253. Mozley descerned the hand of providence at work in the Tractarian conversions, which "made Oxford contribute abundantly to the spiritual needs of the poorest Roman Catholics" living in "wretched Irish colonies established in the worst quarters of our cities and towns" (*Reminiscences,* 2: 445). Such evidence as exists suggests that the contribution was less abundant than he imagined.

and he found himself again in a minority, surrounded now by Irish barbarians instead of English philistines.

Newman did his best to promote ethnic harmony among the Oratorians, but an appreciation of the nature of English Catholicism had to wait for Henry Edward Manning, who observed in 1890 that of an estimated 1.2 million Catholics in the country, a million were Irish. Unlike Dalgairns, the cardinal saw in his savage coreligionists the key to the Church's future victories. "I have spent my life in working for the Irish occupation in England," he said. "That occupation is the Catholic Church in all the amplitude of faith, grace, and authority." The Oxford Movement had grown out of the most conservative political instincts, but the Victorian public associated it in its Catholic incarnation with the most extreme political danger—Irish revolution.[59]

So far history has proved Manning right. Of the estimated 4.2 million Roman Catholics who made up some 8 percent of the English and Welsh population in 1984, about 80 percent were probably of Irish extraction.[60] In 1985, *Crockford's Clerical Directory* noted that "surveys suggest about as many Roman Catholics are at Mass on Sunday in England as there are worshippers in the Anglican parish churches."[61] If the Church of Rome now threatens to overtake the Church of England, credit must go to the Irish savages whom the Tractarians did their best to ignore, or else to Anglicanism itself, whose suicidal tendencies the Oxford Movement did its best to excite.

Historians of nineteenth-century English Catholicism, overwhelmed by the mass of Irish immigrants, have discounted conversion as "statistically a neglible part of the Catholic expansion."[62] This is unfair. Without the Irish invasion, Catholicism would still have made a respectable Victorian sect in competition with the YMCA or with spiritualism.

---

[59] Edmund Sheridan Purcell, *Life of Cardinal Manning* (London, 1896), 2: 678. "If we ask, what harm could Rome do to England? the answer was that it might make Ireland rebel" (G. M. Young, *Victorian Essays* [Oxford, 1962], pp. 146–47).

[60] The British *Catholic Directory* gives an annual estimate of the number of English and Welsh Catholics but makes no attempt to break these down by ethnic groups. Manning's ratio—one English Catholic for every five of Irish extraction—may be set too high, but is probably still roughly accurate.

[61] *Crockford's Clerical Directory*, 1985/86 ed., p. 66.

[62] Edward R. Norman, *Roman Catholicism in England From the Elizabethan Settlement to the Second Vatican Council* (Oxford, 1985), p. 72. Norman echoes Philip Hughes, "English Catholicism in 1850," in *The English Catholics*, p. 53: "If ever our story is told, it will be, inevibably, the story of the achievement of a poor, working-class population, in

In August 1833, while the Oxford Movement was in formation at
Hadleigh, Alexis de Tocquevi.le chatted with a Catholic priest in
Portsmouth:

Q: Is the number of Catholics in England increasing?

A: Yes, we often have converts. But on the other hand the number of those
who do not believe in Christianity is growing. The sect of Unitarians has
made decided progress.

In the backwaters, away from the theological warfare of the universities,
Catholicism more than held its own, and the priest of Portsmouth rightly
noted that his competition came not from the Anglican establishment but
from novel forms of dissent like Unitarianism. But Catholicism was a
match for the Socinians, and Nicholas Wiseman rejoiced in 1843 to
receive Mr. Richards, a Unitarian astronomer who promised to bring
fifteen pupils over with him.[63]

In the next months, while the first Tracts were appearing, Tocqueville
visited Lord Radnor, who admitted that while "your dogmas do not seem
to me reasonable," the number of English Catholics was increasing
because Roman doctrines "are precise and give rest to minds tired with
controversy." In 1825, ten years before Froude summoned the ghost of
Thomas à Becket in the pages of the *British Critic* to demonstrate the
virtues of medieval Catholicism, Cobbett had sold forty thousand copies
of *The History of the Protestant Reformation,* in which the sixteenth-
century settlements were denounced as roundly as any Tractarian could
wish. Catholicism made an appeal to ordinary people independent of the
Tractarian converts. Among an increasingly rootless and distracted
population that felt no compulsion to practice the religion sanctioned by
government, Rome would have picked up its share of the lost Anglican
trade with or without the Oxford Movement. In fact, the Newmanites
may have slowed the pace of the Catholic revival by embroiling a
fundamentally popular enterprise in the esoteric and divisive intrigues of
theological politics. Some people thought so. "Newman's conversion is

---

the main Irish by birth and by descent." But John Bossy, *The English Catholics from 1570–
1850* (London, 1975), makes a case for the importance of native English conversions and
cites the growth of Catholicism in Birmingham, which the Irish immigration hardly
reached, pp. 309–10.

[63] Tocqueville, *Journeys to England and Ireland,* pp. 54, 57. Gwynn, *Wiseman,* p. 133.

the greatest calamity which has befallen the Catholic Church in our day"
was a saying Manning disavowed without much conviction.[64]

The Irish immigration and routine conversions account for virtually the
whole growth of English Catholicism from 1800 to the present. What
remains is a minuscule addition of disaffected converts from the better-
educated classes. Their accession to Catholicism has attracted attention
wildly disproportionate to its importance.

Catholic conversions among the clerisy began before the Tractarian
influence was felt. Twenty-year-old Kenelm Digby converted in 1820 as
a result of his studies of the middle ages at Cambridge. His eleven-
volume *Catholicism, or, The Age of Faith,* began to appear two years
before Keble's Assize Sermon. George Spencer, youngest brother to
Lord Althorp of the Reform Bill, left Anglican orders in 1830 and made
himself Wiseman's lieutenant in the Catholic reconquest of England. In
1817, when he was eighteen, R. W. Sibthorp—Newman's "poor
Sibthorp"—almost converted after two days in retreat with Bishop John
Milner, the leading English Catholic of the day. Sibthorp was rescued by
the police. Later, he took Anglican orders, converted to Roman Catholicism, relapsed, was readmitted to the Anglican priesthood, and then
converted to Roman Catholicism again. When he died in 1879, the
confused survivors gave him two funerals, one Anglican, one Catholic.
Though his career is a parody of the conflicting impulses that beset certain
Anglican sensibilities, it is hard to believe that the Oxford Movement
made much difference in a life whose disposition was well marked twenty
years before Newman's *University Sermons.*[65]

After Newman went over to Rome, the pace of distinguished conversions quickened. By one estimate, "between 1840 and 1899 no less than
446 Tractarians joined the Roman Catholic Church."[66] That the number
can be stated with such precision indicates the weakness of the Oxford
Movement. Its appeal was so narrow that its influence can be traced down
to the last convert. A ship arriving from Dundalk probably added more

[64] Purcell, *Manning,* 2: 310.

[65] Sibthorp certainly read Newman's *Apologia* before his second conversion to Catholicism in 1864 but was emphatic in denying its influence on his actions: "Dr. Newman never
in any degree influenced me, nor would his reasoning in this 'Apologia' at all influence me,
but I greatly esteem and reverence him" (John Fowler, *The Life of Richard Waldo Sibthorp*
[London, 1880], p. 141).

[66] Davies, *Worship and Theology in England,* 4: 117.

members to the English Catholic community in an afternoon than the Oxford Movement did in fifty years.

Some may object with Dalgairns that the accession of a Manning or a Gerard Manley Hopkins cannot be compared to the debarkation of a boatload of ignorant peasants. However well such a judgment comports with Catholic ethics, Manning was surely right that in terms of historical success, it was the quantity of Irish immigrants, not the quality of its Tractarian converts, that made the difference for English Catholicism. But if the quality of its converts were the standard of assessing the success of Tractarianism as a force in English Catholicism, here too the verdict would be doubtful.

There were a number of model converts who reached Catholicism by a religious logic such as Newman recommended in his *Grammar of Assent.* Some of these, like James Hope-Scott or Gerard Manley Hopkins or Sir Peter Renouf or Lady Herbert, went directly from Anglicanism to Catholicism in the best Tractarian tradition. Others, like the Marquis of Ripon, shopped in the open market before taking the plunge—he was a Freemason and Grand Master of the Lodge before his conversion in 1874. Once converted, the Catholicism of these model converts was steady and orthodox, their careers notable and productive. Hope-Scott married Sir Walter Scott's daughter and settled down to rebuild Abbotsford with the proceeds of a lucrative career as a parliamentary lobbyist for the railways. Hopkins became an exemplary Jesuit who demonstrated the fullness of obedience by burning his poems on entering the order. Renouf became keeper of Egyptian antiquities in the British Museum. Lady Herbert was a prolific author of Catholic fiction,[67] and the Marquis of Ripon distinguished himself as Governor-General of India. These were the converts Dalgairns and Faber had hoped for, the spiritual cream of the influential classes.

But these solid citizens found themselves in mixed company. Coventry Patmore converted to Catholicism in 1864 after the death of his first wife.

---

[67] A. O. J. Cockshut, *The Art of Autobiography* (New Haven, 1984), discusses several English Catholic converts, pp. 178–214. His treatment is sometimes more pious than accurate. Lady Herbert, for instance, appears as a rich but distraught penitent, who, though "not a gifted writer" (p. 186), found peace in the Church. In fact she was a spirited controversialist who inundated the future Cardinal Vaughan with letters full of gossip and theological opinion, and her writing is well above the average, as in her fictional *Thekla: An Autobiography* (London, 1887), whose heroine displays the same verve as her creator.

When his second wife died, he endowed a new Catholic church at Hastings in her memory—Saint Mary Star of the Sea. After his dealings with its clergy, drawn from the Pious Society of Missions, he decided that priests were cheats and liars. In later life he was given to deflating their sanctity with truculent witticisms:

> q: Weren't you sorry to hear that Father ———— was dead?
>
> PATMORE: No, I was very glad.[68]

Still, a vexatious convert like Patmore was a net gain for the Church both in prestige and cash (the issue over which he had fallen out with the fathers of the Pious Society was their promise not to mortgage the church building he had donated; they promptly took a loan on it). More problematical are converts like Lord Bute or Anna Kingsford, for whom Catholic dogma merged imperceptibly into spiritualism or neurosis. Lord Bute, whose conversion provided Disraeli with the plot of *Lothair*, funded the Society for Psychical Research in its efforts to prove the existence of a Scottish ghost. Kingsford converted from Anglicanism after a noctural visit from Saint Mary Magdalene. Manning himself officiated at her confirmation in 1872. She later had interviews with the Virgin Mary and Apollonius of Tyana. On reflection, she found that Catholic dogma was "identical with the teaching of the Hermetic science, and with the tenets of the Kabala, Alchemy, and the purest Oriental religion." She died in 1888 with a nun in attendance.[69] If by the end of the nineteenth century the Catholic Church was receiving between five and ten thousand converts a year, how many of these were orthodox Hopkinses and Hope-Scotts, how many heretical Kingsfords and Butes?

[68] Basil Champneys, *Memoirs and Correspondence of Coventry Patmore* (London, 1901), 2: 36.

[69] Lord Bute was the nominal co-author, with A. Goodrich-Freer, of *The Alleged Haunting of B— House* (London, 1899). B— is Ballechin in Scotland, where the tenants were driven off by metallic bangings in the night. After an "objective" visit, Miss Freer determined the house was indeed possessed. She had more experience with ectoplasms than plumbing; a central heating system had been installed just before the poltergeist took up residence. Edward Maitland records the spiritual odyssey of his friend and partner in theosophy in *Anna Kingsford* (London, 1896), 1: 15, 369, 2: 304. What would Newman have made of high-toned twentieth-century English converts like fellow Oxonian Dom Bede Griffiths, for whom all religions are "different expressions of the one Truth of revelation" (*Return to the Center* [Springfield, IL, 1977], p. 107), or Radclyffe Hall, for whom Catholicism was the complement of homosexuality, magic, and fascism?

The addition to the Roman communion of worshipers who could not distinguish between the religions of Newman and Madame Blavatsky reflects little credit on the work of the Oxford Movement.

The indiscriminate zeal with which Catholics solicited converts among the upper classes not only favored the accession of heretics but offended sensitive souls who might otherwise have been friends to Roman Catholicism. On a visit to Italy, Augustus Hare was alienated by "Roman Catholics who made a vehement effort for my perversion," and in 1890 Aubrey de Vere, who had gone over to Rome with Manning in the wake of the Gorham decision of 1851, importuned Patmore to undertake the conversion of Ruskin, then secluded at Brantwood in the grips of mental illness.[70] And some Catholics were lost through "leakage." In the open market of nineteenth-century religion, if the Catholics gained converts, they also lost communicants to dissent and apathy, though the bulk of lapsed believers, like the bulk of all English Catholics, was to be found in the working classes, where they attracted none of the attention lavished on the fashionable converts.[71] What was just as bad, many of the illustrious converts were unable to pass their new faith along to another generation, and so their influence ended with their lives. All but one of Lady Herbert's children rejected her faith, and their "confirmations, communions, and marriages in another Church were as ashes to her soul."[72] Manning was right to pin his hopes for the future on the breeding Irish rather than the high-toned native converts unable or unwilling to produce a second generation of the faithful.

And many were unwilling. Some found in Catholicism the sublimation of a homosexual impulse. For these the Oxford Movement was a strong, often a decisive influence. At Eton in the sixties the young poet Digby Dolben wrote of his two secret infatuations, Catholicism and his classmate Archie. Only Catholicism reciprocated. When he visited Llanthony Abbey, the Anglo-Catholic brothers showed him every kindness, and the Welsh inhabitants of the neighboring village were startled to find the

[70] Hare, *Story of My Life* (New York, 1900), 1: 463. As might be expected, Monsignor Talbot played a leading part in the "most ridiculous scene" where Hare was proselytized. Champneys, *Patmore,* 2: 342.

[71] For the problem of "leakage" among nineteenth-century English and Irish Catholics, see J. A. Jackson, *The Irish in Britain* (London, 1963), pp. 139–48, and Bossy, *Catholicism in England,* pp. 314–16. In 1851, Newman's one-time mentor Whately, by then Anglican archbishop of Dublin, founded the Society for Protecting the Rights of Conscience. Its mission was to aid converts from Catholicism to Protestantism.

[72] *Letters of Herbert, Cardinal Vaughan, to Lady Herbert of Lea* (London, 1942), p. viii.

eighteen-year-old poet galloping through town in the full habit of a Benedictine monk. In 1866 he traveled to Birmingham and made a pilgrimage barefoot to see Newman at the Oratory. Newman was away, and Dolben's reception into the Roman Church was postponed.[73] He drowned the next year at age twenty before his formal conversion, but many others—Frederick Rolfe, Lionel Johnson, John Gray, Lord Alfred Douglas, Sir Edmund Backhouse, and most famously, Oscar Wilde—lived long enough to complete the passage. For Wilde as a Magdalen undergraduate the Catholic Church was "the Scarlet Woman," apocalyptic excess raised to a sacramental mystery, and "that divine man" Newman was her English oracle. The ironies and paradoxes of Wilde's Oxonian wit owe as much to Newman's theology as to Pater's aestheticism, and when in Reading Gaol he sent for his books, the list included the *Apologia, The Idea of a University, A Grammar of Assent,* and *Two Essays on Miracles.* As Sebastian Melmouth he became "a violent Papist" and was received on his deathbed.[74]

Newman would have repudiated what Wilde's sensibility made of Catholicism, and, at any rate, conversions like this did little to strengthen the Catholic community: they were individual acts of aesthetic judgment rather than submissions to the universal truth of the Roman Church. But Newman's appeal to artistic temperaments like Dolben or Wilde opens yet another line of defense for proponents of Newman's importance. Newman, it is said, combined religion and Romanticism to make an aesthetically intoxicating elixir for delicate modern sensibilities.

## Newman the Romantic Apostle

Newman is allegedly important because he led a spiritual revival that expressed itself not merely in particular religious movements but in the aesthetic or cultural proclivities of a whole age.

This is essentially a claim for Newman as some sort of a Romantic. In this view, Keble and Newman belong to a "minority tradition" of

[73] Dolben's story is told in Robert Bridge's introduction to the *Poems of Digby Mackworth Dolben* (London, 1915). Bridges, Dolben's schoolmate, estimates that out of eight hundred students at Eton in 1862, there were perhaps "some ten or twelve" Puseyites (p. xv). The figure is probably a fair reflection of the Tractarian influence on the upper classes.

[74] Wilde, *Letters,* ed. Rupert Hart-Davis (New York, 1962), pp. 33, 825.

Romanticism whose chief figure is Coleridge. If the Oxford Movement failed to achieve its avowed aims, still it lives on as a revisionist fantasy in the larger spirit of the age. "The literary expression of the Movement, and the poetry in particular, is as much cause and symptom as it is result of the Movement. . . . It was the religious manifestation of a change in sensibility, a new kind of awareness made possible in large part by the European-wide phenomenon of Romanticism."[75]

The Tractarians would have considered it a tragic paradox that their movement, which sought to revive the dormant spirit of the Church Universal, should be remembered as an epicycle in retrograde motion around a galaxy of Romantic ideas, most of which they detested. But is there any truth to the notion?

In fact, Newman's opinions and the Tractarian spirit are very consciously the antithesis of everything the modern world would call Romantic. Newman had little appreciation of those authors who now occupy the first place in anthologies of Romantic literature. Blake he seems not to have known, Shelley was an atheist, and Byron he could hardly bear to name except in a paraphrase:

> We have seen in our own day, in the case of a popular poet, an impressive instance of a great genius throwing off the fear of God, seeking for happiness in the creature, roaming unsatisfied from one object to another, breaking his soul upon itself, and bitterly confessing and imparting his wretchness to all around him. I have no wish at all to compare him to St. Augustine; indeed, if we may say it without presumption, the very different termination of their trial seems to indicate some great difference in their respective modes of encountering it. The one dies of premature decay, to all appearance, a hardened infidel; and if he is still to have a name, he will live in the mouths of men by writings at once blasphemous and immoral: the other is a Saint and Doctor of the Church.[76]

So much for the man who in his own time embodied European Romanticism.

If scholarship is determined to reconcile the movement of 1833 with the Romanticism of the early nineteenth century, it must concentrate on the Tractarians' debt to Wordsworth and Southey, Coleridge and Scott. Tractarians actually read and enjoyed these authors: "I wish I could get to know something of Southey and Wordsworth," Froude wrote to New-

---

[75] Stephen Prickett, *Romanticism and Religion,* p. 7; Georg Tennyson, *Victorian Devotional Poetry* (Cambridge, MA, 1981), pp. 8–9.

[76] "Conversion of Augustine," *Church of the Fathers,* in *H.S.,* 2: 144.

man in 1833, "and unCambridgise, unProtestantise and unMiltonise them. I think they are our set."[77] The Tractarians wanted an English Romanticism purged of the elements that define it—Protestant self-reliance, Cambridge rationalism, and Miltonic vision. To take these away would not have been to emend the Romanticism of Wordsworth or Coleridge but to abolish it, which was properly the Tractarian objective.

Finally, the Oxford Movement's claim to represent a tradition of Romanticism must rest on the apparent intellectual fellowship between Coleridge and Newman. Both were steeped in Anglican theology. Both sought to preserve Christian thought amid the assaults of modernism, and both shared a habit of pursing truth through a tangle of verbal distinctions and qualifications. But on close examination, the apparent fellowship of Coleridge and Newman is illusory. Newman hardly ever mentions Coleridge and then hardly ever without objecting to his abstract metaphysics. Coleridge, complained Newman, viewed creeds and sacraments "rather as symbols of a philosophy than as truths"—the usual Protestant heresy disguised beneath a farrago of German metaphysics. In old age Newman had his joke at the expense of those dim enough to imagine that he might have borrowed from such a corrupt source. He pretended "never to have read a line of Coleridge," in spite of the fact that Coleridge is cited in both the *Apologia* and *A Grammar of Assent*.[78]

For all the benefit Newman derived from Coleridge, he might as well not have read him. In the *Grammar of Assent*, he quotes Coleridge's *Aids to Reflection* only to note that "few readers will enter into either premiss or conclusion" of Coleridge's proof of God's existence from the moral nature of man.[79] So little did Newman share the common language of Romanticism that he continued to use the word "imagination" in a strictly scholastic sense in spite of anything he had read in Coleridge.

And how could Newman have had any sympathy with Coleridge, when their aims were totally antagonistic? Coleridge wrote to preserve the marriage of Church and state as the guarantee for the survival of

[77] *L.D.,* 4: 113. It was characteristic of Froude that he was acute enough to describe English Romanticism in three precise terms and vain enough to believe he could change its direction by having a conversation with Wordsworth and Southey.

[78] *Ward,* 1: 49, 58. See John Coulson, *Newman and the Common Tradition* (Oxford, 1970), pp. 254–55, for the argument that Newman and Coleridge shared a "fiduciary" sense of language.

[79] *G.A.,* p. 198, and see also I. T. Ker's sensible discussion of Newman and Coleridge in this edition, p. 349.

Christian civilization. "That to every parish throughout the kingdom there is transplanted a germ of civilization," he writes in the *Biographia Literaria,* "that in the remotest villages there is a nucleus, round which the capabilities of the place may crystallize and brighten . . . *this,* the inobtrusive, continuous agency of a Protestant church establishment, *this* it is, which the patriot, and the philanthropist, who would fain unite in the love of peace with the faith in the progressive amelioration of mankind, cannot estimate at too high a price."[80] To Newman this was rank liberalism—the worship of civilization at the expense of faith. Newman rejected what Coleridge accepted as obvious, that civilization, "the progressive amelioration of mankind," is valuable and divine. "The world, though stamped with Christian civilization, still 'in maligno positus est,' " Newman wrote to Allies in 1860.[81] For Newman, civilization is at best an accident of faith, at worst an obstruction to it. Coleridge produced *On the Constitution of Church and State* to defend the unity of Christianity and civilization. Newman's reply to this liberal heresy can be read in his *Letter to the Duke of Norfolk* of 1874, where he argues that Christianity need not, and probably ought not, have much to do with civilization. The true Tractarian disciple of Coleridge was Gladstone in his *State in Its Relation with the Church.*

Like everyone else, Tractarians read Romantic authors, and like everyone else they were influenced by Romantic ideology. But the Tractarians eviscerated Romanticism even while they borrowed from it. Bagehot characterized the process in his quip that Keble's *Christian Year* is Wordsworth translated for women.[82] The Oxford Movement wanted an emasculated Romanticism, and Milton was the incubus its leaders hoped to exorcise from the bed of English culture. A detestation of Milton as man and poet distinguishes true Tractarians from mere fellow travelers. In Keble's estimation, Milton is below Jeremy Taylor "as pride is

---

[80] *Biographia Literaria* (Princeton, 1983), 1: 227.

[81] Allies, p. 112. "The whole world [including what the liberal means by civilization and culture] lieth in wickedness" (1 John 5:19).

[82] "Mr. Keble, for instance, has translated him for women. He has himself told us that he owed to Wordsworth the tendency *ad sanctiora,* which is the mark of his own writings; and in fact he has but adapted the tone and habit of reverence, which his master applied to common objects and the course of the seasons, to sacred objects and the course of the ecclesiastical year,—diffusing a mist of sentiment and devotion altogether delicious to a gentle and timid devotee" (Bagehot, "Hartley Coleridge," in *Literary Studies,* pp. 62–63). *The Christian Year* is what Romanticism would look like with Protestantism, Cambridge, and Milton removed.

below humility." "I was hardly ever so shocked," he said of reading the poet whose ubiquitous influence defines genuine English Romanticism.[83] At Eton the schoolboy Digby Dolben instinctively understood that Oxford principles and Miltonic verse were incompatible, and he resented the tutor who inflicted *Paradise Lost* on him for his Sunday devotions.[84] Newman regarded Milton as an example of the depths to which Socinianism could sink, and the appearance of Milton's lost *De Doctrina Christiana* in 1827 under the editorship of Bishop C. R. Sumner merely confirmed his suspicions about both the poet and the prelate.[85]

Hopkins was amused that Newman rated Southey's *Thalaba* above *Paradise Lost,* but this preference is only the logical result of Newman's premise that "poetry is the refuge of those who have not the Catholic Church to flee to and repose upon, for the Church herself is the most sacred and august of poets."[86] Far from asserting the oneness of poetry and faith, Newman's view opposes the two and reduces art at best to a therapy for "the overburdened mind," at worst to a species of unbelief. Anyone holding such a view is sure to prefer Southey to Milton or Keble to Wordsworth, but can such a person be claimed as a Romantic, unless Romanticism encompasses everything written in the nineteenth century? The Oxford Movement mounted an attack on the leading ideas of Romanticism—the religious awe of selfhood, the sacramental value of art, the divine inspiration of individual vision. This attack often borrows the language of its opponents, as Keble adapts the style of Wordsworth, but a similarity of language does not mitigate the underlying enmity.

This much Oxford and Newman shared with Romanticism: that their Catholicism could only have existed in the kind of pluralistic society where Romanticism is also free to develop. Newman decried the Romanticism and rationalism of an age which indulged him on the theory that

---

[83] J. T. Coleridge, *A Memoir of the Reverend John Keble* (Oxford, 1869), pp. 68, 121.

[84] "Milton was to Digby as Luther to a Papist," Dolben, *Poems,* p. xxx.

[85] *L.D.,* 6: 203. It is a mark of how little Hugh James Rose, the high-church divine at whose rectory in Hadleigh the Tractarians had their inaugural meeting, shared in the Tractarian spirit that he quoted Milton with approbation in his *Christianity Always Progressive* (London, 1829), p. 20, but then Rose was a Cambridge man. The Oxford Tractarians tolerated him because of his connections: he was editor of the *British Magazine* and a conduit to the ecclesiastical publishers on whom the movement of 1833 depended.

[86] "John Keble," *Ess.,* 2: 442. Hopkins's ability to remain faithful both to his vows and his critical instincts is remarkable: "The Lake School expires in Keble and Faber and Cardinal Newman"—not a compliment (*The Correspondence of Gerard Manley Hopkins and Robert Bridges and Richard Dixon* [London, 1955], 2: 99).

every view ought to be allowed to have expression, and the liberals against whom he railed often gave Newman a fairer hearing than his coreligionists. Newman's autobiography filled the future Cardinal Vaughan "with pain and suspicion,"[87] but the *Apologia* "breathed much life" into George Eliot, who had read the *Lectures on the Position of Catholics* "with great amusement"—"they are full of clever satire and description."[88] The Unitarian James Martineau and the agnostic Leslie Stephen took the Oxford Movement seriously even as they subjected it to public rebuttal. In the Catholic England the movement itself envisioned, Manning and Talbot would simply have had Newman's books put on the Index.

Newman shared nothing substantial with the Romantic culture in which he had his being. His work is a sustained but failed attack on the whole Romantic enterprise, and the attempt to resurrect Newman's reputation by allying it with a movement whose extermination was his life's ambition is a cruel proof of how singularly he failed in his mission.

## Newman the Modern Thinker

Some have attempted to prop up Newman's reputation by allying him with other modern movements to which the tenor of his thought is entirely inimical.

The Oxford Movement praised the virtues of chastity and celibacy. By one of the ironies of scholarship, it is now sometimes recalled as a prototypal gay alliance. This is only one of several modern strategies intended to extricate Newman and the Tractarians from the failure of their stated religious objectives. Each of these strategies would have repelled the Tractarians themselves. What would Newman have said to the proposition that the Oxford Movement provided "a religiously-sanctioned alternative to marriage" for "young men who were secretly troubled by homosexual feelings"?[89] Here the eternal verities of Catholi-

---

[87] Vaughan knew how to pay a compliment. He said of the *Apologia*, "The egotism may be disgusting, but it is venial." (J. G. Snead-Cox, *The Life of Cardinal Vaughan* [London, 1912], 1: 215).

[88] George Eliot, *Letters* (New Haven, 154–78), 4: 160.

[89] "At the heart of the correlation between Anglo-Catholicism and homosexuality was an affinity in outlook between a sexual minority and a minority religious movement within the

cism sink beneath the waves of sociological analysis, the habitual procedure of the liberalism that Newman despised.

Newman would have been no more amused by attempts to salvage his ideals by repackaging them as literature, which he regarded as an undertaking much inferior to the dogmatic theology to which he devoted his life. Newman's place is not really in the prose tradition that runs from Carlyle to Wilde—placed here he is the odd man out. He was very consciously not a literary figure and very distinctly not a man of anything as genteel as letters. His writing was designed to resist consistency with the prose, as with the thoughts, of those whom we consider the great Victorian essayists.

One school tells us that Newman is significant because, apart from his historical connection with failed religious movements, his thoughts on education made a major contribution to a great tradition. No doubt *The Idea of a University,* originally a series of lectures in defense of the educational system of the newly founded University of Dublin, contains a grand and enduring vision of education. But is it Newman's vision? University training, Newman wrote in the famous seventh discourse, "aims at raising the intellectual tone of society, at cultivating the public mind, at purifying the national taste . . . , at facilitating the exercise of political power, and refining the intercourse of public life." The product of these sublime endeavors is that nineteenth-century marvel, the gentleman. Here we have a Newman whose words seem to deserve an honored precedence in the anthologies of Victorian prose as the fountainhead of Matthew Arnold and one school of modern thought on liberal education.

---

established church. . . . [I]t provided an environment in which homosexual men could express in a socially acceptable way their dissent from heterosexual orthodoxy'' (David Hilliard, "Unenglish and Unmanly: Anglo-Catholicism and Homosexuality," *Victorian Studies* [Winter, 1982]: 209–10). The grandfather of modern attempts to link the Oxford Movement and homosexuality is Geoffrey Faber in the "Secret Forces" chapter of *Oxford Apostles,* 2d ed. (London, 1974): "Both Froude and Newman may have derived the ideal of virginity from a homosexual root'' (p. 218). The connection was not lost on the movement's contemporaries. Samuel Wilberforce's friend Charles Anderson, a high churchman, complained that Cuddlesdon College, where Liddon prepared young men for the priesthood, promoted "effeminancy and sentiment repugnant to English taste" (Standish Meacham, *Lord Bishop: The Life of Samuel Wilberforce* (Cambridge, MA, 1970), p. 198). And Kingsley's sneer at Newman in his famous review of Froude's *History* contained an oblique charge of homosexuality: "cunning is the weapon which Heaven has given to the saints wherewith to withstand the brute male force of the wicked world which marries and is given in marriage." See *Apo.,* p. 341.

The difficulty with these elevated thoughts is that they do not square with Newman's own most basic beliefs. Given the choice of refining the intellectual tone of public life or preserving the doctrine of the trinity in riotous squalor, can anyone doubt that the thinker who would rather that the sun and moon fall from their orbits than that one soul should commit a single venial sin would have chosen squalid faith? Measured against the genteel standard that *The Idea of a University* seems to celebrate, Saint Athanasius was a brute, yet Newman never doubted he was the model Christian hero. The most Newman ever claimed for liberal education was that it is no worse than learning a trade or a profession—it is "as useful as the art of wealth or the art of health."[90]

It is tempting to regard the best-known portions of *The Idea of a University* as exquisite specimens from a lifetime's labor in irony. These noble meditations on gentlemen and refinement—what are they but Newman toying with the pious sensibilities of his Irish hosts and revenging himself upon the secular snobbery of his Oxford contemporaries? In the end, the university is only ordinary, merely useful—no better, in fact, than the Tamworth Reading Room. Newman the educator was sure to lead his followers into a wilderness of contradictions and satires. This Newman is not sufficiently sober or straightforward to take his place in the anthologies.

Nor does Newman's theology really fit comfortably in the tradition of English thought that runs from Locke to Mill or Berkeley to Bradley. His topics—the Arian heresy, the development of dogma, the grammar of assent—are on their face alien alike to the common tradition of modern philosophy, to the great majority of ordinary twentieth-century readers, and if the truth be told, to the great majority of twentieth-century scholars as well. Nor does he argue with what the modern world accounts as much philosophical rigor. A clever undergraduate could pull Newman's best theological arguments apart in an afternoon.

If Newman was contemptuous of Coleridge's proof of the existence of God from man's moral sentiments, what are we to make of his own? In its fully elaborated form, Newman's proof can be found in the *Grammar of Assent* of 1870, but its outline is preserved more clearly in Newman's preparatory notes to that essay. He wrote in his notebooks, "All men know what the feeling of a bad or good conscience is, though they may

---

[90]*Idea*, p. 154. "It is ironic," Dwight Culler rightly says of Newman's passage on the gentleman, "that this portrait should be taken as a serious expression of Newman's positive ideal" (*The Imperial Intellect* (New Haven, 1955), p. 238).

differ most widely from each other as to *what* conscience injoins." If the ubiquity of conscience is granted, said Newman, then the existence of God becomes a certainty because "conscience implies a relation between the soul and something exterior, and that moreover, superior to itself." Thus, "there is a God because there is a moral obligation."[91]

But it is by no means certain that all men know the feeling of a bad or a good conscience, unless this feeling is tautologically defined as what all men know. Even granting the universal sensation of conscience, however, it does not follow that moral feelings imply "a relationship between the soul and something exterior." In the first place, the introduction of "soul" at this point begs the question, since it is the existence of the soul Newman was seeking to prove. But assuming that there is a soul, it may be constituted so as to create sensations of good and bad conscience without reference to anything outside itself, either higher or lower. And so the moral sense proves only that some people believe that they have a moral sense. This proof of God is a specimen of Newman's solipsism. Finally, God must exist because "I have a certain feeling on my mind, which I call conscience. When I analyze this, I feel it involves the idea of a Father and a Judge." Newman's defective logic has provided a warehouse of fallacious syllogisms which philosophers have used to train fledgling atheists or to caution aspiring philosophers.[92] Newman's great strength was his ability to dissect liberal arguments according to a standard of logic which he was unable to apply to his own positive theology.

If he failed as a philosopher in the modern tradition, Newman has no claims on our attention as a modern historian either. G. M. Young said that "of historical evidence, as of the methods of historical inquiry, it may be safely affirmed Newman knew nothing." Newman himself freely admitted that he borrowed his history from Gibbon and the Benedictines.[93]

As a poet, he will be remembered by the pious as the author of "Lead,

[91] Adrian J. Boekraad and Henry Tristram, *The Argument from Conscience to the Existence of God According to John Henry Newman* (Louvain, 1961), pp. 112–13. On Newman's "autocentrism," see Henri Brémond, *The Mystery of Newman,* trans. H. C. Corrance (London, 1907), pp. 30–33.

[92] *The Argument from Conscience to the Existence of God,* p. 56. In his demolition of specious philosophical proof for the existence of God, Antony Flew recurs to Newman more often than to any other theist except Aquinas (*God: A Critical Enquiry,* 2d ed. [La Salle, IL, 1984]).

[93] For Young, the history contained in the *Essay on Development* was "a compost of sophistry and superstition" (*Victorian Essays,* p. 152). Thomas S. Bokenkotter, *Cardinal*

Kindly Light'' and ''The Dream of Gerontius.'' Nor is it very flattering to Newman's reputation to suggest that he should be numbered among the Victorian greats because, though lacking in any single distinction or success, his various failures collectively comprise a major career.


## Newman the Prophet of the Second Spring

Newman at any rate was content to accept the apparent failure of his causes in a spirit of submission to the divine will. He would be the first to accept honest defeat rather than victory achieved by the legerdemain of liberal scholarship. What if the Tractarian cause lay in ruins with the infidels in possession of the field? The Vandals had once extinguished Christianity in a whole continent and yet the faith survived. ''He needs no dwelling-place, whose home is the Catholic Church; he fears no barbarian or heretical desolation, whose creed is destined to last unto the end.''[94] Imitating his patience, some of Newman's modern followers have attempted to rescue his message by relocating the triumph of Newmanism from the nineteenth to the twentieth century, or to some century yet to come when the mission that began with the Oxford Movement will bear fruit in the reconciliation of Rome and Canterbury or in the decrees of some future council of the Church in which Newman's theology will become dogma under the inspiration of the Holy Spirit.[95]

Newman himself came to recognize that the Oxford Movement could not effect a reconciliation of the Roman and Anglican positions. When in 1841 he attempted this marriage in his infamous Tract 90, he succeeded only in alienating English churchmen and persuading himself that he

---

Newman as an Historian (Louvain, 1959), provides a very thorough survey of Newman's historical borrowings.

[94] The continent was Africa. ''Its five hundred churches are no more. The voyager gazes on the sullen rocks which line its coast, and discovers no token of Christianity to cheer the gloom.'' *Church of the Fathers, H.S.* 2: 140–41.

[95] The habit of seeking vindication for the Oxford Movement in some future renaissance of the Church Universal began early. After Newman's defection in 1845, his disciple Marriott resolved his confusion with the formula, ''We are in a state of appeal—appeal to a general council.'' When fellow Tractarian David Lewis heard this, he said, ''Didn't Marriott know that an appeal must be lodged within thirty days?'' (Pattison, *Memoirs,* pp. 213–14). Keble also believed that the Church's problems would be solved by an appeal to the next general council; see Coleridge, *A Memoir of the Rev. John Keble,* p. 435.

must ultimately choose between Rome and Canterbury. Newman's partisan zeal could make little sense out of a rapprochement between Anglicanism and Roman Catholicism. He was more at ease when choices presented themselves starkly. As an Anglican, Newman freely denounced the Romans as schismatic. As a Roman Catholic, he reviled the Anglicans as heretics. Keble, whose saintly memory inspired Lord Halifax and the English Church Union in their abortive attempts at rapprochement with Rome, cherished an Anglican independence in which the Church of England was a co-equal branch of Catholicism with its Greek and Roman counterparts. There is no hint in Keble that the trunk should devour the limb.[96] Pusey wrote an eirenicon to reconcile the Catholic and Anglican positions. Newman rightly said of it, "You discharge your olive-branch as if from a catapult." Newman's Oxford Movement brought not peace but a sword. Its followers, who could hardly agree amongst themselves what was orthodox, agreed at least in assuming that truth is too exact, too holy to admit of compromise. Newman the Catholic addresses Pusey the Anglican as one of those "who love you well, but love truth more."[97] Newman as a Catholic was willing to concede that the Church of England was the least objectionable form of heresy available to Englishmen outside the one true faith, but he had no patience with the notion that the Roman Church ought therefore to embrace and support a schismatic communion dead in its sins.

The one player in the Oxford Movement to dabble in the politics of ecclesiastical union—and he is a very minor player—was William Palmer of Magdalen College, who devoted his adult life to establishing the reciprocity of Anglican, Orthodox, and Roman orders. He traveled to Russia and applied to the Metropolitan of Moscow to be admitted to communion in the Orthodox Church, on the ground that the Church of England maintained the same apostolic succession and Catholic dogma as the Eastern communion. This exercise in ecumenism ended when the metropolitan and his synod informed Palmer that the Thirty-Nine Articles contained forty-four heresies.

Another defense of Newman and the movement of 1833 sees their vindication in the gradual enlightenment of contemporary Catholicism. In this view, Newman's theology, silenced in the age of Vatican I, began to find its voice in the teachings of Vatican II. "Through Newman, the

[96] See Keble, *Sermons Academical and Occasional*, p. xlv.
[97] Newman, "Letter to Pusey," *Diff.*, 2: 6–7.

Anglican tradition of Coleridge has become part of the heritage of the Roman Catholic Church itself.''[98] But the modern popes have treated Newman and his ideas with a circumspection that Pius IX would have applauded, and while the Church has acknowledged Father Dominic's credentials for sainthood, it qualifies the memory of his illustrious convert with faint praise. If Newman is a forerunner of the Modernists and Hans Küng, then the Church has already pronounced his doom. If he is orthodox by the standards of Pius IX and John Paul II, then he is no harbinger of a Catholic renaissance. If he is some third thing, then the Church has yet to determine the acceptability of his theological currency, much less sanction its circulation. The teaching that emanates from the Holy See bears little or no trace of Newman's influence.[99]

What remains of Newman's cause? He failed in all his worldly and even intellectual objectives. He was, as he himself acknowledged in the motto he chose for the Library of the Fathers, *vox clamantis in deserto.* But what a voice! Non-partisan critics without any brief to defend Newman the Anglican or Newman the Catholic have located a victory for Newman not in what he said, but in how he said it. If Newman propounded an unheeded theology, he did so in the silver voice of the best Victorian fiction.[100] But Newman, I think, would not have taken much solace from the conclusion that the *Apologia* is one of the great nineteenth-century novels, and the scholarly methods that attempt to sustain Newman's reputation merely on the strength of his brilliant style do so at the risk of turning him into the Sir Thomas Browne of the nineteenth century—grand but empty, all sound and no sense.

[98] Prickett, *Romanticism and Religion,* p. 267, and see *Apo.,* p. xiii, where Martin Svaglic argues that "the Catholic revival in England and especially the second Vatican Council" are Newman's vindication.

[99] In his allocution on the beatification of Father Dominic, Pope Paul VI approved the theology of the Passionist missionary, whose piety had anticipated the decree of papal infallibility. The pope went on to speak of Newman as the convert whose road was "the most toilsome, but also the greatest, the most meaningful, the most conclusive, that human thought ever travelled during the last century." But he implies that the Church prefers the "humble religious" whose books "do not always, alas, reach a high literary standard," to the famous Englishman who "raised so many religious questions" (*Herder Correspondence* 1: 1 [January 1964], 28–30).

[100] George Levine examines "how Newman's history and his beliefs can be seen as relevant to a whole range of problems raised by Victorian cultural history and, for the purposes of this book, to the problem of fiction and Victorian literary failure" (*The Boundaries of Fiction* [Princeton, 1968], p. 174). Here the whole culture of the nineteenth century is implicated in Newman's failure.

## Newman the Modern Athanasius

Newman's failure was comprehensive. It touched every aspect of his life and continues to subvert the defense of his reputation. He might have been an influential scholar, but he rejected the intellectual trends of his time. He might have been a prominent Anglican, but he renounced the Church of his birth. He might have been an important Catholic, but he alienated his adopted coreligionists. After his conversion, he might have enjoyed the friendship of Britain's best minds. Instead, "it was a general wonder how Newman himself could be content with a society of men like Bowles, Coffin, Dalgairns, St. John, Lockhart, and others."[101] Swinburne rightly judged that Newman was not merely out of the mainstream of nineteenth-century life but in monstrous opposition to the whole enterprise of the nineteenth century. In a poem of 1876, Swinburne addressed Newman and Carlyle as the Eumenides of liberal society, two Furies whom modern civilization must appease to overcome: "With all our hearts we praise you whom ye hate," Swinburne writes,

> Go honored home, go home
> Night's childless children; here your hour is done;
> Pass with the stars, and leave us with the sun.

Aeschylus' Athenians were able to mollify the wrath of the Eumenides, but Newman was adamant in his repudiation of the nineteenth century's liberal culture. In 1843, when he had resigned his living and found himself everywhere accused of treachery and error, he drily cited Lucan: "Victrix causa diis placuit, sed victa Catoni" (the victorious cause pleased the gods, but the vanquished one pleased Cato).[102] For another half century he would stoically maintain the lost cause of the old religion in the face of a triumphant liberalism that seemed to please the gods.

It would be easy to find psychological explanations for the apparently self-destructive way in which Newman ruthlessly extracted defeat from every occasion for victory. But psychology is only another manifestation

[101] Pattison, *Memoirs,* pp. 209–10.

[102] Swinburne, "Two Leaders," *Complete Works* (London, 1925–1927; Bonchurch ed.), 3: 99. These lines are Swinburne's free translation of the Athenian chorus in the *Eumenides,* 1032–33. Newman and Carlyle were both alive when Swinburne wrote. There is a sexual slur in Swinburne's epitaph as well: the Greek makes clear that the chorus addresses old women. Lucan, *Pharsalia* 1.128; see *Apo.,* p. 193.

of the liberal spirit against which Newman battled all his life, and it seems only fair to his memory to explain his failure on his own terms, as a failure of his own intellectual and moral choosing.

The magnitude of Newman's failure is the measure of his intellectual achievement. The pitiful paragraph in the *Apologia* that ends the chapter explaining his conversion and recounting his departure from Oxford is instructive: "On the morning of the 23rd I left the Observatory. I have never seen Oxford since, excepting its spires, as they are seen from the railway."[103] Here is Newman the modern Athanasius, an exile and a wanderer for truth who, having given up the comfort of one observatory, continued to be a watcher from afar of the intellectual world he had renounced. Newman prized this distance. Under the spires of Oxford, Newman would have been refined, dazzling, distinguished. On the railway line to Birmingham, Newman was an absurd ecclesiastical vagabond. But from this absurd distance he could see what his brilliant contemporaries beneath the spires could not. It is this distance that makes Newman valuable today, even as it makes him ludicrous.

Newman the modern Athanasius is no mere reactionary—a reactionary after all has to be engaged with the intellectual system against which he reacts. This Newman is a lone voice standing outside the first principles of the whole age. And this is the Newman who belongs in the anthologies: the Newman who is the single unwavering but articulate voice raised against liberalism in all its incarnations, the Newman whose true counterpart in intellectual history is not Carlyle or Arnold so much as Nietzsche or Lenin, the Newman who is invaluable for a description of nineteenth-century thought by his acute refutation of its major premises.

Newman recognized that he opposed a party which constituted, by his own account, "the educated lay world."[104] Today that party comprises very nearly the entire Western world, educated and uneducated, lay and clerical. The victory of everything Newman despised makes his defeated and unfashionable view of Western civilization interesting not merely as a consistent critique of what has come to pass, but as one of the few intelligible alternatives to the ideological monopoly of liberalism. It was Newman's resolute purpose to have nothing in common with the liberals and Romantics who now stand in print on either side of him in the anthologies—small wonder then that his work has come to seem par-

---

[103]*Apo.*, p. 213.
[104]*Apo.*, p. 234.

enthetical in nineteenth-century studies. If Newman still belongs in the anthologies, it would be best to place him either at the very front or the very back of the book by himself in a section called "The Great Dissent."

The modern world will find Newman's great dissent objectionable in substance and obscure in method. There is no help for the substance— Newman did not want the approval of liberals and his candid indictment of them assured that he would not get it. But Newman's hostility to modernism was so pervasive that he chose not even to speak the language of liberalism, on the theory that to adopt an enemy's vocabulary is already to have conceded a major point. Liberalism wants to discuss knowledge; Newman prefers to talk about dogma. Liberalism wants to discuss behavior; Newman prefers to talk about justification. The modern world wants to examine rationality; Newman would rather investigate Socinianism. The very words he chose to discuss modern problems announce his repudiation of liberalism, but at the same time they make his thoughts inaccessible to the great majority of modern readers whose only vocabulary is that of Romanticism or liberalism.

Two heretics in particular stimulated his almost inexhaustible capacity for intellectual outrage, and his dissent from liberalism took shape as a reply to their errors. To understand Newman it is necessary to examine his chief antagonists, Renn Dickson Hampden and Arius of Alexandria.

# 2

# Odium Theologicum:
## *The Liberal as Antichrist*

The pontificate of Pius IX was troubled. Everywhere papal authority was assailed by the forces of liberalism. As the pope's opinion of contemporary society darkened, so did his opinion of converts like Newman. Newman had defected from the Anglican ranks a year before Pius's election. In the pope's eyes, he was fatally tainted by the errors of the modern world he professed to be escaping. At least so Pius's chamberlain, Monsignor Talbot, interpreted the papal mind, and Talbot made it his business to isolate the contagion. He blocked Newman at every turn, thwarting his plans for a Catholic college in Oxford and confining his activities to the backwater of the Birmingham Oratory.[1]

[1] It is hard to believe that any portrait as amusing as Lytton Strachey's of Newman's antagonist Monsignor Talbot could be accurate, but what little evidence there is suggests that Strachey erred on the side of understatement. "Monsignor Talbot's name disappears suddenly and forever—like a stone cast into the waters," Strachey wrote in 1918 (*Eminent Victorians* [London, 1948], p. 112). This certainly is no exaggeration. Talbot is a non-person in Catholic reference works. The longest entry on him anywhere is the telegraphic résumé in the index to Newman's *Letters and Diaries*. Henry Purcell's *Life of Cardinal*

In 1878 Pius IX died. His successor, Leo XIII, had chafed under the paranoia and absolutism of the old regime and was sympathetic to its victims. In 1879 he rehabilitated Newman by raising him to the cardinalate. "It has all come too late," Newman sighed. "I am old and broken." He was seventy-eight. His conversion was thirty years in the past. He had been an old man when he defended himself against Kingsley's slanders fifteen years earlier, and the summa of his intellectual activity, the *Essay in Aid of a Grammar of Assent,* was a decade behind him. For fifty years he had stood against heresy in all its incarnations, and, what was harder, he had defended the truth from the intrigues of Monsignor Talbot, the malice of Cardinal Manning, and the megalomania of Pius IX. The vindication of a red hat came late—perhaps too late—but it came, Newman decided, "in God's good Providence." "The cloud is lifted from me forever," he said, and accepted the unexpected honor.

The frail old man traveled to Rome to receive his reward. There on May 12, in the palace of Cardinal Howard, he received the Vatican's messenger bearing the *biglietto,* the offical notice of his appointment. Looking "ill and faint," he nonetheless insisted on addressing the throng of well-wishers who had gathered for the occasion. "He made a beautiful little address," the Reverend Mr. Wagner of Brighton reported.[2] Exhausted by his celebrity, His Eminence made a slow return to Birmingham. His remaining eleven years there were uneventful.

Had the well-wishers in Cardinal Howard's apartments listened to Newman's "beautiful little address," they would have heard a comprehensive and succinct indictment to liberalism to which Pius IX could have added nothing. "It is an error overspreading, as a snare, the whole earth." It is the "great *apostasia*"—"there never was a device

---

*Manning* (London, 1896) provides the main evidence for his life in the form of his letters to Manning. Like Newman, Talbot was a convert to Catholicism. After a career of clerical intrigue at Rome, he "was unfortunately obliged to exchange his apartment in the Vatican for a private lunatic asylum at Passy," *Eminent Victorians,* p. 74. He flits like a mischievous shadow through the despatches of Odo Russell, Britain's unofficial envoy to Rome between 1858 and 1870. Talbot went mad in 1869 during the preparations for Vatican I. He was discharged sometime before March 1878, when the future Cardinal Vaughan notes receiving a letter from him. Thereafter he disappears. See *The Roman Question: Extracts from the Despatches of Odo Russell* (London, 1962), pp. 131–32, 368, and *Letters of Herbert, Cardinal Vaughan to Lady Herbert of Lea* (London, 1942), p. 297.

[2] *Ward,* 2: 453, 438, 452, 463.

of the Enemy so cleverly framed and with such promise of success."[3]

The Biglietto speech is the culmination of a lifetime's dissent. Its anathemas are plenary, visited on contemporary civilization root and branch. But Newman's vision of universal apostasy had been achieved only after long battle with a host of seemingly unrelated heresies. His general indictment of the modern world emerged from the welter of individual contests with liberalism in which he engaged at Oxford between the time of winning his Oriel fellowship in 1824 and his conversion in 1845.

Oxford provided abundant opportunities for this intellectual combat. In print, Newman confronted two hundred years of Anglican theology, riddled with the errors of Protestant thought. In person, he met daily with the most distinguished contemporary practitioners of this tradition. Many were his colleagues at Oriel—men like Pusey, Keble, Whately, and Hawkins.

Little of this intellectual heritage passed before Newman's mind without a challenge. By the time he was twenty-eight, he had already identified the major types of error in the English tradition. He classified their advocates in an 1829 letter to his mother. They included deists, republicans, utilitarians, schismatics "in and out of the Church," latitudinarians of all descriptions, Baptists, "the high circles in London," and "I might add the political indifferentists, but I do not know enough to speak." As this list suggests, Newman did not distinguish between secular writers like Hobbes, Locke, or Bentham and their clerical counterparts like Tillotson, Hoadly, or Warburton. Whatever their topics or their calling, they were all advocates of a single Anglican culture deeply infected by a "spirit which tends to overthrow doctrine."[4] A faithful rendition of Newman's opinions will use the terms Anglican thought and English philosophy interchangeably.

A few years more study convinced Newman that this spirit of sacrilege pervaded even the most orthodox ranks of the established church. The Evangelicals had sinned by "the profaneness of making a most sacred doctrine"—the Incarnation—"a subject of vehement declamation." The Latitudinarians of the seventeeth and eighteenth century had bequeathed the modern world "a chilling, meagre, uncompassionate,

[3] *Ward*, 2: 460–62.
[4] *L.D.*, 2: 130.

secular divinity indeed.'' The moderate party of Anglican intellectuals who had dominated ecclesiastical politics since the settlement of 1688 were no better. The ''fashionable high Church (so to call it!) divinity of the last century was the divinity of the Revolution''[5]—and Newman was no friend of that revolution. For him, English liberalism had matured in the tolerant atmosphere of seventeenth-century rebellion, and Newman's sympathies were all with the old regime of Charles I and Archbishop Laud. His opinions placed him far to the right of nineteenth-century Tories like Peel—Peel was only a closet liberal in the Latitudinarian tradition. By nineteenth-century standards, Newman was not a Tory at all; he was a Jacobite in the spirit of 1745.

Long before his conversion, Newman had found it almost impossible to discern any coherent pattern of truth in Anglican thought. ''Saving truth lies in a narrow compass,'' he wrote to James Stephen in 1835. The truth was exclusive, and those who were not for the truth were against it. But in the Anglican tradition, truth had been made eclectic. The spirit of free inquiry encouraged a multitude of conflicting opinions that tore apart the fabric of belief and authority. The result was a ''secular divinity,'' which is what English thought had produced in the hands of Locke, Hoadly, Paley, and their intellectual descendants Bentham and John Stuart Mill.[6]

Not surprisingly, in proportion as he rejected the impure tradition of Anglicanism, he became disenchanted with its contemporary exponents. By 1833, Newman doubted ''whether I ought to sit down to table'' with Richard Whately, by then Archbishop of Dublin but a few years earlier Newman's Oriel mentor.[7] Whately was an incarnation of the corrupt Anglican tradition. He might seem orthodox enough to an uncritical observer—he defended the miracles of Scripture, he believed in angels, and he had taught Newman how to use Aristotelian logic in defense of Christian faith. But Whately advocated toleration for dissenters and held ambiguous views on the Trinity. Although these views were well within

---

[5] *L.D.*, 5: 45.

[6] *L.D.*, 5: 45.

[7] *L.D.*, 4: 27. Newman might have had other reasons besides Whately's religious opinions for declining an invitation to eat with him. ''Like Macaulay, he had a healthy appetite, possibly because he had not been playing with it during the day. To provide against the danger incident to those who talk and eat at the same time, when he was to dine at Oriel, a large dish of currie, or calf's head hash, or other soft and comminuted meat was provided'' (Thomas Mozley, *Reminiscences, Chiefly of Oriel College* [London, 1882], 1: 25).

the broad limits of "fashionable high Church divinity," they fell far outside Newman's narrow compass of truth, and Newman kept his distance from his old teacher. When Whately felt Newman's coolness, he wrote a frank and genial letter from Dublin to clear the air: "I, for my part, could not bring myself to find relief in avoiding the society of an old friend, with whom I had been accustomed to frank discussion, on account of my differing from him as to certain principles." Like most moderns, Whately preferred living friendship to abstract doctrine. This spirit of toleration was precisely what made him suspect in Newman's eyes. For Newman, every living act had a doctrinal component. A friendship based on the dissociation of belief and action proposed by Whately was in Newman's eyes dishonest and heretical, and he rejected it when it was offered.[8]

Similar dogmatic difficulties poisoned Newman's relations with the eminent Anglican Edward Hawkins, provost of Oriel, with the editors of the leading Anglican journals, and eventually with nearly all his Anglican associates. If Newman found fault with these, it was only natural that he would react more violently still to the views of those more obviously liberal. For free-thinkers like Thomas Arnold or Blanco White he had nothing but pity or contempt. Arnold would have welcomed dissenters to the established church. Newman wondered whether a man who would allow Baptists to kneel at the communion rail could properly be called a Christian.[9] When Blanco White espoused Unitarianism,

---

[8] Jane Whately, *Life and Correspondence of Richard Whately* (London, 1866), 1: 239–40. It is an easy step from Whately's latitudinarianism to the epicureanism of E. M. Forster's famous epigraph on betraying friend or country. Whately's strong suits were logic and humor, both illustrated in an interview of 1851 with the pious but dim-witted convert, Father Ignatius, youngest brother of Lord Althorp. As the Reverend George Spencer he had been chaplain to Bishop Blomfield of London. Father Ignatius, dressed in his monk's habit and adorned with reliquaries and crucifixes, paid a courtesy call on Archbishop Whately in Dublin.

After the usual salutations had been exchanged, the Archbishop remarked to Mr. Spencer that he had called upon a day of the week when he would be always sure of finding him at home and attended by his chaplains, "for," said his Grace, "these gentlemen are all, my chaplains, though they are not, all my chaplains." "I see," said Mr. Spencer, taking his seat, that you have not forgotten your Logic." "Talking of Logic," said the Archbishop," you know, I suppose, that my work on Logic has been prohibited by the Pope?" (*Life*, 2: 199).

[9] The history of Newman's famous jest is found in *L.D*, 4: 105–8. It original form was "'How are we to know that Dr. Arnold is a Christian?' or words to that effect." Newman

Newman was more charitable—he ascribed his conversion to insanity.[10]

Such dangerous latitudinarians were obviously outside the compass of Newman's theology, but his nominal friends were not spared, either early or late in his career. What Newman called "the Church party"—apostles of high Anglicanism like Joshua Watson and Christopher Wordsworth—he described as "poor in mental endowments." Newman's treatment of Bishop Richard Mant will serve as an example of his dismissive attitude toward churchmen who were supposedly his allies. Mant, an Oriel fellow of an earlier generation, had done battle with the Unitarians while Newman was still a schoolboy. When his *Clergyman's Obligation* appeared in 1830, Newman dismissed it as "a twaddling—so to say— publication."[11] In time, Newman's exclusive dogmatism estranged him from even his two closest Oxford associates, Keble and Pusey. Those who were not for him—the "indifferentists"—were against him, but even those who were for him were found wanting.[12]

So Newman defined himself by separating himself from everyone else, and he formed his opinions by contesting the tainted liberalism he saw around him, even in the purest-minded of his associates. One of these theological contests stands out as being more bitter, more protracted, and therefore more instructive than the others. The combat with Renn Dickson Hampden epitomizes the process by which Newman determined the narrow compass of truth and formed his reply to the heresies of liberalism.

---

improved this in his *Apologia*, p. 42. Despite his public sangfroid in the face of Arnold's umbrage, Newman was vexed to be called to account for a flippant remark he had made while on holiday in Italy. He took his frustration out on Hurrell Froude, who had said much worse about Arnold and gotten away with it. "Only think how mildly I have always spoken of Arnold, and how bitterly you" (*L.D.*, 4: 270).

[10] "It is like a madness–I do not think he is quite right" (*L.D.*, 5: 123). Newman may have been correct. Blanco White's doctor, the distinguished Henry Holland, recorded that White "lived in an atmosphere of doubts and gloomy thoughts" (*Recollections* [New York, 1878], p. 255).

[11] *L.D.*, 2: 130, 185. "Twaddling" was a favorite term of abuse for Newman and Froude, especially as applied to weak-minded high-church figures.

[12] On September 17, 1865, Pusey, Keble, and Newman had a reunion at Keble's vicarage at Hursley. They had not seen each other for twenty years. "They meet round a table, but without a common cause or free outspoken thought; kind indeed, but subdued and antagonistic in their language to each other, and all of them with broken prospects" (*Ward,* 2: 96). This melancholy description is Newman's own.

## Renn Dickson Hampden: The Harbinger of Antichrist

It was Newman's fate always to be harried by some maniacal alter ego, identical in attainments but opposite in belief. Wherever the Catholic Newman might turn, there was Manning like his shadow, casting darkness where Newman had hoped to shed light. Manning played Quilty to Newman's Humbert. These two opposed natures shared a single object of passion: their Lolita was the victory of Catholic truth. They were both Oxford men, both eminent defectors from Anglicanism, and both, to the other's disgust, princes of the Church.

Before Manning was, Hampden had been. From 1830, when Newman was an obscure Oxford don, to 1845, when he made his celebrated conversion, Hampden was Newman's ever-present rival. The contest with Hampden coincided with the development of Newman's exclusive theology. It hardened him in his opposition to all things liberal and compelled him to clarify his own contrary positions. In the course of this great combat, Newman found his polemical style as well as his critical theme. The story of Newman and Hampden is as much a personal as an intellectual drama—it was the essence of Newmanism that belief and action are complementary—and to understand what Hampden thought, it helps to remember what he did—or what Newman thought he did. In these actions Newman found a paradigm of the liberal heresy.

Even his place of birth testified to Hampden's liberalism. He was born in Barbados, the oldest son of a family of political refugees. The Hampdens were descended from the seventeenth-century parliamentary leader John Hampden, who had defied Charles I's exaction of ship money and died in 1643 leading the parliamentary forces in battle against royal absolutism. The family had fled England after the Restoration. The liberal principles for which John Hampden had died were a matter of family honor for his descendants, and Renn Dickson Hampden's daughter records that "from his earliest years, it was a traditionary counsel in the family that no member of it should do anything to disgrace Hampden's great name." Hampden took this counsel to heart. In 1843, while Oxford debated the Tractarian revival of Archbishop Laud's Anglo-Catholicism, he attended the bicentennial commemoration of John Hampden's death in the battle of Chalgrove Field and praised his revolutionary ancestor as "another Miltiades standing on the field of

Marathon." By implication the Royalists and their Tractarian descendants were barbarians.[13]

The battles of the seventeenth century were just as alive in the minds of Newman and his party as they were in Hampden's. Keble hated the memory of John Hampden[14] and Newman was a champion of the lost Stuart cause. In a letter of 1830 to Hurrell Froude praising the *British Critic* for publishing two articles on Laud, Newman doubted "whether we *can* consider our King as *proprietor* of *land* on the old Tory theory—the rightful heir was lost in the Revolution—then the nation took (usurped?) the property of the island—(time has sanctioned their violence)."[15] Just as Newman was the successor of Laud and the nonjuring bishops of the Revolution, Hampden considered the Whig tradition a patrimony to be defended at all costs, and the contest between Newman and Hampden was on both sides a conscious continuation of the seventeenth-century Revolution.

Hampden was raised in England and in 1810 went up to Oxford, where Whately, Keble, Pusey, Hawkins, and Thomas Arnold were his contemporaries or colleagues. He was made fellow of Oriel in 1814, eight years before Newman achieved the same honor; in 1816, the year Newman entered Trinity College, however, Hampden married and gave up his fellowship for a succession of curacies and a home in London.

By 1829, when Hampden returned to Oxford as a public examiner, Newman had yet to write a book, while Hampden had already produced two volumes of theology, *An Essay on the Philosophical Evidence of Christianity* (1827) and *Parochial Sermons Illustrative of the Importance of the Revelation of God in Jesus Christ* (1828). But both these tracts were secured from celebrity or criticism by Hampden's diffuse and overpunctuated style. Meanwhile the bookless Newman had lived at the center of English learning. Newman was a tutor of Oriel and vicar of the university church, Saint Mary's. He was a star pupil of Whately and an intimate of Keble and Pusey. Colleagues and students came to Newman for his charm and grace, while undergraduates remembered Hampden as

[13] Henrietta Hampden, *Some Memorials of R.D. Hampden* (London, 1871), pp. 1, 134.

[14] In 1832 Hurrell Froude suggested to Newman that they begin a quarterly magazine and solicit from Keble an article on John Hampden, "a subject K would take to with zest, as he hates that worthy with much zeal and more knowledge than your humble servant" (*L.D.*, 3: 18).

[15] *L.D.*, 2: 185–86 (Newman's punctuation).

a churlish pedant, "not so much repulsive as utterly unattractive," who could "make one thing as dull as another."[16]

Newman and Hampden did not always hate each other. Between 1829 and 1831, they maintained something like cordial relations. In these years Hampden lost two infant daughters. Newman buried them both at Saint Mary's, and Mrs. Hampden always remembered the vicar's "remarkable power of giving expression to the grand words of the burial service."[17] In the first three years after Hampden's return to Oxford, he and Newman were often together, but it must have been the older man who was flattered when the eloquent young tutor joined him in the Oriel common room. Newman recognized Hampden for a liberal—was he not one of that reforming crowd that would "exclude Aristotle and bring in modern subjects?"—but he hardly distinguished him from a dozen such men with whom he maintained civil relations, and Newman's diary records frequent dinners with Hampden.[18]

But whatever amicability existed between the two ended in the spring of 1832 when the university selected Hampden to deliver the annual series of eight Bampton lectures, meant as Oxford's contribution in the battle "to confirm and establish the Christian faith, and to confute all heretics and schismatics." Hampden chose an esoteric topic: "The Scholastic Philosophy Considered in Its Relation to Christian Theology." Thomas Mozley, Newman's pupil and later a high-church clergyman and editorial writer for the *Times,* claimed that few people returned after Hampden's first stultifying address on dogma and scholasticism, but one lecture sufficed for an attentive listener alert for heresy, and the latter part of this chapter will discuss how the errors latent in Hampden's early work were to Newman's mind fully developed in these lectures of 1832.

[16] Mozley, *Reminiscences,* 1: 380.

[17] *Some Memorials,* p. 22.

[18] *L.D.,* 2: 186. Newman's identification of Hampden as an enemy of Aristotle is revealing. Hampden was arguably the most distinguished student of Aristotle at Oxford, and his article on Aristotle in his *Fathers of Greek Philosophy* (1862) is an homage to his Greek master. Newman was alarmed not that the reformers would ignore Aristotle, but that they would take him seriously enough to institute an Aristotelian program of curricular reform stressing science over theology. According to Mark Pattison, this was in fact what happened in the university reforms of the 1850s. Oxford's "scientific period" began with "a survey of the whole Aristotelian system"—that is, a reading of Artistotle beyond the logical books to which Newman would have confined Aristotle's influence. *Essays* (Oxford, 1889), 1: 465.

Newman sat through Hampden's first Bampton lecture in horror.[19] What
had been obscure or unread in the *Philosophical Evidence* was here
broadcast to the Oxford community as scholarship with the imprimatur of
the university. Now Newman saw Hampden for what he was—the
harbinger of Antichrist.[20] In June of 1832 when Provost Hawkins invited
Newman to join him and Hampden for dinner, Newman pointedly
declined. A decade of theological warfare ensued.

Their disagreement was more bitter for their similarities. Both were
Oriel men. Both were expert in Aristotelian logic. Both regarded Bishop
Butler's *Analogy of Religion* as the bulwark of true religion. Both were
students of the first Christian era. Both were obsessed by dogma. Their
early bibliographies might be the work of twins, each concerned to
establish Christianity on a solid foundation of credible evidence.

Their intellectual similarities naturally led to professional rivalry. In
1833, while Newman was making his reputation as editor of the Tracts,
Hampden became principal of Saint Mary Hall and set about reforming
the curriculum in just the way Newman had predicted he would. In the
same year, the term of the professor of moral philosophy was about to
expire. Newman was not without ambition. "As to my scheme," he
wrote Froude in September, "it is a purely selfish one. If you burn this, I
will tell you. I suppose the Moral Philosophy professorship falls next
Spring. Don't you think I would make a good Professor?" As the election
neared, Newman's hopes rose. He thought he had "a fair chance."

On March 7, 1834, the electors chose Hampden instead. "I give you
without delay intelligence of an important event," Newman wrote to
Henry Wilberforce three days later, "viz. my having been floored as
regards the Professorship—*triakteros oichomomai tuchon*—in the person

---

[19] "It was the delivery of his Bampton Lectures in 1832 which caused my dislike of
him. . . . I protested against his FIRST Lecture to Isaac Williams, as I came out of Church
on hearing it, as I. W. afterwards reminded me"—a clarification written by Newman in
1850 (*L.D.*, 2: 250). See also *L.D.*, 2: 222, 3: 58.

[20] It was four more years before Newman called Hampden *prodromos Antichristou* in a
letter to Thomas Mozley (*L.D.*, 5: 210), but he treated Hampden in this spirit from the time
of the first Bampton lecture. Newman picked up the phrase "forerunner of Antichrist" from
Cyril of Jerusalem's catechumenal addresses, delivered in 348 at the height of the Arian
controversy. Hampden was a type of Antichrist, as Arius or Julian the Apostate had been
before him. In 1835, Newman expatiated on the character and coming of the Antichrist in
four lectures, "The Patristical Idea of Antichrist." He refers to Cyril's language explicitly
in *D.A.*, p. 58. The conflict with Hampden only intensified the apocalyptic frenzy of these
lectures.

of the Principal of St. Mary Hall.''[21] The quotation, adapted from the
Agamemnon, contains a bitter jest. Aeschylus' chorus descibes how
Kronos, having toppled Uranos, in turn "chanced upon a trivictorious
contestant and departed.'' Aeschylus had compared Kronos to a wrestler
overthrown by a rival who wins three falls in the ring. Newman altered
the original to identify himself with the vanquished Titan. In his mind,
the struggle with Hampden was explicitly a classical *agon*—a wrestling
contest as well as a titanic tragedy. Hampden had won the first fall. In his
Bampton lectures, Hampden insulted God and Newman snubbed Hampden. But by winning the professorship of moral philosophy, the heretic
had insulted Newman, and sterner measures were demanded. Newman
waited for his occasion. It came soon enough.

In 1834, the university was debating whether to relax its rule that all
students must subscribe to the Thirty-Nine Articles of the established
church, a regulation that closed Oxford to dissenters. Four months after
winning the moral professorship, Hampden joined the controversy on the
side of toleration. "Is there not room left for debate in our present terms
of communion?'' he asked in his pamphlet, *Observations on Religious
Dissent*.[22] Newman thought Hampden's *Observations* went so far beyond the narrow compass of truth that he could now enlist the support of
even the most twaddling Oxford churchmen against Hampden's overt
heterodoxy. He sent Hampden a letter which he later called "the
beginning of hostilities in the University'': "While I respect the tone of
piety which the pamphlet displays,'' he wrote his rival, "I dare not trust
myself to put on paper my feelings about the principles contained in it,
tending as they do in my opinion altogether to make shipwreck of
Christian faith.''[23]

Hampden checked his temper and made a civil reply to Newman's
letter, but he had the militant spirit of his revolutionary ancestors, and
only one additional provocation was necessary to bring him on to the field
of theological battle where Newman wanted him. The provocation came
in the spring of 1835 and took the form of a collection of pamphlets on the
subscription question edited by Newman. His unsigned preface alleged
that the professor of moral philosophy was a Socinian heretic who cared
no more for the Trinity than a Unitarian. "Socinian'' was one of the most
dreadful epithets in Newman's vocabulary. It implicated the offender in

[21] *L.D.*, 4: 40; 4: 188, 4: 201. The quotation is from the *Agamemnon*, 171–72.
[22] *Dissent*, p. 35.
[23] *L.D.*, 4: 371.

all the crimes of skepticism and dissent, and Hampden understood the gravity of Newman's accusation perfectly. He had no trouble unmasking the author of the preface and proceeded to write his antagonist just the kind of furious response Newman had hoped to elicit:

> Sir,
>
> I have ascertained to my great disgust that you are the Editor of a Collection of Pamphlets professing to be on the Matriculation-Question just put forth, and the Author of some remarks prefaced to them. . . . I charge you with dissimulation, because you have concealed your name in the background. . . . I charge you with falsehood, because you have sent out to the public what you know to be untrue. . . . I charge you with malignity, because you have no other ground for your assault on me but a fanatical persecuting spirit.[24]

In deference to Hampden's outrage, Newman omitted the offending accusation from a second edition of the pamphlets. He could afford this concession, having already accomplished his mission by making Hampden lose his composure. It would be easier in the coming battles to defeat a hysterical opponent, and Newman wrote Froude, "We have had a triumph over Hampden."

To Hampden himself Newman replied with glacial indignation: "Mr. Newman observes, in answer to the Principal of St Mary Hall's letter received yesterday, that he cannot enter at length into the details of it without doing violence to his own feelings of self respect."[25] So Newman maneuvered for psychological advantage in preparation for the final, apocalyptic confrontation with the harbinger of Antichrist.

Once again Providence supplied the occasion. On January 19, 1836, Edward Burton, the regius professor of divinity, died unexpectedly at the age of forty-two. By January 23, the rumor had spread through Oxford that Hampden would be appointed to the vacancy. The regius professorship of divinity was the most estimable prize in the academic hierarchy of early nineteenth-century Oxford. It was wholly in the gift of the Crown—in reality, of the deistical prime minister, Lord Melbourne. It paid well and, since a license from the regius professor of divinity was a common prerequisite for clerical employment, it was a position of power and influence in a university whose main business was to provide clergymen for the Church of England. Burton had been ideal for the job. He was

[24]*L.D.*, 5: 81.
[25]*L.D.*, 5: 89; 5: 83–84.

devout and scholarly and belonged to the conservative Anglican tradition of the seventeenth-century divine, Bishop Bull. Like Bull, he wrote to defend the dogmatic truth of the Trinity against Socinians ancient and modern. The prospect of the uncouth and unorthodox Hampden as Burton's successor made the Tractarians desperate with rage.[26] On February 10, they met in the Christ Church common room and formed a committee of resistance to Hampden's appointment. They raised money. They sent a petition with seventy-three signatures to King William IV. They enlisted the eloquent Pusey to put their case before Lord Melbourne. They petitioned the Heads of Houses, the universtiy's executive committee, to initiate an inquiry into Hampden's anti-Trinitarian opinions.

One task remained. Someone had to draw up a bill of particulars against Hampden, a task that would require navigating the "palpable obscure" of the enemy's prose. As "prime of those heaven-warring champions," Newman volunteered for the assignment. Following the meeting of the committee for resistance, he spent the whole night writing his *Elucidations of Dr. Hampden's Theological Statements,* a fifty-page syllabus of errors culled from the pages of Hampden's published works. In the coming struggle, moderates were more likely to read the fifty pages of Newman's digest than the thousand pages of Hampden's theology, and so the *Elucidations* proved crucial in persuading undecided opinion that Hampden was in fact a heretic.

Hampden was not idle in this crisis. He was, after all, born from warrior stock. When the Heads of Houses met on February 11 to discuss his opinions, he attended in his capacity as principal of Saint Mary Hall. " 'Strange,' said the Dean of Christ Church, 'very strange that *you* should be here, Mr. Principal: we have met to talk about you. Do you mean to stay?' 'I do,' was the reply."[27] The motion to examine Hampden for heresy failed on this occasion by a single vote—Hampden's own.

Meanwhile, William IV had been disturbed by the petition he received

---

[26] Typically, while Tractarians publicly hailed Burton as a model high churchman, Newman was privately ironic. "His pamphlet on the five points, (baptism, marriages, church yards, universities, and church rates) is very good, but he gave up church rates, on the ground that 'what is thought a grievance, is a grievance.' Some one told him how much this part of the pamphlet was objected to; to which he replied—'Oh is it? indeed? then I will leave it out of the 2nd Edition—I am very sorry—I had no notion' etc etc." (*L.D.,* 4: 271). In other words, Burton suffered from the twaddling disease rampant among high-church types.

[27] Henry Lewis Thompson, *Memoirs of Dean Liddell* (London, 1900), p. 33.

from the holy men of Oxford. Lord Melbourne, however, was unmoved. He told the king that to abandon the appointment would insult the blameless Hampden, diminish the royal prerogative, and subvert the principle of toleration. "Viscount Melbourne has some practical knowledge of universities," he explained to his monarch in a letter of February 15, "and in his opinion there is in those bodies as much bitterness, as much faction, as much violence, as much prejudice, as there ever was in any public assembly." Melbourne had two additional reasons to stick with his nominee. Hampden was one of the few Whigs at Oxford and Melbourne had read enough of his work to know that they shared the liberal principles of the Glorious Revolution. In addition, Melbourne was honor-bound to do something for Hampden. In October of 1835 he had asked Whately, Hampden's one-time Oriel colleague, to see if Hampden would accept a poorly paid bishopric. "To an ambition of this kind, I must plead guilty," Hampden had replied. Melbourne was pledged to do something to satisfy this ambition, and the necessity of filling the regius professorship—a prize the ambitious cleric might covet more than the possession of an obscure see—coincided with an outstanding obligation. But Melbourne was not completely honest when he portrayed Hampden to the king as blameless: It was Hampden in his glee who leaked word of his impending appointment and so caused all the trouble.[28]

On February 17, Hampden's appointment to the professorship was officially announced in the *London Gazette*. But his opponents refused to yield. There were more Tories than Whigs at Oxford, and now they made their numbers felt. The regius professor of divinity had several *ex officio* duties within the Oxford community. He sat on the board that elected the university's select preachers, and he advised the vice-chancellor in disputes about religious orthodoxy. If his enemies could not deny him his office, they could try to make it worthless to occupy. In March, they moved to strip Hampden of his *ex officio* functions. They persuaded the Heads of Houses to bring a motion to this effect before Convocation, the legislative assembly of the university made up of all professors and most degree holders. The M.A.'s would make the difference at such a conclave, and the Tractarians meant to import hordes of disgruntled old Oxonians to register their hostility to Hampden's opinions.

At this moment, the prosecution of Hampden took on a special urgency

---

[28] *Lord Melbourne's Papers,* ed. Lloyd C. Sanders (London, 1889), pp. 497–98; Hampden, *Some Memorials,* pp. 45–46.

in Newman's mind. The rise of the heretic Hampden coincided with the decline of his friend and confidant Froude. News of Hampden's appointment to the regius professorship and Froude's impending death from consumption reached Oriel within twenty-four hours of each other in February of 1836. While he lived, Froude had incited Newman's tendencies to intrigue and malevolence. In his letters to Froude, Newman held nothing back. Here only he freely expressed his ambitions, his fears, his hatreds, and his passions. "No one is there else in the whole world but he whom I could look forward to as a contabernalis for my whole life," Newman wrote Samuel Rickards the day he learned of Froude's death.[29] It was natural that he should associate Hampden with the sinister forces that had snatched his tentmate from him at the height of battle, and Newman now fought his rival with the fury of Achilles avenging Patroclos. The trial of Hampden became the funeral games for Froude. Within days of Froude's death, Newman was working to assure that the forthcoming meeting of Convocation would be packed with Hampden's enemies. "We are going to bring men from the Country," Newman wrote to Robert Wilberforce on March 15.

A week later Convocation met with some 450 members present—a huge turnout for an assembly so obsolescent that all its business was still conducted in Latin. As it happened, another bit of medievalism defeated the Tractarians on this occasion. Two proctors, elected annually, supervised all meetings of Convocation. They retained the immemorial right of vetoing any motion brought to the floor. After the anti-Hampden statute of disabilities had been approved by the assembly, the two proctors rose "and uttered, or seemed to utter (for the noise was too great for them to be heard), words which had been unknown in Congregation House for centuries—'Nobis Procuratoribus non placet.' "[30]

The meeting of Convocation had attracted a host of country clergymen to Oxford. A mere handful had come to support Hampden. At Rugby, Hampden's friend Thomas Arnold gave the liberal young Oxonians on

---

[29]*L.D.*, 5: 247. *L.D.* gives the spelling *contabernalis*—this is either Newman's exotic variant on *contubernalis* or a faulty transcription of Newman's hand. Newman wrote to Froude in 1834 on the strategy of Tractarianism: "At present however men are *sore;* therefore, having established a raw, our game is to keep it from healing. I am projecting then a pamphlet, not for any specific measure, but generally on Church grievances, to *irritate*, and shall (if so) write it as rhetorically and vehemently as I can" (*L.D.*, 4:270). This could be Trotsky or Lenin. The death of Froude closed forever Newman's one avenue of unreserved candor. All the rest was discretion and irony.

[30]*L.D.*, 5: 260; *Some Memorials*, p. 67.

his staff a holiday to join this freethinking minority, among them Algernon Grenfell. While in Oxford, he ran into his old friend and teacher Keble. He crossed the street with hand extended to greet his mentor but was rebuffed. "Grenfell! You have sacrificed at the altar of Jupiter, and I renounce your friendship from this day," Keble thundered. The proctors' veto had only hardened the Tractarians' resistance.[31]

But when the proctors' term of office expired later in April, Hampden's enemies had no trouble securing the election of more cooperative men. By May, with a new set of proctors in place, Convocation met and passed the statute of disabilities, 474 votes to 94. It did Hampden little real harm. His appointment to the professorship was untouched. In practice, his privileges were virtually undiminished. Many bishops continued to refuse jobs to Oxford clergymen without a certificate of fitness from the regius professor of divinity, and by 1842, the Heads of Houses had appointed Hampden as the chairman of a theological board of examiners, a virtual repeal of their former condemnation.

Besides, if Hampden lacked charm, he could rely on his own tenacity and the eloquence of his liberal supporters. Between the two convocations of 1836, Arnold dubbed Hampden's enemies "the Oxford conspirators" in the pages of the *Edinburgh Review*. Privately he called Newman and his party "idolators." From Dublin, Whately interposed himself between Hampden and the "furious bigots" in letters to Lord Melbourne, and the readers of London's liberal evening paper, the *Globe*, would have read of the first Oxford convocation in an account by the economist Nassau Senior, which began, "Oxford today has exhibited the appearance of a Spanish town at an auto-da-fé, with this difference, that the visitors who crowded to it from the rural districts came in the hopes not only of enjoying the triumph of Holy Church over a heretic, but of actually contributing to his suffering."[32]

Hampden himself took legal advice and was assured he could overturn the convocation's statute in court. He chose not to sue, but he did not

[31] See Francis Newman, *Contributions Chiefly to the Early History of Cardinal Newman* (London, 1891), p. 81—usually an unreliable source, but here perhaps acceptable because not directly about his brother.

[32] Stanley, *Life and Correspondence of Thomas Arnold*, 5th ed. (London, 1845), 2: 42; Hampden, *Some Memorials*, p. 66; Whately, *Life*, 2: 355; "The Oxford Malignants," *Edinburgh Review* 63 (April, 1836), p. 235. The title—not Arnold's but the contribution of the editor, Macvey Napier—is another proof how the seventeenth-century background constantly intruded into Victorian theology: Charles I's most loyal supporters had been dubbed the Oxford Malignants by the revolutionaries.

hesitate to exact other retribution from the Tractarians. In spite of his self-proclaimed toleration, Hampden could be as petty as his opponents, and he attacked Newman through his less-talented disciples. When one of these, the Reverend Richard Macmullen, was required as a condition of his Corpus Christi fellowship to defend the orthodoxy of some proposition given him by the regius professor of divinity, Hampden compelled him to argue for the exclusive authority of Scripture and against the doctrine of transubstantiation—in Tractarian theory the two most objectionable articles of Anglican belief. Macmullen acquiesced only after protracted litigation.[33]

## The Heretic as Bishop

The Hampden controversy flared up twice after 1836. In 1842 the Heads of Houses proposed that Convocation lift Hampden's disabilities and admit him to the privileges revoked in 1836. Once again both sides summoned their followers from the countryside. The prohibition was retained by 334 votes to 219. In spite of this renewed insult, Hampden's life seemed settled. He lectured. He examined candidates for divinity degrees. He gardened or played with the family's pet magpie at the rectory at Ewelme, the living that accompanied the regius professorship. And then Lord John Russell became premier and in 1847 nominated Hampden to the see of Hereford.

There was no apparent reason for Russell to make such a divisive appointment. Hampden expected nothing. There were other competent churchmen of liberal sympathies who could have filled the bishopric of Hereford without provoking the storm of protest that inevitably came with Hampden's nomination. But Hampden had one qualification that made him irresistible to the new prime minister. Russell was a historian and the biographer of his illustrious Whig forebear, Lord William Russell, executed in 1683 for his alleged participation in the Rye House Plot against Charles II. Arrested with Lord William was John Hampden,

[33] Walter Walsh, *History of the Romeward Movement in the Church of England* (London, 1900), p. 65–66. Walsh's is a biased and amusing account of the whole Tractarian movement, with special attention to its most ridiculous moments. Walsh's dates are often wrong. Macmullen went on to join the Puseyite clergy as Saint Saviour's, Leeds, and thence to Rome.

one of Russell's most loyal supporters and grandson of the parliamentary martyr who had died on Chalgrove Field. A century and a half later, the party of liberty was at last triumphant in the person of Lord John Russell, and what was more natural than that a latter-day Russell should repay a family debt of honor and support a latter-day Hampden? If they suffered the calumnies of Tories and the slander of religious bigots, what was that to men whose ancestors had died for freedom on the scaffold or the battlefield? It appealed to Russell to recreate, and then to rectify, the political catastrophes of the late seventeenth century.[34]

Precisely because it was a reenactment of his forefather's political struggles, Russell took vindictive pleasure in the commotion occasioned by Hampden's appointment. William Howley, the archbishop of Canterbury, complained of the "explosion" Hampden's nomination would cause in the Church. Russell responded as if he were addressing Laud, not Howley, haranguing the archbishop about "Confessions, and Rosaries, and Articles taken in a non-natural sense, and monkish legends of saints." Thirteen bishops remonstrated against the appointment. Russell answered that he would not give royalist Oxford a veto over "the supremacy, which is now by law vested in the Crown"—by which he meant the Parliament as embodied in himself.[35]

In the face of this liberal onslaught, Hampden's enemies fell back on the intricacies of ecclesiastical law. A bishop might be nominated by the monarch, but he also had to be elected by the diocesan chapter of his prospective see. Although no chapter since the Reformation had failed to ratify the royal nominee, the dean of Hereford, a high churchman and no friend of Hampden, took a literal view of the election process and

[34] "He never forgot that Lord William Russell, who was the founder of the family greatness and whose life he wrote, had died on the scaffold for conspiring against Charles II; for the sake of his ancestor, Russell, too, had to be on the side of radicals and rebels" (A. J. P. Taylor, *Essays in English History* [New York, 1976], p. 69). Lord John had written a history of the Reformation and the Revolution, and he may have remembered that the bishop of Hereford appointed by Charles II, Herbert Croft, had like Hampden been savaged for his Latitudinarian views. "Nothing hath caused more mischiefe in the Church, then the establishing new and many Articles of faith, and requiring men to assent to them, with divine faith," Croft wrote in his treatise, *The Naked Truth* (1675). Croft's sentiments were echoed 160 years later by Hampden in his *Observations on Religious Dissent*. By the appointment of Hampden, Lord John recreated seventeeth-century history down to the most minute detail of theological controversy.

[35] Spencer Walpole, *Life of Lord John Russell* (London, 1891), 1: 494–95.

vowed in a letter to Russell that "no earthly consideration shall induce me to give my vote in the Chapter of Hereford Cathedral for Dr. Hampden's elevation to the see of Hereford." Russell replied, "Sir—I have had the honour to receive your letter of the 22nd inst., in which you intimate to me your intention of violating the law."[36] It is the kind of letter a man waits a lifetime to write, and Hampden's appointment offered the happy occasion for Russell's bravado. The prime minister knew his English law better than the dean: failure to elect Hampden would subject the dean and the chapter of Hereford to the terrible penalties of the ancient statute of Praemunire, under which anyone guilty of derogating from the royal prerogative of ecclesiastical appointment was subject to loss of civil rights, forfeiture of property, and imprisonment at the royal (or in this case, the prime ministerial) pleasure. It was 1683 all over again for Russell—he was fighting against Rome and superstition, for liberty and law. So the appointment of a Victorian bishop was staged as a revival of seventeenth-century politics and enforced by the terrors of a medieval statute.

In the end, the chapter of Hereford cathedral elected Hampden by a vote of fifteen to two, but still the Oxford opposition would not relent. Two additional formalities stood between Hampden and his see and the Tractarians made the most of them. The election of a bishop had to be confirmed in the Court of Arches, the archbishop of Canterbury's ecclesiastical court at Bow Church, London. Keble and Pusey spared no expense to contest the validity of Hampden's election. Acting through surrogates, they spent some two thousand pounds on a host of lawyers, who on January 11, 1848, appeared at the Bow Church to oppose Hampden. It was the first substantial challenge to an episcopal candidate since the reign of James I, but the archbishop's vicar general refused to hear the objectors and proceeded to certify Hampden's election.[37]

Still Hampden's enemies persisted. Hampden would not officially be-

[36] Walpole, *Russell*, 1: 480; Walsh, *Romeward*, p. 79. Even the Tractarians' litigious attorney Badeley was afraid of the statute of Praemunire. See Henry Liddon, *Life of E. B. Pusey*, 4th ed. (London, 1898), 3: 160–61.

[37] On January 8, 1848, three days before Hampden's appearance at the Bow Church, Gutteridge, a Birmingham surgeon, had attempted to object to the election of James Prince Lee as bishop of Manchester. Not being represented by counsel nor resident in the bishop's diocese, he was summarily dismissed. A complete record of the litigation surrounding Hampden's appointment is preserved in Richard Jebb, *Report of the Case of the Right Reverend R. D. Hampden* (London, 1849). For the legal costs of the Hampden affair, see Liddon, *Life of Pusey*, 3: 161.

come a bishop until consecrated by his metropolitan, the archbishop of Canterbury. The Tractarians sought to forestall this sacred formality by petitioning the Court of Queen's Bench for a writ of mandamus ordering the archbishop to reopen the confirmation hearing and entertain charges of heresy against Hampden. They seemed to have a point. The confirmation process required the vicar general to summon any opposers, but having summoned them, he had ignored their accusation.

The case was argued for three days before four judges by eleven lawyers. Hampden prevailed once again. The Tractarians had little chance of success in the court of Queen's Bench, where they had to argue their case before the chief justice, Lord Denman, a Cambridge man who had defended the Luddites in 1812 and Queen Caroline in 1820. He was as firm a believer as Russell in the state's supremacy over the Church. On this occasion, his liberal convictions took the form of judicial witticisms at the expense of Oxford Anglicanism. The power to make a bishop lay wholly in the Crown, he said, and the election, confirmation, and consecration were "going through a form, and acting a farce." If the clerical actors in this farce were thereby exposed to mockery, Lord Denman reminded them "of the Roman augurs, who were said never to meet one another without laughing." If the accusation process were more than a formality, why had it never before been used? Had there been no unsound nominees before Hampden? "Was envy dead, was faction banished from the world? Where were the sons of Belial at that time?" The non-appearance of opposers, he suggested, "is as much a part of the proceeding as any other part of it." Denman saved his most poignant sarcasm for his last. He suggested that if the archbishop could not in good faith consecrate Hampden, then he must behave like any other conscientious civil servant and resign.[38]

Archbishop Howley did better than that. He died, thereby delaying Hampden's consecration yet again. But in a few weeks Russell had appointed the low-church John Bird Sumner as archbishop and on March 26 at Lambeth Palace Renn Dickson Hampden received his rochet and chimere as bishop of Hereford.

In December of 1847, when news of Hampden's election by the chapter of Hereford reached Woburn Abbey during the Russells' Christmas festivities, Lord John was "radiant with satisfaction." Hampden's cause had aroused all Russell's Whig zeal. Hampden briefly

[38] Jebb, *Case of Hampden,* pp. 482–96.

became a symbol of Protestant liberties for both the classes and the masses. When Hampden stepped out of the Bow Church after his contentious confirmation hearing, he was greeted by a crowd of cheering cockneys.[39] But Hampden's appointment was not the only popular cause of 1848. Between the time of Hampden's nomination and his consecration, Louis Philippe abdicated in France, Metternich fell in Vienna, and revolutions swept Europe. About the time Lord Denman was handing down his satiric judgment in the matter of Hampden, Karl Marx was dropping the manuscript of the *Communist Manifesto* into a mailbox in Brussels, destined for London. In the seventeenth century the victory of Hampden and Russell would have been a milestone on the road of political progress. By 1848, Hampden's installation already seemed ludicrously irrelevant. The Tractarians' opposition to Hampden's liberalism was a medieval reaction to seventeenth-century revolutionary ideals that in their moment of triumph were already assailed by the specter of nineteenth-century socialism.

What did the Hampden affair mean to the participants of 1848? To Russell it was an occasion to revenge the ancient wrongs done to family and party. For Hampden it meant vindication, for both himself and his latitudinarian principles. For Marx, if he had deigned to notice it, the Hampden affair would have been one more symptom of the exhaustion of bourgeois society. The forces that had once beheaded a monarch and conquered an empire now frittered away their ideological capital in ecclesiastical inanities. Here was proof that the age of capital was spent, the age of labor beginning. The modern observer is liable to agree with the Marxist position, at least to the extent of finding the Hampden affair silly.

And Newman? For Newman, the Hampden affair was neither an end nor a beginning but only a further manifestation of the defective idea pervading Western culture. The latitudianarian spirit that carried Hampden to Hereford and the socialist upheaval that toppled Louis Philippe were for him developments of a single doctrinal mutation. The expression of this heresy was liberalism, and its root was an aberrant notion of the Trinity almost as old as Christendom. Hampden became a bishop and Louis Philippe an exile because the world had denied the Catholic dogma of the Trinity. In Newman's view, Hampden's election was a symptom of

---

[39] Frances Bunsen, *A Memoir of Baron Bunsen* (London, 1868), 2: 155; *Some Memorials,* p. 156n.

liberalism rampant. Liberalism was the social expression of Socinianism, and Socinianism was only a mutation of the Arian heresy. The world is only as good as its beliefs, and the beliefs of the modern world are heretical.

Nothing seems more peculiar about Newman than this insistence that action can be explained by reference to dogma. But this peculiarity is what distinguishes Newman's thought and makes it worth studying. This view, so alien to the conventions of modern thought, deserves a respectful hearing, not only because it is the basis of Newman's indictment of modernity, but because it presents the most determined defense of the primacy of belief yet devised.

The Hampden case provides a means of gauging the scope of Newman's theory of belief. What in Newman's mind was the liberalism that Hampden represented? How was it related to the religious movement called Socinianism? What connection did either have with the theology of a fourth-century Alexandrian heretic? Assuming that the connections exist, is it not a large order to believe that ideas so ancient and obscure should in any way be connected with the ordinary practices of modern life? In this view, what is the relation between belief and action? In short, how do we draw the narrow compass of truth? To understand Hampden's heresy and the Arianism out of which Newman believed it grew is to see how Newman formed the standards of truth by which he condemned the modern world.

## Hampden's Heresy

Newman and Hampden owed their celebrity to each other. Outside Oxford, people noticed Newman because he opposed Hampden and Hampden because Newman opposed him. Their long struggle ended in a moment of notoriety for each—for Newman at his conversion in 1845; for Hampden at his appointment in 1847. After the moment passed, each receded from public consciousness and pursued his new religious duties at Birmingham or Hereford.

The parallelism of their careers is matched by the symmetry of their thought. In part, this was predictable: they started with the same teachers and the same texts. But even allowing for similar backgrounds, the counterpoint of their intellectual development is remarkable.

Each enjoyed controversy and formed his opinions best in opposition. The articles each wrote in the 1820s and 1830s for the *Encyclopedia Metropolitana* were often incursions into what ought to have been the other's territory. The scholastic Newman wrote about the humanist Cicero; the humanist Hampden wrote about the scholastic Aquinas. In 1832 Newman prepared a book on the Arian heresy, which he abominated; at the same time, Hampden was preparing his Bampton lectures on scholasticism, which he despised. The 1830s find Newman and Hampden working along such similar lines that each seems to write in response, or even in anticipation, of the other. In his lectures as professor of moral philosophy, Hampden proposed an instinctual theory of ethics; Newman countered with a dogmatic reply in his *Lectures on Justification*. Newman's University Sermons and his *Lectures of the Prophetical Office of the Church* refute a line of nominalist thought developed by Hampden in his Bampton lectures. Hampden refuted Newman's refutations in his "Lecture on Tradition" of 1839. Each read the other's work carefully— we have Newman's *Elucidations of Dr. Hampden's Theological Statements,* the fifty-page critique of the professor's whole opus produced in a single night, and Hampden's "Lecture on Tradition" is explicitly an attack on Newmanism, while his other works are implicitly so. It was natural for each to see in the other a model of intellectual evil. In the eyes of each, the other confounded truth.

After 1836, Newman relinquished his leading role in the persecution of Hampden. His sudden indifference arose in equal parts from personality, policy, and principle. In spite of Newman's determined opposition, Hampden had become regius professor. Newman was comfortable, even pleased with this setback, since he had seen all along that his party had more to gain from defeat than victory. "The Ministry will be at open war with the Church," he prophesied with grim satisfaction after Hampden's elevation to the chair of divinity. "The Archbishop will be roused, and large numbers of waverers in this place will be thrown into our hands."[40] This is an early example of Newman consciously preferring failure to success. It would be easier to define his own opinions in rebuttal to those of a triumphant heretic.

Strategy also dictated that Newman not pursue Hampden further. By

[40] *L.D.*, 5: 237. Even Ker has to admit that Newman, having to choose between success or failure in the Hampden affair, "inclined to the latter alternative" (Ker, p. 126). Elsewhere, Ker's narrative is careful to disguise Newman's almost pathological detestation of Hampden.

the time the reconsideration of Hampden's disabilities came up in 1842, Newman had become the victim of the same inquisitorial machinery that he had earlier employed against his rival. In Tract 90 Newman had asserted the congruity of Anglican and Roman Catholic doctrine and now it was Newman whose orthodoxy was debated by the Heads of Houses. "It did not become me, being myself under Hebdomadal censure, to take a forward part now against Hampden,"[41] he wrote to Keble in 1842. And if in 1836 the death of Froude had made Newman ferocious, like Achilles he became in time magnanimous through grief. He saw that his objection to Hampden was not so much personal as cosmic. In such a fundamental confrontation of views, continued debate was pointless. Already Newman had begun to stand outside the field of combat where Hampden and Russell, Howley and Pusey contended. Hampden the man gradually ceased to matter, and increasingly it was Hampden's ideas against which Newman exclusively directed his attack.

These attacks did not stop Hampden's ascent from the professorship of moral philosophy to the ranks of the Anglican episcopate. But Newman did succeed in reducing Hampden's ideas to theological slogans, thereby assuring that they would never again receive serious consideration on their philosophical merits. In the *Elucidations,* Newman made himself simultaneously Hampden's oracle and executioner. Thanks to Newman's syllabus, it became unnecessary actually to read Hampden. In 1847, at the height of the agitation surrounding Hampden's appointment to Hereford, Arthur Stanley was shocked to learn that "not one copy of Hampton's 'Bampton Lectures' had been sold since these disturbances had begun,"[42] and nothing Hampden ever wrote was republished after his death in 1868.

What had Hampden really said? When scrupulous churchmen examined Hampden's theology, they were likely to conclude with Bishop Wilberforce that it "contained a good deal that was disagreeable, a great deal that was obscure, and nothing that was heretical."[43] They were wrong. Hampden was in fact the heretic that Newman portrayed in his

---

[41] Mozley, *Reminiscences,* 2: 355.

[42] Rowland E. Prothero, *Life and Correspondence of Arthur Penrhyn Stanley* (New York, 1894), 1: 349.

[43] Written in 1847 during Wilberforce's agonies over Hampden's appointment to Hereford. See Standish Meacham, *Lord Bishop: The Life of Samuel Wilberforce* (Cambridge, MA, 1970), p. 156. Wilberforce's soft line on Hampden confirmed the Tractarians in their characterization of him as Slippery Sam. In the same year, Provost Hawkins of Oriel

*Elucidations*. His epistemology ends in logical positivism and his morality in relativism. If Hampden is no great stylist, he is a central link in the chain of English thought connecting Ockham, Bacon, and Locke with Russell, Wittgenstein, and Ayer. It is altogether fitting that his thought should be the handmaiden to the philosophy of Bertrand Russell—as he was the ally of Lord John Russell, so he was the ally of Russell's grandson in the cause of liberalism. The heretic bishop deserves to be remembered by something more substantial than a footnote to Newman's *Apologia*.[44] If nothing else, Hampden's work is important as a reagent in the process that called Newman's fluent prose into being. But more importantly, his thought epitomizes the liberal premises that in Newman's mind constituted the heresy of modern civilization.

## The Relative Deity

Taken together, Hampden's 1832 lectures on scholasticism and his *Course of Lectures Introductory to the Study of Moral Philosophy* published three years later contain two distinct philosophies, one orthodox, one heretical. The first of these is a plodding rendition of eighteenth-century Anglican Latitudinarianism; this unoriginal theology earned Hampden his ecclesiastical preferments. The second is a radical pursuit of Latitudinarianism to its logical conclusion in relativism; this heterodox philosophy earned him the enmity of Newman, who saw that Hampden was the epitome of liberalism, and that, fully understood, his philosophy repudiated the Christian values it pretended to defend. In order to see what Newman saw and Wilberforce missed, it is necessary to examine Hampden's Anglican commonplaces with the inquisitorial eye of Newman himself.

According to Hampden's orthodox Anglicanism, the mind is fashioned to perceive regularity in the physical events of the universe.

---

also reexamined Hampden's work and detected no heresy. In 1856, Gladstone recanted his part in the 1836 opposition to Hampden. Twenty years after the fact he wrote the bishop to confess that "by my resistance, I had condemned myself" (Hampden, *Some Memorials*, p. 200).

[44] Hamish Swanston, *Ideas of Order: The Mid-Nineteenth-Century Revival of Anglican Theology* (Assen, Netherlands, 1974), devotes several pages to Hampden as a Baconian philosopher. This is one of the very few contemporary books to treat Hampden in detail.

Hampden calls these events facts. To the regularity of these facts the mind gives names such as "gravity" or "red." Similarly, the mind is fashioned to perceive order in the Gospels. The historical events that make up the Gospels are also facts, and once again, the mind supplies names for these facts, such as "the Trinity" or "baptismal regeneration." But these names are not in Scripture any more than the terms "gravity" and "red" are in nature. We know, said Hampden, that there are three Persons in the Godhead, "because we read the fact in the pages of scripture," but the names we give to this fact and the opinions we form about it are circumscribed by our limited powers of reasoning. The fact of the Trinity is real and imperishable, but the God whom we perceive in our own linguistic formulations is "a relative Deity"—relative to our own fallible interpretations.[45] Just as the scientist has to revise his linguistic descriptions to accord with the facts of nature, so the believer ought to adjust his theological vocabulary to accord with the facts of the gospel. Otherwise theology loses its relation to gospel facts and becomes a series of opinions in the mind, and "no system of faith deserves the name of a religion, which is founded merely on a collection of *opinions.*"

Fortunately, says Hampden, "the whole revelation of Christianity is eminently historical in its nature," providing us with a complete factual foundation for belief.[46] What makes the historical facts of the gospel any more reliable than those of the Donation of Constantine or the life of Saint Anthony? Here Hampden repeats Locke. The gospel validates itself by its miracles. "A revelation of the divine wisdom must ultimately rest on the credit of miracles wrought in confirmation of it." This, the opening statement of Hampden's *Philosophical Evidence,* is merely a paraphrase of Locke's *Reasonableness of Christianity.*[47] Any eighteenth-century Anglican would have found this argument tediously familiar.

These Latitudinarian opinions are the foundation on which Hampden erected his Bampton Lectures of 1832. Nothing in them seems to depart from the reputable Anglican theology of Locke, Butler, and Middleton. Hampden's orthodoxy rests on his explicit premises that mankind has two sorts of knowledge—natural and revealed—and that these two sorts

[45] *P.E.,* pp. 22, 24.

[46] *Sermons,* pp. 20, 22.

[47] "Miracles being the basis on which divine mission is always established, and consequently that foundation on which the believers of any divine revelation must ultimately bottom their faith" (*Reasonableness of Christianity* [Stanford, CA, 1958], p. 86).

of knowledge are the objects of two distinct disciplines—science and theology. But on close examination, Hampden's orthodoxy is perfunctory.

Hampden's heterodoxy arises from his implicit negation of the Latitudinarian premises he seems to defend. For Hampden, there are not really two forms of revelation; there is only nature and nature is understood only by science. Theology and science share a single method of investigation: the method of science. They also share a single body of evidence: the facts of science. The study of revelation is only a speciality within science and theology disappears as an independent intellectual inquiry. Having reduced theology to science, the heretical Hampden goes on to point out that science itself can give no certain or enduring answers about eternal truths. The only God we can ever know is the "relative deity" of scientific language. In the end, everything is relative—dogma, ethics, politics, and knowledge itself. When Leslie Stephen reached similar philosophical conclusions forty years later, he felt compelled to leave Anglican orders—and he was a Cambridge man. It is a tribute both to Hampden's ambiguity and to his perseverence that, having transformed Latitudinarianism into agnosticism, he soldiered on to become professor of divinity and bishop.

The first clue that the Bampton lectures might contain something more than a rehash of eighteenth-century Anglicanism is the zeal with which the author hurled himself on his scholastic opponents. The Bampton lectures are Hampden at his best and worst. Their style is turgid and they are tedious, even by the standard of the nineteenth-century lecture hall. Most of Hampden's audience melted away before the eighth lecture, a nine thousand–word excursus on the nature of dogmatic theology. But a handful of adepts understood that these prolix effusions concealed a revolutionary message. A single lecture convinced Newman he was in the presence of the Antichrist. Thomas Mozley saw Hampden as "a man almost carried off his legs by the sudden sense of a great discovery and a delightful emancipation." And for nineteen-year-old Mark Pattison, Hampden's "tone of omniscience" coupled with his "dissolving power of nominalist logic" was an intimation of an intellectual freedom Oxford would not experience again for another twenty-five years.[48]

The modern reader tempted to browse through Hampden's Bampton lectures will find these reactions bizarre. His apparent topic is "The Scholastic Philosophy Considered in Its Relation to Christian Theology"

---

[48] Mozley, *Reminiscences,* 1: 361; Pattison, *Memoirs,* p. 170.

and on this subject he seems to do no more than state the modern commonplaces about medieval thought. If this were all the lectures did, they would still deserve respect—Hampden helped establish the modern commonplaces. When the Bampton lectures were delivered in 1832, H. H. Milman's *History of Latin Christendom* was still twenty-five years in the future. An Englishman who wanted some account of scholasticism would have had to rely on what he could learn from Henry Hallam's disparaging survey in *Europe during the Middle Ages* or what he could piece together from the German scholars Mosheim and Brucker.[49] Before Hampden the English-speaking world had no coherent version of medieval philosophy.

But medieval philosophy was only the apparent subject of Hampden's lectures. Like most scholarly enterprises, Hampden's erudition had a contemporary objective. His Bampton lectures were an attack on the traditional foundations of knowledge and a demand for intellectual toleration and a new era of humanism on the scientific model. The Bampton lectures of 1832 were a program for a liberal revolution in Anglican thought. Their covert relativism coincided with what Newman called liberalism in the broadest sense: "the doctrine that there is no positive truth in religion."[50] It was their liberalism that made the Bampton lectures of 1832 controversial.

The intellectual vigor of the lectures is so unlike the derivative and deferential theology of Hampden's earlier works that Thomas Mozley assumed he must have stolen his ideas from some greater spirit. Mozley had no trouble identifying a candidate: Blanco White—Newman's "poor Blanco."[51] In 1832 White was a fifty-seven-year-old refugee from the

[49] Gibbon had dismissed scholasticism in a phrase: "Before the revival of classical literature the barbarians in Europe were immersed in ignorance" (*Decline and Fall of the Roman Empire* [London, 1910; Everyman ed.], 6: 391). The adjectives Hallam applied to scholasticism give the measure of his judgment: "repulsive," "obsequious," "barren" (*Europe in the Middle Ages* [London, 1869], pp. 684–85). The French scholar Victor Cousin's studies in scholasticism were still in the future when Hampden prepared his Bampton lectures. The only systematic accounts of medieval philosophy were those of two Lutherans, Johann Brucker, whose *Historia Critica Philosophiae* (1742–1744) appeared in an English translation in 1791, and Johann Mosheim, whose four-volume *Institutionum historiae ecclesiasticae* (1726) was familiar to Victorian theologians from two English translations. Newman drew on it.

[50] *Ward*, 2: 460 (the Biglietto speech).

[51] Mozley, *Reminiscences*, 2: 352–53. Canon Liddon also charged Hampden with "great obligations" to Blanco White (*Life of Pusey*, 4th ed. [London, 1898], 1: 363). Neither was impartial.

Spanish Inquisition comfortably lodged among the liberals of Oriel College. He had been raised in Spain, where he had entered the Roman priesthood in 1800. An extensive education in Catholicism made him expert in scholastic philosophy and sexual repression. He learned to despise both. After ten years in the Roman priesthood he fled to England and became an Anglican. For the fellows of Oriel, he was a revelation. Their theological horizons had been bounded by Butler, Hooker, and Saint Augustine. Suddenly they found themselves in the company of a man who conversed comfortably about Abelard, Anselm, and Aquinas.

Each of the Oriel scholars drew his own conclusions from this revelation. To Whately and Arnold, a nearer acquaintance with scholasticism merely confirmed their prejudices against medieval superstition. But for Newman and Hampden the discovery of scholastic philosophy was an intoxicating challenge.

White was in part responsible for their volatile reactions to medieval thought. He was volatile himself. Having begun as a priest in a Spanish cloister, he ended his days as a Unitarian in Liverpool. No doubt the animus that he brought to his account of Catholic theology was partially responsible for the spirit of Hampden's attack on scholasticism. But there was nothing in the Bampton lectures that was not a consistent development from the latitudinarian principles of Hampden's first two books, and the ponderous relish with which Hampden pursued his medieval victims indicates how much he had identified his topic with his own philosophical agenda. That this agenda was revolutionary fully accords with Hampden's professed desire to continue the revolution of his seventeenth-century ancestors. They had fought to eradicate political absolutism. He would fight to abolish philosophical absolutism.[52]

In his mind, this absolutism rested on three pillars: a belief that humans acquire truth from some source beyond nature; a belief that language can reveal this truth; and a belief that reason guarantees the validity of this revelation. Hampden set about destroying each of these positions by reducing doctrine to ideology, language to mind-game, and reason to delusion. This for Newman was liberalism in its philosophical essence.

[52] Martin Murphy, *Blanco White: Self-Banished Spaniard* (New Haven, 1989), pp. 155–56, gives a judicious account of Blanco White's influence on Hampden and discounts the notion that White made any direct contribution to the Bampton lectures of 1832.

## Dogma as Ideology

Hampden's demolition of philosophic absolutism began as a historical survey of medieval philosophy. The boundaries he assigned scholasticism were generous: it embraced at least twelve hundred years of Western thought from the third-century Alexandrian school of Christian hermeneutics to the fourteenth-century nominalism of Ockham. But scholasticism had not stopped there. In the modern era, "the spirit of Scholasticism still lives among us." Even from the time of the Reformation, "the minds of men had been trained to think and speak of divine things, in the idiom of Scholasticism."[53] When Hampden rejected scholasticism, he repudiated by his own standards the main tradition of Western philosophy. This tradition pretends to propound divine truths, but in Hampden's view its own origins are suspiciously mortal, and Hampden asserted that, since scholasticism is wholly within nature, it cannot claim a knowledge that transcends nature. The term ideology was not in Hampden's vocabulary, but the modern sense of the word underlay his analysis of scholastic thought. Dogmas and doctrines arise from the material facts of human life; they have no metaphysical sanction.

For Hampden, scholasticism arose from the forces of history. Scholasticism, like the Latin Christianity of which it is the voice, was a desperate attempt to impose order on the "colluvies of barbarism," an intellectual attempt to overcome historical disorder. It alone was harmonious in a world of "discordant materials"; it alone was consistent in a world of "promiscuous assembly."[54]

Hampden did not hesitate to explain dogma as the effect of social conditions. Pelagius's refutation of original sin, he said, could only have assumed the appearance of unorthodoxy in the late fourth-century atmosphere of social disintegration. "The uniformity of the general state of things in the Eastern Empire" gave Pelagius's ideas no foothold there, but in the anarchy of the Western empire, his theory that individuals are

---

[53] *S.P.*, pp. 386–87.

[54] *S.P.*, p. 32. Although in 1832 Hampden would not have known Hegel's lectures on the philosophy of history, delivered a generation earlier, he often seems to repeat them. "Mere empty understanding," "a rubbishy metaphysic," and "baseless combinations of categories" are Hegelian epithets for scholasticism which Hampden would happily have endorsed. But Hampden is not entirely an echo of the Hegelian *Zeitgeist*. For Hegel scholasticism was an expression of Northern German "barbarism and perversion"; for Hampden, it was the desparate intellectual resistance of Latin civilization to this barbarism (Hegel, *Lectures on the History of Philosophy* (London, 1955), 3: 95–96).

free to find their own salvation appeared as "the disenthroning of Providence." At this moment in history, Pelagius's views seemed to support the general attack on the law of the state and the order of the Church, and so they attracted the wrath of Augustine.[55] In a happier era Pelagius would have been revered as a philosopher, not reviled as a heretic. Scholasticism was for Hampden relative to the material conditions of social life. It was ideology.

Like any Marxist, Hampden acknowledged that ideology is necessary. It is impossible to have civilization without a network of doctrines and theories to sustain it. But though he admits its necessity, Hampden stressed the evil of ideology. Its creeds and dogmas are "the penalties of social religion." Mankind is doomed to suffer under a succession of conflicting dogmas and doctrines, each claiming absolute validity. The only constant in this equation is human nature itself, which unfailingly requires *some* ideology. In politics, only "the social principles of our nature" are permanent; in religion, only the "truths of the Gospel" endure.[56] For a moment it seems that Hampden was offering an escape from relativism. If dogmas and governments are not absolute, at least human nature and gospel facts are. But when humans try to put these absolute "principles of our nature" or "truths of the Gospel" into words, they are doomed to failure. Words like dogmas are social constructs: they are relative and will never lead to absolute truth. Language itself was the second object of Hampden's attack on absolutism.

## Language as Mind-Game

For Hampden, the "social religion" that was scholasticism had many virtues but one overriding vice—"the evil of a Logical Theology." Medieval philosophy confused words and things, and this confusion is what denotes scholasticism, ancient or modern. Athanasius and Ockham shared a single fallacy: "They applied the analytical power of language to the interpretation of nature," thereby falling into the most common error of human thought: "We believe that we have combined real facts in

[55] *S.P.*, 156–59. Hampden was the champion of Pelagius. They had much in common. Pelagius was supposed to have been a Briton. Like Hampden, he espoused a latitudinarian philosophy and suffered the consequences.

[56] *S.P.*, p. 383.

nature, when we have only explored and marked connexions which our own minds have woven together."[57]

The scholastics' ambition was "to reduce the variable truth connected with human life, to the same exactness which belongs to truth purely metaphysical."[58] According to Hampden, the scholastics believed that it was as wrong to say that man could be saved without grace as it was to insist that two plus two equals three. In scholasticism one kind of absolute truth reigns always and everywhere, embracing variable behavior as well as abstract mathematics. In place of this scholastic theory, Hampden insisted that there are two types of truth: the truth of ideas, which is human truth, and the truth of facts, which is divine truth.

Facts simply are. They embrace everything that is, from the Trinity to the caterpillar. They are true by definition. Together they constitute "divine truth." The human mind, however, forms ideas about these facts, and while these ideas may be more or less true, there is an unbridgeable gulf between the mind and the facts to which it responds. In their attempt to bridge the gulf, humans have developed "a symbolic language, derived from the operation of the mind about the objects of the natural world." This symbolic language may be mathematical or linguistic—any system of signs is a symbolic language that comprises what Hampden called "ideas." Ideas organized with a high degree of intellectual rigor constitute what Hampden called "human truth." But since these mental constructs interact only with each other and never with the facts they pretend to represent, "it is evident, that conclusions drawn from these terms are nothing more than further connexions of that symbolic language."[59] Human truth is a mind-game.

This mind-game can produce highly developed species of human truth, either in science or in philosophy. To use a modern example that thoroughly accords with Hampden's view, in one symbolic language atomic events behave like waves; in another they behave like particles. According to the logical rules of our mind-game, both ideas cannot be

---

[57] *S.P.*, pp. 54, 86–87. Hampden sounds like a disciple of William of Ockham, but in fact he condemned Ockham along with Scotus—both thought they could understand nature by understanding language. *The Cambridge History of Later Medieval Philosophy* says that Ockham identified "universals with really existent abstract general concepts" (Cambridge, 1982), p. 438. Hampden denied this identity. He was a modern in his treatment of universals.

[58] *S.P.*, p. 355.

[59] *S.P.*, p. 363–64.

simultaneously correct, but Hampden would be as happy as any modern physicist to accept quantum mechanics anyway, since the facts that comprise divine truth are not bound to follow the laws of human reason.

> These facts belong to an order of things, of which we do not directly know the general laws. The more indeed we approximate to a knowledge of these general laws, the more will such objections disappear. But as we never can arrive, in this state of our being, at a proper knowledge of them; numerous anomalies, the evidences in truth of our real ignorance of the subject, must always exist.[60]

According to Hampden, human ideas are relative to the human mind and therefore always open to revision.

The error of the scholastic philosophers was to equate the symbolic language of the mind with the reality it pretends to describe. In this situation, "the conclusions of human reason will naturally be intruded on the sacred truth. The fact will be accommodated to the theory."[61] In its intellectual arrogance, scholasticism pretended to state divine truths that by the very nature of language are unstatable.

Hampden was not opposed to philosophical speculation. He only insisted that all dogmas, creeds, and doctrines are as tentative and defective as the language in which they are stated. The language of dogma may claim permanence or infallibility, but the claim is mere ideology. In fact, doctrines owe their apparent certainty to "the agreement of a community." Society guards this agreement with the same tenacity with which it protects its domestic institutions. Community demands continuity and defends itself from "a latitudinarianism which could virtually annul it." But the commonsensical right of the community to devise rules for its preservation ought never to be mistaken for a power to state divine truths, which are unknowable and therefore unutterable.[62] In 1817, Jeremy Bentham had dismissed the Church's

[60] *S.P.*, pp. 366–67.

[61] *S.P.*, p. 367.

[62] *S.P.*, p. 383. Here is a case of Hampden developing an idea of Locke (*Essay Concerning Human Understanding* 3.11) which would find its fullest expression a hundred years later in Wittgenstein. Locke insisted that men "must also take care to apply their words as near as may be to such ideas as common use has annexed to them." Hampden developed this prescription into the theory that doctrines are social constructs made of words. Wittgenstein applied Hampden's observation to the whole universe of knowledge: "It is not single axioms that strike me as obvious, it is a system in which consequences and premises give one another *mutual* support," Wittgenstein observed (*On Certainty* [Oxford, 1969], p. 21e).

invocation of the Father, the Son, and the Holy Ghost as "a short string of sounds."[63] Bentham was only more concise than Hampden.

These subversive reflections on language and dogma were Hampden's own. His supposed Svengali, Blanco White, held completely opposed views on language. After White had become a Unitarian, he wrote in his journal for 1839, "God would not employ human language to say what, according to his laws, human language cannot express. This appears to me an unanswerable objection to the doctrine of the Trinity." White still assumed with the schoolmen that all facts must be reducible to language. He wanted to make philosophy perfect by forming "a consistent metaphysical nomenclature. My principal guide shall be the old nomenclature of the Schoolmen."[64] Hampden had no patience with this cryptoscholasticism masquerading as free thought. He wanted once and for all to sever the ties between language and metaphysics and to deal with scholasticism in the same spirit in which his ancestors had dealt with the Stuart monarchs.

In his critique of the scholastics' theory of language, Hampden developed the philosophy of Locke to the point where it could, with some final adjustments, be converted into the principles of logical positivism. He did this by purging out of English empiricism the greater part of its scholastic residue. Hampden explained his method in his *Lectures on Moral Philosophy*. Hobbes, Locke, and Paley "were carried out of the proper orbit of moral truth, to seek a system of rules in the abstractions of the human mind; and hence perversely represented the procedure of the moral judgment as the mere intellectual calculation of consequences." They perpetuated the scholastic fallacy of confusing human truths reached through reason with divine facts among which we actually live.[65] Locke's failing had been to treat the word ideas seriously, as if judgments about facts could be made by an examination of the symbolic language to which they are reduced in our heads. Hampden rejected the procedure as confusing word-games with morality: "To inquire into the *nature* of ideas, is an arbitrary speculation on what has no existence but in the

[63] *Church-of-Englandism* (London, 1817), pt. 2, p. 53.

[64] *The Life of the Reverend Joseph Blanco White* (London, 1845), 3:55, 3: 75. Hampden would have said Blanco White was to nineteenth-century Anglican theology what Ockham had been to scholasticism—a nominalist, but still trapped in the delusion that language had a real connection with things.

[65] *M.P.*, p. 169.

nomenclature of science." Locke's error "gave occasion to the idealism of Berkeley, the skepticism of Hume, and the materialism of Priestley."[66] Hampden wanted to remove all "arbitrary speculation" from philosophy.

But if Hampden reduced revelation to science and then deprived science of the linguistic tools that enable it to state truth, he still believed that there was a divine truth to be scientifically investigated. The gospel is a self-validating record of sacred revelation:

> Assuming, however, that there is a clear case of inspiration established in regard to our sacred Books,—that they are a complete volume of inspiration,—and that this inspiration extends to all matters pertaining to the kingdom of God, which we are concerned to know,—it follows, that whatever is recorded in those books is indisputably true; and that nothing independent of these books, or not taken from them, can possess the same authority,—not to say in *degree* only,—but even in *kind*. For this is *divine* truth; whatever is distinct from it, is *human*.[67]

Here Hampden narrowed to the finest of fine points the Latitudinarian theology of his eighteenth-century predecessor in freethinking, Conyers Middleton. In his *Free Inquiry* of 1748, Middleton courted the wrath of high churchmen by arguing that the claims of the early Fathers of the Church to "a divine and infallible interpretation of the Scriptures" were "unworthy of any credit." But if tradition were corrupt as early as the second Christian century, where should the believer draw the line of credibility? At A.D. 100? At the time of the Gospels themselves? Middleton maintained that "after our Lord's Ascension, the extraordinary gifts, which he had promised, were poured out in the fullest measure on the Apostles."[68] So Middleton left intact a century of revelation in which the gap between human and divine knowledge had been bridged. Hampden felt that Middleton had been too generous by half. For him, the Apostles deserve no more deference than the Fathers and perhaps less. How could "the air of divine truth" be breathed "amidst an atmosphere charged with heathen profaneness; and the carnal prejudices of Judaism?" Without ever saying so, Hampden tacitly included the entire

[66] *M.P.*, pp. 264–65.

[67] *S.P.*, pp. 356–57. A curious passage. Hampden nowhere says he acquiesces in the assumption that "there is a clear case of inspiration in regard to our sacred books." His supposed orthodoxy rested on a hypothesis to which he may or may not have assented.

[68] *Free Inquiry* (London, 1748), pp. xxxiii, xxviii.

Old Testament in this exclusionary rule. All that is left of revelation is the New Testament, which Hampden characterized as a "sacred
inclosure."[69]

What is left inside this sacred inclosure? Only facts, according to
Hampden. The Gospel records no opinions. It states "revealed facts,"[70]
and to the obvious objection that these facts only make sense when
interpreted by the human mind, a process that looks very opinionated,
Hampden replied that the human impulse to interpret facts is precisely the
scholastic fallacy he was trying to put behind him. Hampden deprived the
priest and the critic of their most cherished function, the power to
interpret with authority. For him, no interpretation can claim anything
more than a relative and imperfect authority:

> The most perfect reasonings founded on the terms of theological propositions,
> amount only to evidences of the various connexions of the signs employed.
> We may obtain by such reasonings, greater precision in the use of those signs.
> But the most accurate conclusion still wants a key to interpret it. There must be
> in fact a repeated revelation, to authorize us to assert, that this or that
> conclusion represents to us some truth concerning God.[71]

Any absolutely valid interpretation requires a "repeated revelation" to
guarantee its validity, and Hampden's point was that such a "repeated
revelation" is both historically and logically absurd. The spirit of
Hampden lives on in the theories of modern criticism, and fashionable
theories of deconstruction have their origin in the detritus of nineteenth-
century theology.

When Newman came to refute Hampden and the tendencies of modern
philosophy, he had to show that the apparent absurdity of a "repeated
revelation" was in fact divinist sense. To do this, he had to rehabilitate
doctrine and language after Hampden's attacks, but most of all he had to
counter Hampden's denunciation of reason itself, for Hampden's attack
on scholasticism rested on three pillars—the reductions of doctrine to
ideology, of language to mind-game, and finally, of reason itself to
solipsistic delusion.

[69]*S.P.*, pp. 357–58.
[70]*S.P.*, p. 391.
[71]*S.P.*, p. 55.

## Reason as Delusion

For Hampden, scholasticism was not only a historical episode in Western philosophy; it was an evil predisposition inherent in all human thought. What the Bampton lectures sought to prove is "the irrelevance of all deductions of consequences to the establishment of religious doctrine."[72]

How is it possible to have a religion without doctrine, language, or reason? Hampden had an answer. Scripture "is instructive to us in point of sentiment and action."[73] Its language is a catalyst between divine facts and human behavior. As in a chemical process, the catalyst provokes the reaction between two elements but is not part of either and is irrelevant in the final product. The point of the gospel is not to create symbolic languages, creeds, or dogmas for the amusement of reason, but to cause a sentimental reaction leading to Christ-like behavior in the course of ordinary human life. The goal of theology, as of science, is not to know the divine truths, which are by definition unknowable, but to act in conformity with them. According to Hampden, we can act on Christian principles even though we cannot believe in them. Here belief is irrevocably separated from action—a divorce that in Newman's estimation characterized liberalism.

For Hampden, reason is not merely irrelevant but iniquitous. Reason leads us into a maze of language. We lose sight of our proper object, the action of Christ's example on our lives. Worse, said Hampden; reason leads us into a brand of solipsism, which is the natural tendency of scholasticism and all rational philosophies from Plato to the present. Assume, said Hampden, that divine truth is rational in the same way the human mind is rational. Then divine truth will operate according to the same laws as human reason. Reason becomes the image of truth, and by an easy step, "The mind becomes everything in fact and reality, as it is everything in its power of conception and generalization." By making these assumptions, scholasticism allowed reason to usurp the place of God: the scholastic worships his own mind. "It is ratiocination that triumphs; and Logic domineers over Theology."[74] Far from achieving a subordination of reason to authority, scholasticism according to Hampden is reason run amok.

[72] *S.P.*, p. 54.
[73] *S.P.*, p. 54.
[74] *S.P.*, pp. 108, 373.

Hampden was an astute intellectual historian, if nothing else. But historical acuity was secondary to his central purpose, to dislodge reason itself from its preeminence in philosophy. In place of reason, which for Hampden constituted a solipsistic and inert world of self-enclosed symbolic systems, Hampden advocated the study of ourselves and our actions as natural phenomena. "The knowledge, indeed, of nature from phenomena, the only knowledge that we are able to obtain, is precisely that which serves for action."[75]

Hampden allowed nothing to stand in the way of this radical pragmatism. He was a priest in a church which venerated the apparently doctrinaire theology of Saint Augustine. But, said Hampden, in reality Augustine held no doctrines. "His very writing, in fact, are so many actions.  . . .  He had too deep an acquaintance with the practical course of things, not to be aware, that the skill of the logician is not omnipotent over the affairs of life; and that he who would rightly avail over men and things, must sometimes be content to wear the guise of paradox."[76] The father of Protestant theology was really, like Hampden, a pragmatist who subordinated reason to action. Hampden claimed that Christianity in the hands of its greatest teachers has always been anti-rational. So Hampden's contempt for the absolutism of reason led him irresistibly to a theory of morals based solely on "sentiment and action."

In the next generation Hampden's ponderous reflections on reason and instinct were served up in more palatable form by the son of his old Oriel colleague Thomas Arnold. Matthew Arnold was ten years old when the Bampton lectures of 1832 were delivered and fourteen when his father came to Hampden's defense with his "Oxford Malignants." Forty years later in *Literature and Dogma* he effortlessly reproduced the anti-scholasticism for which Hampden and his father had contended. Ancient Judaism, he argued, understood God poetically, not rationally. The Israelite's religion was true so long as "he felt and experienced," false as soon as he began to speculate. "God is here really, at bottom, a deeply moved way of saying *conduct* or *righteousness*."[77] Whether this observation represents the primitive Jewish view, it certainly reflects Arnold's own. If he had not learned it from Hampden's lectures on moral philosophy or on scholasticism, he had absorbed it in the family circle,

[75] *M.P.*, p. 67.
[76] *S.P.*, pp. 20–21.
[77] *Literature and Dogma* (New York, 1873), pp. 33, 47.

and in Arnold's fluent and popular prose Hampden's philosophy went forth to become the orthodoxy of modern liberalism.

But while Arnold's style was more graceful than Hampden's, his philosophy was less daring. If in logic Hampden was the precursor of Wittgenstein, in ethics he anticipated Nietzsche. In the Bampton lectures all that remains of Christian revelation is the "sacred inclosure" of Scripture. On inspection, however, this "sacred inclosure" is either empty or nonexistent. Nothing can come out of it, since the mind cannot validly infer anything about the Gospels' divine facts, and nothing can enter it, since the mind is forbidden to impute any human idea to the divine facts. The gospel is a philosophical black hole in the firmament of nature. Hampden only appeared to leave revelation in place. His revealed religion is an empty and incomprehensible phantom, and all that remained in his universe was nature and man confronting nature. "Strictly to speak, in the Scripture itself there are no *doctrines*. What we read there is matter of fact." Even the Epistles, which appear to be a tissue of doctrine, are for Hampden addressed not to the reason or intellect but to the will. They tell man "what remains for him to *do,* now that Christ has done all that God purposed in behalf of man."[78]

Hampden only said in the dignified language of Latitudinarian thought what Nietzsche announced with more candor in *The Anti-Christ:* "Only Christian *practice,* a life such as he who died on the Cross *lived,* is Christian." Nietzsche agreed with Hampden that Christianity was at bottom pure instinct; he only disagreed with him over the nature of that instinct. "The 'Christian,' that which has been called Christian for two millenia, is merely a psychological self-misunderstanding. Regarded more closely, that which has ruled in him, *in spite of* all his 'faith,' has been *merely* the instincts—and what instincts!"[79] Hampden anticipated Nietzsche in embracing a theory of morals as instinct. Our religious impulses, Hampden said, are "the expansions and elevations of those instincts of right which exist in the heart." Hampden felt himself to be hovering on the brink of heresy in this sentence, and he drew back: "I am wrong, perhaps, in speaking of our moral ideas by the name of instincts, because it is not necessary for the argument. It is enough that we have moral ideas, however obtained."[80] But in this retraction he had to fall

---

[78] *S.P.,* p. 374.
[79] *The Anti-Christ* (New York, 1978), p. 151.
[80] *M.P.,* p. 13.

back on the language of ideas which he had so conclusively rejected in
Locke and the scholastic philosophers. He was between a rock and a hard
place. Either we go with reason and accept a universe of language and
interpretation, or we go against reason and accept a universe of instinct.
In practice, Hampden did not hesitate to accept the universe of instinct.

Either the instincts are "right" (Nietzsche would have said healthy) or
they are not "right" (Nietzsche would have said shallow). How do we
know if our instincts are right or wrong? By comparing their effects with
the gospel. How do we judge the result of this comparison? By our
instincts. Hampden's ethic ends in a tautology governed by instinct.

So Hampden refuted scholastic rationalism in its ancient and modern
incarnations, but still he admired the spirit of the schoolmen. If scholasticism ended in "the irresponsible, infallible, authority of the Latin
Church," it nevertheless kept alive "an internal principle of liberty in the
soul of man superior to all external constraints." Because it was founded
on the primacy of reason, scholasticism could never stop questioning its
own self-created symbolic language, and sooner or later the restless spirit
of scholasticism would challenge its own first premises and destroy itself.
Eventually, the scholastic philosopher "was assailed within his own
territory: his own arms were hurled against him."[81]

And so the rationalistic and freedom-loving spirit of scholasticism
compelled itself toward the very conclusions it was designed to evade:

> All great things bring about their own destruction through an act of self-
> overcoming: thus the law of life will have it, the law of the necessity of "self-
> overcoming" in the nature of life—the law-giver himself eventually receives
> his call: "patere legem, quam ipse tulisti." In this way Christianity *as a
> dogma* was destroyed by its own morality; in the same way Christianity *as
> morality* must now perish, too: we stand on the threshold of *this* event. After
> Christian truthfulness has drawn one inference after another, it must end by
> drawing its *most striking inference,* its inference *against* itself; this will
> happen, however, when it poses the question, *"what is the meaning of all will
> to truth?"*[82]

This is Nietzsche in the *Genealogy of Morals,* but it could be Hampden if
he had written better. In fact, Nietzsche might be describing Hampden.
Hampden described how scholasticism as a dogma was destroyed by the
arrogance of its own rational morality, and in Hampden nineteenth-

[81] *S.P.,* pp. 30, 46–47, 368.
[82] *Genealogy of Morals* (New York, 1968), p. 597.

century Christianity drew the inference against itself that there is no absolute foundation to truth other than the human instinct to insist on truth. Hampden's philosophy is the very thing he set out to destroy: a freedom-loving investigation of truth that ends in its own refutation.

It is not hard to see why Hampden became an object of Newman's hatred. Hampden truly was the harbinger of Antichrist. He proclaimed a philosophy of the will in which dogma becomes ideology, truth becomes ineffable, divine realities are inaccessible to human reason, and belief is an irrelevancy subordinated to feeling. In Newman's mind these were the tenets of liberalism.

At first glance, Hampden's turgid reflections on medieval philosophy seem far removed from the usual concerns of liberalism. In Newman's day as in ours, people thought of liberalism as a movement for individual rights, free markets, and material progress. But for Newman, these aspirations were only the trappings of liberalism. He never doubted that liberalism rested on a series of heretical beliefs, that its political program was merely a symptom of a deeper evil rooted in more basic principles. The satanic virtue of Hampden was that in him the heretical roots of liberalism were fully exposed. Hampden's liberalism was only a modern version of the Socinian error of the Reformation, and the Socinian error was a version of the Arian heresy of the fourth century. Through Hampden, Newman was able to see how the evils of modern culture arose from the aberrations of ancient belief. Were not the Arians the root of Hampden's philosophy and of all modern evil?

# 3

# Heresy and Liberalism:
# Cicero, Arius, and Socinus

In the Arian heresy Newman found the historical example that vindicated the preeminence that his mind accorded to belief as the master category of human affairs. But he was predisposed to judge the past by its ideas even before he discovered the Arian thread running through Western history. The historical view that crystalized in his study of fourth-century heresy was already apparent in his early essay on Cicero.

## Cicero

In 1824, eight years before Hampden's lectures on scholasticism, Newman was a twenty-three-year-old tutor of Oriel and curate of Saint Clement's, Oxford. He was still the protégé of Richard Whately, who, like a good mentor, strove to advance his pupil's career. Whately was a leading contributor to the *Encyclopedia Metropolitana,* volumes of which had been issued since 1817 as an Anglican riposte to the rationalism of its rival, the Scottish *Britannica.* In 1824 the *Metropolitana's* editor, Edward Smedley, asked Whately if he could find someone who in two months could produce a piece on Cicero to replace the unpublishable effort of the prolix divine Julius Hare. Whately bestowed this choice assignment on Newman. It was the first of several such commissions, all readily accepted. Newman was then making forty-five pounds a year at Saint Clement's and Smedley paid him fourteen guineas for his piece on Cicero. When three encyclopedia articles earned a curate's salary, the opportunity of contributing was coveted.[1]

Cicero's busy life was the pivot on which the Roman state turned from republic to empire. Later Victorians like Trollope venerated him as the model of civilized humanity—the man of letters as statesman, the *novus homo* as champion of order and light. In his article for the *Metropolitana*, Newman showed no interest in this Cicero. "Willingly would we pass over his public life altogether; for he was as little of a great statesman as of a great commander."[2] Cicero's career, which occupies the bulk of Plutarch's life, Newman dismissed in ten pages. The Cicero who was the devoted friend and urbane correspondent of Atticus, the Cicero who charmed even his enemies, he dispatched in a paragraph. Instead Newman devoted forty pages to Cicero the philosopher and rhetorician. At twenty-four, Newman instinctively shunned the derivative world of civilization for the primary universe of thought.

Since Cicero had studied in Athens and his dialogues reflect the thought of the Academy, Smedley asked Newman to find an occasion in his article to survey the development of Platonic philosophy in the three centuries after the death of the master. Newman fulfilled his assignment, and from his summary the Platonists of the Middle and New Academy emerge as the prototypes of Locke, Hume, and Butler, the Anglican philosophers with whom Newman was struggling in the formation of his own opinions. In Newman's account, the chief question of Academic philosophy conveniently coincided with his own central preoccupation—the how, what, and why of belief.

[1] In 1828 Hampden asked Whately if he too could participate in the lucrative exposition of knowledge undertaken by the *Metroploitana,* and by one of the ironies of Oxford politics, it was Newman who was instructed to pass this request along to Smedley: "Dr. Whately requests me to inform you that his friend Mr. Hampden lately editor of the Christian Remembrancer, is not unwilling to have his name added to the list of contributors to the Encyclopedia, if you have employment for him, and he considers you will find him a great acquisition" (*L.D.,* 2: 73). The *Metropolitana* appeared over twenty-eight years from 1817. For Newman's salary and his pay from the *Metropolitana,* see *L.D.,* 1: 174–75.
[2] *H.S.,* 1: 256.

According to Newman, Arcesilas, who had headed the Platonic
Academy in the middle of the third century, had insisted that true
philosophy must suspend judgment on all subjects. He had mistaken "the
profession of ignorance, which Socrates had used against the Sophists on
physical questions, for an actual skepticism on points connected with
morals."[3] In the system of Arcesilas's Academy, truth and belief vanish
together and man is left alone with phantoms of reality—the same bleak
legacy bequeathed to Hampden and the liberals by those latter-day
Academicians, the English philosophers of the eighteenth century.

But if the Academy had arrived at a version of Hume's skepticism, like
eighteenth-century Anglicanism it had recoiled from its own conclusions. According to Newman, Arcesilas's second-century successor,
Carneades, saved the Academy from the consequences of its skepticism
much as Bishop Butler had salvaged English empiricism for Anglican
theology.

> Although we find Carneades, in conformity to the plan adopted by Arcesilas,
> opposing the *dogmatic* principles of the Stoics concerning moral duty, and
> studiously concealing his private views even from his friends; yet, by allowing
> that the suspense of judgment was not always a duty, that the wise man might
> sometimes *believe* though he could not always *know;* he in some measure
> restored the authority of those great instincts of our nature which his
> predecessor appears to have discarded.[4]

The Academicians under Carneades arrived at a qualified sort of belief by
the same method approved by Locke and perfected by Butler: "Since we
cannot arrive at knowledge, we must suspend our decision, pronounce
absolutely on nothing, nay, according to Arcesilas, never even form an
opinion. In the conduct of life, however, probability must determine our
choice of action; and this admits of different degrees."[5]

As Newman presented it, the philosophy of Carneades and the later
Academy could be summarized in a sentence: "Most of the propositions
we think, reason, discourse, nay, act upon, are such as we cannot have
undoubted knowledge of their truth; yet some of them *border so near*
upon certainty, that we *make no doubt at all* about them, but *assent* to
them *as firmly,* and act according to that assent as resolutely, *as if they
were infallibly demonstrated."* The sentence is from the chapter "On

[3]*H.S.,* 1: 264.
[4]*H.S.,* 1: 268.
[5]*H.S.,* 1: 271.

Probability'' in Locke's *Essay on Human Understanding*. It would fit effortlessly into the article on Cicero, just as it provided a point of departure for the *Grammar of Assent* forty years later.[6]

In order to make the philosophy of the Academy an occasion to expound his own opinions about belief and morality, Newman often had to compel the evidence to fit his argument. His assertion, for instance, that Carneades maintained ''the wise man might sometimes *believe* though he could not *know*'' is supported by Newman's footnote referring the reader to Cicero's *Academica*. In that passage, Cicero observes in a parenthesis that Carneades admitted the wise man ''sometimes assents.'' This is very slender evidence on which to attribute a theory of belief to the Platonic skeptics, but excellent evidence of Newman's inclination to make his subject-matter respond to his own preoccupation with belief.[7]

At the heart of this preoccupation was the challenge offered by skepticism, ancient or modern. If skepticism were correct and all belief is uncertain, then men could never know that anything is true or that any act is right. Newman was disgusted by the facile acquiescence of Cicero and his liberal descendants in this philosophical agnosticism. For Newman, action unguided by belief was mere expediency, while belief severed from its moral consequences was mere sophistry. In his encyclopedia article, the young Newman was hard on the sterile urbanity of classical humanism: ''Intellectual amusement, not the discovery of Truth, was the principal object of their discussions,'' he said. ''The motives and principles of morals were not so seriously acknowledged as to lead to practical application of them to the conduct of life.''

Newman borrowed something from Plato and much from Aristotle, but he was never the disciple of any classical philosopher. Whatever their attainments, Plato and Aristotle, like Cicero, lacked a correct view of life, and because they did not believe rightly, they neither acted nor taught rightly. The ancient world had no sense of the correspondence between belief and action. They regarded ''the perfectly virtuous man as the creature of their imagination rather than a model for imitation.''[8] For Newman, the conjunction of right ideas and right actions constituted truth, and Cicero's life was of little interest to him not for its lack of event but for its lack of application of belief to event. The English philosophers

[6]*G.A.*, p. 106; Locke, *Essay Concerning Human Understanding*, 4.15.2.

[7]''Carneades non numquam secundum illud dabat, adsentiri aliquando: ita sequebatur etiam opinari, quod tu non vis, et recte, ut mihi videris'' (*Academica* 2.21).

[8]*H.S.*, 1: 258–59.

of the eighteenth century had rediscovered the skepticism of the Academy and relapsed into the moral poverty of classical civilization. So Newman projected the errors of modern thought upon Cicero's classical humanism. Ancients and moderns alike were strangers to truth and morality because they were incapable of belief.

## The Arian Connection

Cicero's skepticism could be explained by his ignorance; he had lived before the Christian era. The modern liberal has no such excuse. His unbelief is a willful rebellion against revealed truth, and his paganism is not ignorance but apostasy. In time, Newman was able to locate the origins of this apostasy. Hampden's lectures on scholasticism coincided with Newman's discovery that the origins of liberalism were to be sought in the Arian revolt against belief.

Late in 1831, while Hampden was preparing his demolition of scholastic philosophy, Newman was also collecting his thoughts on dogma and tradition. Newman was known to be eloquent, and his encyclopedia articles had won him the respect of the orthodox churchmen associated with the *Metropolitana*. In 1830, two of these divines, William Lyall and Hugh James Rose, undertook the publication of a Theological Library to expound the authentic teaching of the English Church. Both were Cambridge men, who may be forgiven for assuming that Newman was another moderate Anglican like themselves. They invited Newman to write an ecclesiastical history of the Church's general councils that would illustrate the place of the Thirty-Nine Articles of the Anglican communion in the tradition of Catholic dogma. Newman accepted this challenge, and Rose arranged for the publisher Rivington to offer Newman one hundred fifty pounds for the first edition. By August, 1831, Newman had outlined a three-volume exploration of Catholic dogma, "1 on the Trinity and Incarnation; 2 on original Sin, grace, works, etc.; 3 on the Church system."[9] For the next ten months he immersed himself in a study of the first general council at Nicaea, which in 325 had condemned the Arian heresy.

While Newman studied the erroneous beliefs that had polluted Christian doctrine in the fourth century of the Christian era, history seemed to

[9]*L.D.*, 2: 320, 324, 353.

repeat itself in the intellectual and political crises of nineteenth-century England. He had hardly begun to compose his book when Hampden delivered his infidel lectures in the spring of 1832. At the same moment, the Reform Bill was moving through Parliament. As Newman wrote, the liberal assaults of 1832 merged imperceptibly with the heretical challenge of 325.

The coincidence of Newman's ecclesiastical researches, the passage of the Reform Bill, and Hampden's lectures made Newman see that liberalism was an error older and more fundamental than Whig theory or English latitudinarianism. "By liberalism I mean the anti-dogmatic principle and its developments," Newman wrote in his *Apologia*. [10] The father of liberalism was Arius, the first of those who had denied the dogmatic principle. The heretic Socinus had revived his error in the sixteenth century, and now Lord Melbourne and Hampden continued their work.

When the Whigs' Reform Bill received its second reading in April 1832, Newman wrote his disciple Simeon Pope, "Whigs are neither fish, flesh, nor fowl. Their policy is liberalism, and their basis is Socinianism." [11] Inspired by this insight into the pedigree of liberalism, he wrote furiously throughout June. On the fourth of the month the Reform bill passed Parliament. On the tenth Newman refused to dine with the apostate Hampden. The conflict between Arian heresy and Christian belief seemed ubiquitous. The savagery of the conflict that he saw in his mind's eye could only have been reinforced by the arrival in Oxford of the cholera epidemic at the end of the month. Plague, heresy, and reform coalesced into a single manifestation of universal depravity. Now his book could no longer be a general history of the doctrinal foundations of Anglicanism. It demanded to be a revelation of liberalism's antecedents in the errors of Arius. That summer he finished his *Arians of the Fourth Century*, "if not fainting, yet feeling as if I were." [12]

Newman had promised Rose and Lyall a panorama of Catholic doctrine. Instead, he presented them with a monograph on a single antique heresy. The editors were perplexed. They declined to publish Newman's book in their Theological Library, and he had to be content with a smaller, less remunerative edition brought out separately by

[10] *Apo.*, p. 54.

[11] *L.D.*, 3: 42.

[12] *L.D.*, 3: 75. When Newman revised the *Arians* for a third edition in 1871, he again felt the strain of the work. See *L.D.*, 25: 209, 211.

Rivington. Newman had disappointed his respectable colleagues. The
public ignored or pitied him.[13] His tome had to wait two years for its first
review. But in his obsession with Arianism, Newman had found the great
if unfashionable themes that constitute his dissent from modernism.
First, he suggested a radical revision of history. The origins of Western
liberalism were to be sought not in seventeenth-century rationalism, or
sixteenth-century Protestantism, or even medieval nominalism, but in
early Christian dogmatics. This hypothesis is startling enough in itself to
earn Newman a place in intellectual history. But above all else, the
Arians provided him the model he required to demonstrate the mastering
influence of belief in human affairs. The story of Arianism would prove
that belief determines the fate of individuals, that belief dominates all
action, that belief shapes history. To understand belief is to understand
life itself. These are the premises of *The Arians of the Fourth Century*.
They are the premises of all Newman's subsequent publications.

From 1832, the Arian controversy was the fixed intellectual point
around which the constellation of Newman's opinions revolved. The
essays of 1833 that later formed *The Church of the Fathers* were balanced
on the Arian question. *The Lectures on the Prophetical Office of the
Church* of 1837 drew their historical parallels from the fourth century and
their logic from Arius's great opponent, Saint Athanasius. *The Essay on
the Development of Christian Doctrine* of 1845 was largely supported by
analogies drawn from the Nicene era of Church history. Newman's
contribution to Pusey's Library of the Fathers was the two-volume *Select
Treatises of St. Athanasius in Controversy with the Arians*. These
Athanasian tracts were his constant inspiration in the troubled years
leading up to his conversion. Sometimes he worked over them for twelve
hours a day.[14] It was the Arian issue that guided him imperceptibly
toward Rome. "The Church in communion with Rome decreeing, and
the heretics resisting. Especially as regards the Arian controversy. How
could I be so blind before!" he wrote a friend in 1844.[15] At last the Arian
question funished him the decisive evidence that determined his conversion: "I saw clearly that in the history of Arianism, the pure Arians were
the Protestants, the semi-Arians were the Anglicans, and that Rome now

[13] "I have read Newman's 'Arians,' " Baron Bunsen wrote Thomas Arnold in 1835. "O
heaven! what a book! . . . I had hoped his inward Christianity and the air of England
would set him right" (*A Memoir of Baron Bunsen* [London, 1869], 1: 414).

[14] Mozley, *Reminiscences, Chiefly of Oriel College* (London, 1882), 2: 336.

[15] *K.C.*, p. 25.

was what it was then. The truth lay, not with the *Via Media,* but with what was called 'the extreme party.' "[16] Rome—the extreme party—had been right about the Arians; it was right about the Anglicans. He went where truth could be found.

After his conversion and during his troubled residency in Rome in 1846 and 1847, he returned to the Arian theme, this time in four Latin dissertations that he hoped would make him better understood in his new Church, since, as Ward puts it with some understatement, "He found his English writings so imperfectly comprehended." But the Vatican could not or would not comprehend Newman's Arian obsession, whether expressed in Latin or English. In 1859 Newman demonstrated in an article for the Catholic *Rambler* that in the Arian dispute it had been the laity, not the papacy, which had unswervingly upheld the true Catholic doctrine. This particular application of Arian studies prompted Monsignor Talbot to observe that "Dr. Newman is the most dangerous man in England," and Pius IX himself was *"beaucoup peiné."*[17] Newman was compelled to recant his libels on the infallibility of the Holy See, but even this inglorious episode did not diminish his passion for Arian studies. His *Tracts Theological and Ecclesiastical* of 1874 was a collection of essays preponderantly on Arian subjects and contained a new article, "Causes of the Rise and Successes of Arianism," written at a time when Newman had lost interest in almost all other scholarly pursuits.

Through forty years of crisis and controversy, Newman indefatigably pursued Arianism as the key that unlocked the mysteries of his own mind and of the corrupt civilization around him. And if the world misunderstood his passion, what else was to be expected from a culture steeped in the very heresy he contested?

Newman's account of the Arian controversy in *The Arians of the Fourth Century* is not so much history as polemic. His first reviewer was correct in saying that "Mr. Newman is in all this a partisan," and modern students of Arianism deplore the bias that warps Newman's scholarship.[18] Newman would have scorned this craven liberal obeisance to objectivity. His Arian researches had revealed a great truth about belief.

[16] *Apo.,* p. 130.

[17] *Ward,* 1.172; 2: 147, 172. "What is the province of the laity?" Talbot asked Manning. "To hunt, to shoot, to entertain. These matters they understand, but to meddle with ecclesiastical matters they have no right at all" (*Ward,* 2: 147).

[18] The first of the few reviews *The Arians* received was by Herman Merivale in the *Edinburgh Review,* 63 (1836). More recently, Rowan Williams praises Newman's skill as a

He could not be impartial about the truth. To see this great truth it is necessary to understand Arianism as Newman understood it.

## The Arian Controversy

On September 18, 324, at Chrysopolis by the Bosporus, Constantine, emperor of the West, defeated Licinius, emperor of the East, and became sole ruler of the Roman empire. Constantine speedily took inventory of his new dominions and was vexed to discover that the Christian community at Alexandria was torn by religious dissension. The Church was an organization which could either complement or confound the bureaucracy of the unwieldy empire Constantine had now to command and Alexandria was a city that controlled the trade of the Mediterranean. The prosperity of the empire depended on the peace of the Egyptian Church. In these circumstances, says his biographer Eusebius, the emperor considered the Alexandrian controversy "in the light of a calamity personally affecting himself," and within weeks of his victory at Chrysopolis he wrote to the warring parties at Alexandria, admonishing them that "as long as you continue to contend about these small and very insignificant questions, I believe it indeed to be not merely unbecoming,

---

controversialist but dismisses his research as "built upon a foundation of complacent bigotry and historical fantasy" (*Arius: Heresy and Tradition* [London, 1987], p. 5). Newman's admirers have tried to forestall such criticisms by arguing that Newman's meditations on the fourth century are "something more true, more deep, and more beautiful than history" (Henri Bremond, *The Mystery of Newman,* trans. H. C. Corrance [London, 1907], p. 117). Newman, I think, would have said that having accurately delineated the essential idea of history he could not honestly be faulted for a few inconsequential errors of fact. I have relied on Williams and other contemporary historians for the facts about the Arian controversy but left Newman's prejudices and interpretations intact. These books contain useful surveys of the events and creeds in dispute by Arius and his opponents: Henry Chadwick, *The Early Church* (New York, 1967); W. H. C. Frend, *The Rise of Christianity* (Philadelphia, 1984); and J. N. D. Kelly, *Early Christian Doctrines,* 5th ed. (New York, 1978). Many of the original sources are translated in *A New Eusebius* (London, 1957), and *Creeds, Councils, and Controversies* (London, 1966), both edited by J. Stevenson. There is also a large literature on Arianism, much of it listed in the bibliography of Williams's *Arius*. Particularly helpful are two volumes in the Philadelphia Patristic Foundation monograph series: Thomas A. Kopecek, *A History of Neo-Arianism,* and Robert C. Gregg, ed., *Arianism: Historical and Theological Reassessments* (Cambridge, MA, 1979, 1983).

but positively evil, that so large a portion of God's people which belongs to your jurisdiction should be thus divided."[19]

The insignificant questions that threatened the tranquility of the Church had been posed by Arius, presbyter of the Egyptian Church and the popular priest in charge of an Alexandrian parish. What was the relation of God the Father to Christ the Son? Arius and his supporters maintained that "God must pre-exist the Son." Arius's bishop, the pious and scholarly Alexander, rejected the views of his presbyter and held that the Son was "eternally with the Father."[20]

To a practical man like Constantine, Arius and Alexander were quibbling over verbal nothings. Because he could find no meaningful tort in the Alexandrian controversy, the emperor's initial response was to dismiss the whole business on the judicial principle *de minimis non curat lex* (the law takes no account of small matters).

The history of the Arian controversy seemed to many worldly minds then as now to be so much hot air. But the Arian controversy refused to yield to the logic of the world, and to resolve it Constantine was compelled to convene the first general council of Christendom, an assembly of some 250 bishops which met in June 325 at Nicaea near Constantine's headquarters at Bithynia. There the fathers of the Church anathematized Arius and asserted the principle now memorialized in the Nicene Creed that Christ is "of one substance with the Father."

But the Arian controversy did not end at Nicaea. A dizzying succession of twenty-five lesser councils followed in the next fifty-six years, some ratifying but most overturning the Nicene formula. Meanwhile, Arianism provoked riots in the streets of Alexandria and Byzantium. It divided the Christian community against itself across the eastern half of the empire and became an endless occasion for intrigue among the habitués of the imperial court. At one time or another, the Arian side commanded the allegiance of numerous bishops, two emperors, and perhaps a pope.[21] Large segments of the working classes took to the streets to defend

[19] *A New Eusebius*, pp. 352, 354.

[20] Williams, *Arius*, pp. 97, 155.

[21] Did Pope Liberius (352–366) apostatize? Newman and Athanasius thought he had. See *Ari.*, pp. 322–23. Modern historians have been slower to judge. Did Liberius subscribe to the *creed* of Sirmium, drawn up in 351 by the orthodox Basil of Ancyra, or to the *blasphemy* of Sirmium, composed in 357 by the heretical Valens? See *Creeds, Councils, and Controversies*, pp. 13–15, 34–37.

Arianism, and two hundred years after his death, Arius's theology lived on in the worship of the Goths, who had been converted to Christianity by heterodox clergymen. On the orthodox side, this formidable coalition of heretics called forth a single great champion, the fanatic Saint Athanasius, successor to Alexander in the see of Alexandria (328–373), who for forty years campaigned across three continents, suffered five exiles, and produced volumes of polemic in defense of the Catholic faith.

For sixty years the children of this world delighted to watch these Christian controversialists sink deeper into a morass of verbal distinctions apparently divorced from any practical application. In the theaters of Alexandria the pagans and Jews mocked the vaporous wranglings of their Christian neighbors, and forty years after Nicaea the apostate emperor Julian could still find amusement by summoning orthodox and Arian prelates to debate in his presence, "that he might enjoy the ageeable spectacle of their furious encounters."[22]

The controversy was entangled in the politics of empire from the start, and its development was Byzantine in every sense. But behind its intrigues and anathemas, the Arian dispute was a simple contest between two irreconcilable views of God and his universe. Arius fought to maintain a strict monotheism in which God's Son must necessarily be the creature of his uniquely omnipotent Father. For Arius, God "alone has none equal to him or like him, none of like glory." Christ "is not equal to God, nor yet is he of the same substance." God is so completely "invisible to all" that He is "invisible to the Son himself."[23] Arius's God is uncreated, unoriginated, uncaused, unequaled, undivided, and unknowable. The human mind can only approach him through negatives. Whatever is created, originated, caused, multiple, or knowable is by definition not God. Logic, Scripture, and Christian tradition testify that Christ was created, that in the language of Arius, "there was when he was not," since a father must obviously exist before his son. Therefore, Jesus was created by and subordinate to the one great God. Arius thought that his theology alone could make sense of the Christian promise of salvation. Only a created Son could redeem the created world. Redemption made no sense unless Christ was a creature like ourselves whom men could emulate with some hope of attaining similar favor in God's sight.

Alexander and Athanasius replied to Arius and his adherents that what-

[22] Gibbon, *Decline and Fall* (London, 1910; Everyman ed.), 2: 372.

[23] Williams, *Arius*, pp. 101–102. Williams says this fragment "has a good claim to be treated as direct quotation" from Arius's *Thalia*.

ever attributes God has, Christ must have too. Both are uncreated, uncaused, and undivided. It is a mistake to think of Father and Son standing to each other as parent to child or cause to effect. Christ and God are like sunlight and sun—inseparable aspects of a luminous unity. Like Arius, Alexander and Athanasius also appealed to the necessities of Christian redemption. Man could not be saved by some creature like himself. Only God in the plenitude of his grace could save the world, and if, as a Christian was bound to believe, Christ had saved the world, then Christ was God in the plenitude of his grace.

Sixty years of bewildering disputation did nothing to alter or enlarge the fundamental issues as first stated by Arius and his Alexandrian opponents, but gradually the weight of the controversy converged on four obscure philosophical terms. Was the Son unlike (*anomoios*) the Father, as Arius's followers held? Or perhaps it would be safer to say that the Son was like (*homoios*) the Father in ways unspecified, or even that he was like in nature (*homoiousios*)? Or was the Son's nature the same as the Father's (*homoousios*), as Athanasius steadfastly maintained?

This dispute over syllables was the more protracted because the contending parties did not agree on the meaning of the three central terms in dispute—*likeness, sameness,* and *nature.* In 325, after the Council of Nicaea anathematized Arius and declared for the Alexandrian ''sameness in nature'' of the Father and Son, the best minds of the Arian party made themselves orthodox by accepting ''sameness of nature'' in their own sense. Athanasius and his party meant by ''sameness'' absolute identity of individual nature—God and Christ were *homoousios,* that is, they were one God. But the word *homoousios* was vague enough to accommodate the Arian sense of general similarity. Two goats may have the same goat nature, and yet a nanny is not identical with her kid. In this sense the Arians believed Father and Son to be *homoousios.* So after Nicaea the Arian bishops accepted ''sameness in nature,'' kept their benefices, and reserved their right of individual interpretation.

Through such equivocations, the Arian dispute became a controversy about language itself. What kind of truth could words express, and with what degree of precision? The underlying question in the Arian controversy was whether words could enunciate transcendant truths with enough precision to command universal conformity of belief—in other words, whether dogma is valid or not. The Arians said no, the Athanasians yes.

The Athanasians won. At the general council of Constantinople in 381, the Church ratified the Nicene formula that declared the Father and Son to be *homoousios*. This decree ended the great era of controversy and established the dogmatic principle so dear to Newman. After Constantinople it was heresy to doubt that Father and Son were consubstantial, but more important, it was heresy to doubt that the Church could speak the truth. Only those whose beliefs conformed to this truth in thought, word, and deed could legitimately claim the name of "Christian." The defeat of the Arians was the victory of dogma.

## The Anatomy of Error

It is as much a mistake to dismiss the Arian controversy because the contestants battled over a diphthong as it would be to dismiss the battle of Gettysburg because the opposing armies fought for possession of an obscure village. The Arian dispute attracted Newman because it was a contest of first principles that addressed the most fundamental issues of human belief. For Newman, the issue in the Arian controversy was not merely what is correct dogma, but whether dogma is valid at all. Like the heretical Hampden, Arius had said no, and this single species of false belief had corrupted the fourth century, as it once again contaminated the nineteenth. Newman labored over the corpse of Arianism so he might learn to treat the virulent error of anti-dogmatism, now reincarnated in liberal thought.

Arius insisted that God is inexpressible—it is the key word of his position.[24] It is easy to see what infuriated Athanasius and later Newman in this doctrine. According to Arius, nothing created can either think or speak meaningfully about God the creator and, since Christ is created and unlike the Father in nature, even he cannot grasp the idea of God. Mortals can say or think nothing true about ultimate reality nor can they learn the truth through Christ. Newman described the Arians as "a party who had no fixed tenet."[25] Arius was the author of the anti-dogmatic principle and

[24] Williams, *Arius*, p. 101.

[25] *Ari.*, p. 231. According to Socrates Scholasticus, ten years after the Council of Nicaea, Arius recanted his heresy and was readmitted to the Church. Was this expediency or only the logical conclusion of his philosophy? According to Arius, words could say nothing meaningful about God. What difference did it make to the faith if some believers adhered to one empty set of terms while others clung to another set equally inane? Pointless word-splitting was a poor excuse to separate from the visible communion of Christian worship.

the features of liberalism were already visible beneath the theological mask of fourth-century Arianism. Arius had proclaimed God to be inexpressible, and after his death in 337, his followers pursued this position to its logical conclusion in the principle of toleration, the creed of all liberal heretics. In 357, the Arian bishops met at Sirmium and proposed to dispel the rancor that arose from terms such as likeness and sameness of nature. If the terms were eliminated, they reasoned, then each individual could retain his own interpretation in an atmosphere of undogmatic forebearance. Did the words *homoousios* and *homoiousios* separate Christians from one another? ''There ought to be no mention of this at all. Nor ought anyone to preach it for the reason and consideration that it is not contained in the divine Scriptures, and that it is above man's understanding, nor can any man declare the birth of the Son, of whom it is written, *Who shall declare his generation?*''[26]

To the modern eye, the Sirmium declaration looks like a statesmanlike compromise. The venerable Ossius, the 101-year-old bishop of Cordova, embraced it as a fair resolution of a half century's discord. But this judicious formula was branded by the orthodox Athanasians as ''the Blasphemy of Sirmium''—and from Newman's perspective the Athanasians were right. Implicit in the Sirmium compromise was the Arian premise that words could not express ultimate realities, that the best statement of dogma was silence. The liberal philosophy of Newman's antagonist Hampden, which rejected dogmatism and embraced toleration, was merely a reprise of the Blasphemy of Sirmium. Like the Arians, the liberals denied the possibility of dogma, and with dogma they discarded truth itself.

Like Hampden and the liberals, the Arians denied that human language could express divine truths while writing volumes to defend their metaphysic of silence. Their garrulity in defense of an ineffable God only seems like a paradox. The Arians believed that while language could say nothing about the uncreated divinity, it could state general truths about his created world with great precision. For the Arians, the created world is a consistent and knowable intellectual whole, instinct with the same logic by which the human mind apprehends order. Humans can describe this created world, and their descriptions are true in so far as they conform

---

By this logic Arius may not have been as craven as his orthodox detractors made him out to be when he affirmed the Nicene faith.

[26]*Creeds, Councils, and Controversies,* pp. 35–37.

to logic. So there is a kind of truth in the world: truth is attained when an intellectual proposition in the mind corresponds to an intelligible event in creation. The heretic Asterius is supposed to have said that men live in an "intellectual world."[27] So long as men confine themselves to speaking about this intellectual world, their statements have a truth guaranteed by the intellect itself. But this kind of truth is abolutely divorced from God; God is above creation and beyond intellect.

The Arians' distinction between God the ineffable Father and Christ the created Son is the theological counterpart of their separation between divine and intellectual truth. Christ is as incapable of sharing in God's nature as words are incapable of expressing it. Christ is the singular, first-made object of the intellectual world and an intellectual nature like ourselves. It is the promise of the gospels that we can know this intellectual world as fully as Christ knows it, and since it is an intellectual world, we will know it as reason, order, logic—in short, as the Logos that Christ represents and that lightens every man that comes into the world.

In one sense, the Arians anticipated scholasticism. For them, reason and logic constituted the royal road to truth. But Athanasius and Newman saw that the Arian notion of truth contradicted the notion of dogma. Unlike the scholastics, the Arians had denied that words could express transcendent realities.

When Athanasius came to refute the Arian doctrine, he argued for the sameness of Christ's nature with God's on the analogy that the Father is in the Son as the word is in the thought.[28] The analogy summarizes the Arian dispute in a nutshell. For the Arians, the transcendent thought was not in the created word at all. "How things are in the world is a matter of complete indifference for what is higher. God does not reveal himself in the world. . . . There are, indeed, things that cannot be put into

[27] This is Newman's translation of an extract from Asterius preserved in Athanasius' *De synodis;* "As in things visible the sun is one among such as show themselves, and it shines upon the whole world according to the command of its Maker, so the Son, being one among intellectual natures, also enlightens and shines upon all that are in the intellectual world" (*Ath.*, 1: 89). "Intellectual world" translates the Greek *noeto kosmo* (*De synodis* 19). If this is Asterius's expression, he may have borrowed it from Philo of Alexandria, whose supreme and inexpressible divinity is, like the Arian God, known through "the intelligible world" (*noeton kosmon*) (*De opificio mundi* 4). Newman would have had no trouble believing that a Jew was behind the errors of Asterius. And did not the Oriel *Noetics*—Whately, Hawkins, and company—take their name from this heretical term?

[28] *Ath.*, 1: 360.

words.''[29] This is Wittgenstein developing a line of liberal thought that runs back through Hampden and Locke, and which for Newman has its origins in Arian sophistry. Newman and Athanasius were zealous in defense of the opposite premise, that transcendent thought is in the human word. Christ is the master thought of creation and he is one with the Father. Because we can know Christ, we can know God. Because we can speak truthfully about Christ, we can speak truthfully about God. Humans can speak divine truths, and dogma is a living expression of divine power.

The orthodox party equated words and actions. If as the Athanasians held, the word contained the thought and the thought was divine, then speaking, writing, and even thinking are directly under the supervision of God and should submit to his will. The Arians, on the other hand, believed the connection between words and ideas was merely conventional. Speaking, writing, and thinking are part of creation, and creation is separate from the ineffable divinity.

In Newman's mind, the Arian separation of divine truth from human words was an invitation to moral anarchy. In his *Arians,* he spoke of the necessity to make action conform to dogma and he reviled the Arians for reducing theology to a ''flimsy artifice'' of intellectual abstractions that ''is decomposed as soon as the principles beneath it are called upon to move and act.''[30] In Arianism, Cicero's ignorant skepticism assumed the form of willful apostasy. In this, the Arians were proto-liberals. Their anti-dogmatic principle led to the deism of Locke and the relativism of Hampden, in which words were mere tools with no fixed relation to action. So the moral anarchy of the modern world was inherent in the denial of Christ's consubstantiality.

If Arius's principles were admitted, there would be no God, no faith, no priests, and no dogma. Arius's religion would end, Newman said, in paganism or else in ''the virtual atheism of philosophy.''[31] Arius maintained the inexpressible transcendence of God. A god about whom nothing meaningful can be said is a god about whom the less said the better, and here monotheism shades off into atheism. Since God takes no part in creation but works through intermediaries, and since we can know nothing of God anyway, it is only natural for men to return the compli-

[29] *Tractatus Logico-Philosophicus* (London, 1961), p. 73.
[30] *Ari.,* p. 147.
[31] *Ari.,* p. 230.

ment and relegate God to the category of venerable but empty classes. This God is more abstract than even the prime mover of deism—at least the wisdom and intellect of the deist divinity could be read in his creation—but the Arian God has no intelligible part in the world, and we can only infer the excellence of his subordinates, not himself, from the glories of heaven and earth.

How much more sensible that we should worship what we can understand, and what understands us—namely those most excellent creatures more perfect than ourselves by whose agency God made and sustains the world. Christ is the most excellent expression of God's inscrutable majesty, which, says Arius, appears to us "in countless manifestations" as "spirit, power and wisdom, God's glory, truth, image, word."[32] All these manifestations also deserve our reverence.

Looked at from Newman's perspective, Arianism is a recrudescence of polytheism that leads to pantheism and then to atheism. According to the tenets of Arianism, we worship Christ, who is only a more exalted creature than ourselves. But Newman might reply, if this is all there is to Christianity, why not worship the excellency of nature—or worship humans better than ourselves? For that matter, why not worship our best selves? This line of thought obliterates God in self-absorption. Once Arianism admitted the worship of any creature, it countenanced the worship of all, and where all things are holy, God is dead.

So Arianism leads to pantheism or atheism. But even if the Arians could maintain that they were theists of some sort, Newman thought that they could not logically ask that their system be called a religion. By its own first premises, Arianism announces that no transcendent statements can be valid, since anything pertaining to God and his will is unspeakable. But to Newman religion was nothing if not the assertion of truths about transcendental realities. At best, Arianism was a philosophy like its successor heresy, liberalism, and for Newman, philosophy divorced from dogma was an empty and perilous undertaking. The Arians were no better than the shallow humanist Cicero. Like him, they had trained in the schools of classical learning. Their humanism had only disposed them to heresy.

At one point in his *Arians,* Newman equated "platonizing" and "arianizing," for him a terrible juxtaposition. Of Aristotle, he is even more contemptuous, recalling the fourth-century source which had called

---

[32] Williams, *Arius,* p. 103.

him "the Bishop of the Arians."[33] The Arians had advanced a Platonic agenda by means of Aristotelian logic. Their Christ is only the demiurge of Plato and they studied the world he had made by the methods of Aristotle. Their heresy, Newman sneered, was "founded in a syllogism."[34] The Arians sought to perpetuate classical philosophy under the guise of Christian theology.

From the Arian dispute the Church learned that religion required not merely a higher order of knowledge than philosophy, but a different order of knowledge altogether—an order fundamentally at odds with the classical tradition from which Christianity seemed to have sprung. The defeat of the Arians formed the prologue to the suppression of the Athenian schools and prepared the way for the clerical philistinism of Gregory the Great. Newman regarded the extermination of Cicero's classical humanism as a noble by-product of the suppression of the Arian error.[35]

The Arians defended their heresy by appealing to the Bible. They asserted against their opponents that while no true Christian could believe less than what the Scriptures revealed, it would have been superstitious arrogance to believe more. Their position was clearly stated in the Blasphemy of Sirmium, where they condemned creeds and dogmas that employed words not found in the Bible. For Newman, this anti-dogmatic literal-mindedness constituted "the principle of liberalism."[36]

For Arians and liberals alike, the truths of the Bible are all creaturely truths, truths that the intellect can comprehend by reason and by logic—there are no other truths available to men. If the Bible seems to speak of God or other superintellectual phenomena, on examination these statements turn out to be negative assertions about what we cannot know: of the Son it is written, "Who shall declare his generation?" In fact, the Bible could not logically and does not actually reveal anything ineffable. The Arians "assumed as an axiom, that there could be no mystery in the Scripture," Newman says.[37] For the Arian, Scripture appeals only to the intellect. Does the intellectual conception we have formed of the scrip-

[33]*Ari.*, pp. 345n., 40, 32. "Do you not think the Fathers on the whole are suspicious of Plato?" (*L.D.*, 26: 159).

[34]*Ari.*, p. 28.

[35]"The overthrow of the wisdom of the world was one of the earliest, as well as the noblest of the triumphs of the Church" (*U.S.*, p. 314). Or, "the effete schools of Athens are stifled by the edict of Justinian" (*Idea*, p. 223).

[36]*Ari.*, pp. 361–62.

[37]*Ari.*, p. 221.

tural meaning agree with what is actually present in the text? Will our idea stand up to logical examination? Does it conform to the universal categories of reason? Do other reasonable, logical, and intellectual creatures, dispassionately employing the same intellectual methods we normally adopt, assent to our conclusions? If we can answer these questions positively, our interpretation of Scripture is true, true in the same way that the assertion ''all men are mortal'' is true, true in the same way the assertion ''lead is heavier than air'' is true. The Bible is a logical document.

In the Arian system, faith is a drab affair. I do not have to accept Christ as a personal savior so much as I have to accept the Bible as a truthful intellectual guide. Having made this initial choice, the rest of Christian belief unfolds a wonderful Platonic universe according to a relentless Aristotelean logic. So the Arian system exalts the Scriptures as the sole expression of Christian faith and simultaneously demeans them as a mere textbook of creation.

Newman did not have to pore over patristic texts to recover the Arian theory of Scripture. He had heard Hampden expound it in his Bampton lectures. In both its ancient and modern incarnations, the Arian theory assailed the dogmatic principle. If dogma pretended to make statements about God and his truths, it would be meaningless, since God and his truths are ineffable. If dogma claimed to reveal the truth of the Gospels, it would be redundant, since this truth was already apparent to the interpretative skills of intellect and the logical systems of philosophy. All that remained for dogma was to proclaim that Scripture is the true point of departure for all Christians, a proposition demanding no dogmatic support, since, in the Arian system as in the philosophy of Locke and Hampden, the Bible attests to its own validity in its clarity and in its miracles. Arianism proceeds from a self-validating axiom supported by the logical necessity of its conclusions. In such a view, dogma is an irrelevance, if not an insult to the intelligence of both man and God.

The corollaries of the anti-dogmatic principle shaped liberal society. Grant that there is no dogma, then all beliefs are entitled to toleration. Grant that the intellect is the pinnacle of creation, then humanism is the highest expression of the spirit. Grant that the truth of Scripture is merely intellectual, then moral relativism follows. Grant that men can enunciate no absolute standard by which to judge their thoughts, words, or deeds, then a pluralistic society ensues.

In the fourth century, Athanasius had defended the Church against the contingencies of error by asserting the dogmatic principle. Newman did the same in the nineteenth century: ''The Church should teach the truth, and then should appeal to Scripture in vindication of its own teaching.''[38] A society dedicated to true belief must have one indefectible oracle to proclaim truth and maintain order. Scripture could never be this oracle. Only the Church speaking dogmatically could preserve the dogmatic authority of truth.

So Newman's dissent from liberalism developed from his anatomy of Arianism. His contemporaries were puzzled or repelled by his habit of decoding modern civilization as a series of theological abstractions and many in subsequent generations have also found the reduction of history to belief either tedious or incomprehensible. But the modern response begs the fundamental question at issue in the Arian controversy: to ignore dogma is not to rise above the quibbles of Alexander and Athanasius, but to take sides with Arius and Asterius. What was at issue at Alexandria and Constantinople was precisely whether the world can or should enunciate and enforce divine truths. Many are likely to agree with Arius in rejecting the dogmatic principle. Newman agreed with Athanasius in defending it. There is no obvious reason for believing one answer to be better than the other, and this at least is a question which history cannot make go away. In the very act of ignoring the Arian controversy, modern man makes his choice for Arianism.

The inevitability of the Arian question attracted Newman to his lifelong study of the fourth century. Newman disliked dealing with trivial and secondary issues. He dismissed ordinary intellectual debate as the wrangling of amateurs:

> Half the controversies in the world, could they be brought to a plain issue, would be brought to a prompt termination. Parties engaged in them would then perceive, either that in substance they agreed together, or that their difference was of first principles. This is the great object to be aimed at in the present age, though confessedly not a very arduous one. We need not dispute, we need not prove,—we need but define. At all events, let us, if we can, do this first of all; and then see who are left for us to dispute with, what is left for us to prove. Controversy, at least in this age, does not lie between the hosts of heaven, Michael and his Angels on the one side, and the powers of evil on the other; but it is a sort of night battle, where each fights for himself, and friend and foe

---

[38]*Ari.*, p. 50.

stand together. When men understand what each other means, they see for the most part that controversy is either superfluous or hopeless.[39]

Newman made it his mission to clarify the night battle of the modern era. Even the language he chose to explain his mission betrays his obsession with the fourth century as the model of all subsequent history. His image of the night battle was lifted from an account of the Arian controversy by the fifth-century church historian Socrates Scholasticus.[40]

Seen Newman's way, contemporary civilization is a contest between the irreconcilable principles of Arius and Athanasius. In the night battles of the nineteenth century, Newman cast Hampden and the liberals as an Arian chorus. For himself he reserved the role of the dogmatic protagonist Athanasius. During his exile from Arian Alexandria, Athanasius justified himself in his *Apologia pro fuga sua;* during his exile from Socinian Oxford, Newman appropriated Athanasius' title for his own exercise in self-justification, the *Apologia pro Vita Sua.* Athanasius had defended a sacred truth, and how did the world repay him?

> Can anyone who has but heard his name, and cursorily read his history, doubt for one instant how the people of England, in turn, "we, our princes, our priests, and our prophets," Lords and Commons, universities, ecclesiastical courts, marts of commerce, great towns, country parishes, would deal with Athanasius—Athanasius, who spent his long years in fighting against kings for a theological term?[41]

The world dealt with Athanasius just as it dealt with Newman—shabbily. And yet failure was a small price to pay for his dogmatic cause, since in Newman's mind all righteousness flowed from correct belief in a theological term.

[39] *U.S.*, pp. 200–201.

[40] "Thereafter, vexatious spirits, armed with quibbles of language, waged war one against the other. The result was like nothing so much as a night battle, in which neither party understood the thinking of the other, and consequently suspected their opponents of slander" (*Ecclesiastica historia* 1.132 [author's translation]). Gibbon also echoes this passage in his description of the Arians' "nocturnal combats." Was Socrates remembering Thucydides' account of the Athenians' Syracusan night battle (*The Peloponnesian War,* 7.44)? By the time Arnold used the expression "clash by night," the image of night-battling had become virtually synonymous with theological warfare.

[41] *Dev.*, p. 185.

## Dogma or Ideology?

In his Bampton lectures, Hampden gave the liberal rejoinder to Newman's theory of belief. Events dictate action, and the Nicene Creed is a social document whose interest is purely historical. Who is right—Newman or Hampden? Do beliefs drive the world or is dogma only a pious name for what the Marxist would call the all-too-human phenomenon of ideology? Newman's Arian paradigm offers an excellent test case for the conflicting claims of dogma and ideology.

In the Arian conflict, the Roman world seems consciously to have articulated its fundamental beliefs, and endowed both these beliefs and their verbal expression with the status of action, subject to the operation of law. The Church and later the state assumed the right to define and enforce divine truths. Nor did the fourth century leave the important work of dogmatizing to priests and intellectuals. Constantine as chief magistrate took a leading role in the proceedings at Nicaea and styled himself "bishop to those outside the church."[42] The eunuchs and women of the imperial court were partisans of the moderate brand of Arianism championed by Constantine's biographer, Eusebius, bishop of Caesarea. The ascetics of the remote Egyptian desert were zealots for the "sameness of nature" championed by their patron, Athanasius, whom they secreted during his long years of exile. The Gothic barbarians of the northern frontiers adopted the doctrine of the Arian missionaries who had converted them and spread Arianism at the point of the sword. Arianism is alleged to have seduced some seven hundred virgins of the Alexandrian church, and Athanasius accused Arius of having composed popular ballads with which to propagate his heresies among sailors, millers, and travelers. By 380, the theological wrangles of the Church had permeated the urban masses, and Gregory of Nyssa records that at Constantinople, "if you ask anyone for change, he will discuss with you whether the Son is begotten or unbegotten. If you ask about the quality of bread, you will receive the answer that 'the Father is greater, the Son is less.' "[43]

The late fourth century is a striking historical instance of a whole civilization participating in the formulation of religious ideology, which,

---

[42] Eusebius of Caesarea recorded Constantine's remark in his life of the emperor. See Timothy Barnes, *Constantine and Eusebius* (Cambridge, MA, 1981), pp. 270–71, for a discussion of Eusebius's reliability and his imputation to Constantine of Arian opinions.

[43] See W. H. C. Frend, *The Rise of Christianity*, p. 636.

according to Marxist theory, is nothing more than an abstraction of the material conditions at the base of social life. The disputants of the fourth century seem to have been dimly conscious that their theology mirrored their society. In his panegyric on the occasion of the thirtieth anniversary of Constantine's accession to the imperial title, Eusebius proclaimed that the empire was the replica of heaven.[44] Modern practice would simply reverse Eusebius's claim: heaven was the replica of empire.

Marxist analysis ought to provide the key to the Arian phenomenon if there is anything to Marxist analysis in the first place. In the process, it ought to be able to topple belief from the eminence to which Newman elevated it, thereby invalidating the whole of Newman's religious position.

Newman's most fundamental principle was at stake in studying the Arian controversy. If he was right, the Arian example proved that belief, freely chosen and willfully pursued, is the source of all human action and the means of salvation or ruin. If his opponents were right, fourth-century dogmatics demonstrated that belief was an accident of various human and natural forces. In Newman's view, history is the free creation of individuals striving for truth. In his antagonists' view, history is an impersonal network of cause and effect that circumscribes free choice and moves to no transcendent purpose. Marxism has taken this antagonistic view to its fullest development and it seems sensible to test Newman's convictions against the most powerful arguments that can be marshaled to rebut them.

The Marxist would argue that the Arian controversy was the ideological reflection of a profound social crisis in the Roman world. Between the time that Arius began his argument with Bishop Alexander and the time that the Council of Constantinople composed the doctrinal language that spelled the defeat of the Arian party, the network of free and slave labor that had sustained the economy of the classical world disintegrated and a new social order emerged. In the Marxist view, the Arian controversy is the ideological echo of these economic upheavals.

Slavery generated neither the manpower nor the enthusiasm to run the sprawling economy of the later empire, and the resulting shortage of labor fed a spiral of inflation and social dislocation that threatened to

[44] Barnes, *Constantine and Eusebius*, p. 254. Anticipating the Marxists, Hampden had seen the Arian controversy as a political and scientific dispute. Unity of faith was demanded by the disunity of the empire, and the relation of Father and Son was another way of inquiring into cause and effect (*S.P.*, pp. 101–102, 118–19).

unhinge the delicate balance of society. Successive generations of imperial administrators met this crisis by attempting to legislate economic equilibrium. At the end of the third century, Diocletian enacted wage and price controls. In the ten years on either side of the Council of Nicaea, the emperors introduced a system of fixed hereditary obligations for various workers, such as soldiers, ships' captains, and tenant farmers. In future, the rural tenant's children were to be bound to the soil and the urban artisan's children to the shop, thereby assuring a continuity of manpower in essential jobs, but at the cost of an open labor market. The substitution of serfdom for slave or free labor was part of an economic reform to end all reforms. The rulers of the empire attempted to arrest the material conditions of life in a perfect moment of tax-generating tranquility by freezing class relations in perpetuity.[45]

The empire that aspired to this economic harmony was in fact a volatile amalgam of competing interests. Virtually autonomous corporations and provinces opposed the bureaucracy at Rome or Byzantium. Dock workers, soldiers, and tenant farmers had to acknowledge the sovereignty of the Roman emperor, but more immediately they were forced to honor their obligations to local magistrates, bishops, generals, and landlords. Practically, every man had two masters to whom in theory at least he owed a single obedience.

The Marxist will be quick to point out the similarity between the worker's obligation to two masters and the Christian's adoration of God the Father and God the Son. In this view, the Arian dispute was not, as Newman thought, a struggle over divine truth, but an ideological hallucination in which economic realities assumed the character of theological quibbles.

What was the relation of the emperor and his central government to his far-flung subjects? Was he an Arian or an Athanasian Father? Either alternative might be attractive to each of the competing social groups within the empire. The emperor might find the supreme and unapproachable godhead of Arius's divinity a suitable analogy for his imperial station. Ultimate sovereignty resided in Caesar, and his lieutenants were as little able to rival him as Arius's created Son was able to know his heavenly Father. The emperors Constantius and Valens were avowed

---

[45] The sources for the reconstruction of the Roman economy of the third and fourth centuries are surveyed in "The Crisis of the Third Century and the Emergence of the Byzantine State," *Roman Civilization*, ed. Naphtali Lewis and Meyer Reingold (New York, 1966), 2: 419–89.

Arians, and Constantine for all his protestations in favor of the Nicene faith, may have espoused the theology of his biographer, the moderate Arian Eusebius.

But was Arianism an entirely safe metaphor for imperial organization? Arius's god was theoretically omnipotent but practically ineffectual. He was absolutely remote and acted only through intermediaries—an uncomfortable reflection of the reality that for most Roman subjects Rome and Byzantium were distant and unavailing political abstractions. In Arius's system the supposedly subordinate Son through whom the Father worked his will might easily usurp the veneration that properly belonged to the Father, just as the supposedly subordinate general or magistrate might challenge the authority of the emperor.

As the implications of the Arian doctrine became clearer, emperors were more and more likely to favor the orthodox alternative. In Athanasius's theology, God the Father and Christ his Son were one undivided substance of authority and power. The emperor might lose something when his subordinates were of one substance with him, but he gained more if the empire was ruled by a single imperial presence operating in several persons. Orthodox Christianity provided an efficient model for the imperial hierarchy, and in time the emperors Constans, Jovian, and Theodosius defended Athanasian orthodoxy with arms as well as arguments.

The leadership class of the empire might also be expected to favor the implications of orthodox theology. The local landlord, general, or magistrate preferred to think of himself as "the same in nature" as the emperor he served rather than merely as one of his creatures, the status to which the Arian model would have reduced him.

Equally attractive to the ruling classes was the theory of justice implicit in the Athanasian position. In the Arian system, the universe operated according to intelligible laws of impartial justice. The justice of Athanasius's God, on the other hand, was arbitrary and mysterious. The emperor and his minions preferred to model themselves on the arbitrary rather than the rational theory. "What the emperor has determined has the force of a statute, seeing that by a royal law which was passed concerning his authority the people transfers to him and upon him the whole of its own authority and power."[46] So the jurist Ulpian explained the imperial authority in the early years of the third century. The Marxist

---

[46] *Roman Civilization*, 2: 538.

would say that the abstractions of Athanasian theology in the next century only mimicked the political rationale underlying Roman autocracy. In law, the people transferred their power to the emperor, who dispensed arbitrary justice. In Athanasius' theology, the people transferred their sins to God, who dispensed arbitrary salvation.[47] So Christian orthodoxy conformed itself to Roman jurisprudence.

By contrast, Arianism appealed to all those antagonistic to the new economic order and its ruling classes. It was the natural theology of second-level bureaucrats, intellectuals, professionals, shopkeepers, slaves, artisans, and men of ambition. Arius maintained a supremely willful and unappproachable divinity who could be treated as a bureaucrat or businessman would have liked to treat his nominal superior—as a necessary irrelevance. For Arius the intelligible business of creation was conducted by a rational and creative Son, whose role was that of a cosmic master craftsman.[48] What workingman would not prefer a kind and skillful foreman like himself to a distant and arbitrary dictator? Arius's Christ was accessible. His laws were rational. Humans could aspire to be like him, and by hard work they could succeed.

The Arian Christ had an obvious appeal to men who despised the new economic order of fixed obligations and wistfully recalled the freedoms of the Hellenistic world—the freedom to seek advancement in the job market, the freedom to argue free of dogmatic trammels, the freedom to advance from class to class. If the Marxist view is correct, then Arianism was a theological expression of nostalgia for the economic laissez-faire of classical civilization. Though they appear to us as the radical element of fourth-century Christendom, by the Marxist analysis the Arians were the apologists for a fading libertarianism which reached its high water mark two hundred years earlier in the age of ambitious Trimalchios and virtuous Epictetuses.

What little is known about the Arian leaders and their followers confirms the Marxist view of Arianism as a coalition of intellectuals, bureaucrats, professionals, artisans, merchants, and freedmen who opposed the orthodox forces of elitism, hierarchy, and feudalism. For

---

[47] "Now the Word had taken on Himself the judgment, and having suffered in the body for all, has bestowed salvation on all" (Athanasius, *Orat.,* 1.60, in *Ath.,* 2: 60).

[48] "What Arius did was return to the original Scriptural and post-Scriptural Jewish conception of God as artisan" (Henry A. Wolfson, "Philosophical Implications of Arianism and Apollinarianism," in *Dumbarton Oaks Papers* [Cambridge, MA, 1958], p. 20).

Newman, the mongrel origins of the heretics was another proof of their theological error. He thought their bad beliefs made them forget their social place. The Marxist would reply that their social place made them adopt their bad beliefs.

At the top of the class structure, Arianism attracted worldly and cultured aristocrats. Arius's episcopal patrons, Eusebius of Caesarea and Eusebius of Nicomedia, both relished the stimulation of an open society and had trouble distinguishing between what they owed to Caesar and what to God. Eusebius of Nicomedia dabbled in imperial politics and traveled in court circles. Eusebius of Caesarea was stigmatized by Newman as a "mere man of letters."[49] They were post-apostolic Whigs. Like their nineteenth-century counterparts, they allied themselves with men socially beneath them but politically compatible.

But the bulk of Arius's support was drawn from the levels of society that men of good birth usually shunned. It was the common sneer of Athanasius and the orthodox party that the Arians were parvenus, arrivistes, and otherwise unworthy to debate about sacred things by virtue of their polluting connection with commerce or labor. There is no reason to doubt his detractors' description of Arius as an ambitious subordinate who took pride in his intellectual attainments—these would be the requisite qualities for an ambitious *novus homo*. Asterius, the early Arian apologist, had been a sophist who took money for instruction. He was tainted by the free market in both labor and ideas. George of Cappadocia, whom the Arians nominated to fill the Alexandrian see from which they had ousted the indomitable Athanasius, is universally reviled in the orthodox histories not so much for his theology, which must have been moderate (he was the protégé of the Eusebean court party) as for his enterprise, which ill comported with his humble origins. He was alleged to be the son of a fuller who had made his fortune (his enemies said by fraud) as a pork contractor to the army. He was said once to have cornered the market in niter, invested shrewdly in papyrus, and even to have a stake in the embalming business. His connection with industry and trade was sufficient in the eyes of orthodox apologists to render his theological opinions worthless, in spite of the fact that George was the owner of a library extensive enough to have excited the envy of the learned emperor Julian, the most erudite of fourth-century rulers. This nouveau-riche clerical entrepreneur died at the hands of a mob of Alexandrian pagans,

---

[49] *Ari.*, p. 256.

and by the fortunes of hagiography became Saint George, or so Gibbon imagined. That an Arian pork-contractor should be the patron saint of heretical England must have seemed apt to Newman.[50]

Aetius, the most logical exponent of Arian theology in the mid-fourth century, is also the most representative example of its class characteristics. He was an ambitious artisan who reveled in social mobility. Newman called him a "despicable adventurer."[51] Before he found his calling as a theologian, he had been a goldsmith, a doctor, and a teacher. His career demonstrates the classes to which Arianism appealed. Not surprisingly, he was the most rigorous and forceful exponent of the strict Arian theology that held the Father to be utterly unlike the Son in nature. By background and training men like Aetius had everything to lose in an ideological system that fixed religious and economic obligations for all time and subordinated every creature, politically and metaphysically, to the will of a despot.

The hypothesis that Arianism reflects a social controversy goes a long way toward explaining the weird coalition that supported the heretics. Here was a doctrine that united interests of Gothic barbarians and Alexandrian virgins with those of learned prelates and ambitious craftsmen. These diverse constituencies had only one thing in common—a desire to open the power and wealth of the empire to enterprise and ambition. Understood in this Marxist light, the Council of Nicaea makes perfect sense as a convocation of ideologues acting in collusion with the ruling classes. Their function was to lend theological sanction to the forces of a new, more rigid Byzantine economic order then emerging to replace what the economist Eric Roll has described as "the strongly individualistic quality of the Roman economic structure." The emperor Constantine himself presided at Nicaea, and the fathers of the Church readily consented to a creed which favored the perpetuation of the ruling elite to which they now belonged. The reverence for gentility so pronounced in the Cappadocian fathers later in the century was already apparent in the alliance of the better classes that dictated the Nicene formulas.[52]

---

[50] "Through a cloud of fiction, we may yet distinguish the combat which St. George of Cappadocia sustained, in the presence of Queen *Alexandra,* against the *magician Athanasius*" (Gibbon, *Decline and Fall,* 2: 472; see also *Ath.,* 2: 29–30).

[51] *Ari.,* p. 339.

[52] Roll, *A History of Economic Thought,* 4th ed. (London, 1983), p. 38. The Cappadocian fathers—Basil the Great, his brother Gregory of Nyssa, and their comrade Gregory of

The best evidence that this is the correct interpretation of Nicaea is its own handiwork: the bulk of the business that occupied the council concerned not doctrine but canon law, and the ecclesiastical legislation illuminates the ideological proclamations of the fathers of Nicaea. The council forbade the translation of bishops, priests, or deacons from one church to another—an ecclesiastical check against upward mobility, the counterpart to the secular prohibition restricting the tenant to his lease-hold. Clergy were forbidden to lend money at interest—a regulation designed not only to take the priest out of the sordid world of commerce, but also, given the growing financial power of the Church, to reduce inflation and restrict the supply of money for new and potentially destabilizing private ventures. And the fathers of Nicaea refused to enact a canon in favor of clerical celibacy, thereby leaving open the possibility that the cleric like the nobleman, the ship's captain, and the serf, might bequeath his social position to his progeny in the new economic system of fixed hereditary obligations. The doctrine and the canons of Nicaea are of piece and all in tune with the enunciation of an ideology for the new, restrictive economic system. George Ostrogorsky said of the Byzantine empire on the threshold of the fourth century, "Compulsion in economic life paved the way for compulsion in political affairs." In a Marxist analysis, it would be fair to add that the empire's economic compulsion also led to ecclesiastical and dogmatic compulsion.[53] Nor will the Marxist be surprised that under the name of Socinianism, the Arian heresy recurred in sixteenth-century Europe at precisely the moment when the individualistic and entrepreneurial forces of the pre-Nicene economy reasserted themselves in the spirit of the Renaissance.

If the Marxist analysis is correct, then the Arian controversy is an example of the subordination of thought to fact, and the labors of the pious from Athanasius to Newman in defense of the Trinity have been nothing more than the displaced defense of a repressive economic system. If Marxism is correct, then freedom as Newman understood it is a

---

Nazianzus—were very conscious of the inferior breeding of the heretics. Gregory of Nyssa sneered at Aetius as a "tinker." See Robert A. Kaster, *Guardians of Language: The Grammarian and Society in Late Antiquity* (Berkeley, 1988), p. 6.

[53] Ostrogorsky, *History of the Byzantine State,* trans. Joan Hussey (1940; New Brunswick, NJ, 1969), p. 30. The remains of the Council of Nicaea are gathered in *The Seven Ecumenical Councils of the Undivided Church,* ed. Henry R. Percival (1899; reprinted, Grand Rapids, MI, Eerdmans, 1977), pp. 1–55.

myth. Neither Arius nor Athanasius, neither Newman nor Hampden freely selected his beliefs. Each merely acted out a part—a part not even written by some divine power, but improvised by the mindless forces of time and circumstance. In such a view the bliss of Newman's heaven and the pains of Newman's hell become either absurd or monstrous. Having no real power of choice, who can earn paradise or deserve damnation?

But the Marxist analysis is open to two objections, one historical and one logical. For the traditional Marxist, ideas must follow material conditions as effects follow causes—and usually they must follow at a considerable remove. "All through history, mind limps after reality," Trotsky said.[54] But in fact orthodox and heretical ideas about the Trinity developed in uncomfortable proximity to the economic events they ought to have followed. The compulsory system, in which the emperor was sovereign, though the subject owed an equal and like obedience to his local master, was embryonic at the time that the Council of Nicaea enunciated the theological equivalent of this political theory in the "sameness of nature" of Father and Son. Only by hindsight can we impute a perfected imperial economy of restrictions to the first decades of the fourth century. When Constantine convened the Council of Nicaea, he had been absolute ruler of East and West for less than a year. He was by no means secure on his throne, much less able to demand the religious articulation of a political ideology that had hardly begun to exist. Constantine's imperial system was so insecure in fact as well as in theory that after his death the empire was convulsed by rival leaders with rival theories of political and economic organization.

And the hierarchical class relations which the doctrines and decrees of Nicaea seem to reflect were no more certainly in place by 325 than was the emperor's supreme authority. If there are intimations of serfdom in the decrees of the third and fourth centuries that bound the worker and his progeny to their jobs, the full implications of serfdom were not worked out until long after Nicaea.

But if the Marxists insist that by 325 the seeds of the restrictive system had been in place for a hundred years or more and that the fathers at Nicaea merely echoed in theological language the realities of the economic sphere, their opponents can with justice reply that the theological issues debated at Nicaea had as venerable a pedigree as the evolving class relations that they were supposed to mirror. Arius's ideas had been anticipated in the third century by those of Lucian of Antioch, who had learned his heresies from Paul of Samosata, who had been a pupil of the great Alexandrian, Origen, who had sewn the seeds of heresy at the same time the emperor Alexander Severus was taking the first steps toward the imperial regulation of trade guilds. No matter how deep into history the Marxist digs to find the economic base on which he alleges the super-structure of Christian ideology was reared, the Christian archaelogist can dig as deep or deeper to find an earlier instance of dogma in formation. And so the Marxist is confronted with two unpleasant possibilities: either the debate about the Father and the Son proceeded in tandem with the economic and political conditions it is alleged to reflect, or the doctrinal controversy preceded the economic realities to which it is so comfortably adapted.

Refined Marxists escape these difficulties by asserting that ideology does not have to be the direct result of economic or political conditions. In this view, ideology and economic conditions are both determined by something still more fundamental. Frederic Jameson, for instance, suggests that ''passionate disputes about the nature of the Trinity'' are best understood as ''vital episodes in a single vast unfinished plot dictated by ''a political unconscious.''[55] Fourth-century Christian ideology may have coincided with or even antedated the imperial economy which it would eventually come to support and yet the ideology would still logically follow the class structure, even while chronologically preceding it. History may be likened to a plot dictated by the political unconscious. To further their plots, authors may place events in their novels in any sequence they like, but the order of events will not alter the denouement toward which they are working. Just so, the unconscious in its historical drama may introduce ideology before economics, yet all the while work toward a political, and not a dogmatic, conclusion. And so for the Marxist, the Arian controversy and the orthodox Christianity that emerged from it may have conditioned the fourth century's political unconscious, but it was politics that drove the society, and not the theology by which the unconscious attempted to understand itself.

This refined Marxism has its logical difficulties. Let it be granted that an abstraction, a guiding spirit, such as the political unconscious may be said to exist at all. If economics and ideology are both products of this

---

[55] *The Political Unconscious* (Ithaca, NY, 1981), pp. 19–20.

guiding spirit, how does such a version of history differ from Newman's view that an unseen force guides history, except that Newman calls the force belief while the Marxist calls it the political unconscious? And if the Marxist insists that his guiding force is purely material and objective, while Newman's guiding force is abstract and unreal, has he not merely pushed the problem one step back by a verbal trick? The political unconscious has then become another name for the material and economic determinism that we encountered and rejected in the first place. Either the Marxist is a pure materialist, in which case Newman would insist that his case was defeated by his own historical facts, or else the Marxist must admit spiritual entities, in which case Newman would ask why the Christian's "belief striving toward God" is a less intelligible form of words than the Marxist's "knowledge striving toward consciousness."

But the Marxist analysis of the Arian controversy runs into a still more fundamental difficulty—the problem of self-reference. Marxism cannot talk about Arianism without talking about itself. It cannot objectively examine the Arian dispute without taking the Arian side because the Arian premises are the Marxist premises.

The religious revolution of Nicaea and Constantinople was not that the Church declared the Son to be "the same in nature" as the Father—the Arians could live with this ambiguity—but that it declared anything at all about God. Here the bishops and the emperor, speaking for the whole Church, declared that there are supermaterial truths that guide human events, that mortals in this world can apprehend these truths, and that they are bound to believe in them. The strict Arians simply denied these premises, and maintained that the only true statements about God are statements about what we cannot know. All real knowledge is intellectual, a correspondence between the created intellect and the created world it apprehends.

Marxists, both vulgar and refined, proceed according to the Arian theory:

> For us, the "real" is not a *theoretical slogan;* the real is the real object that exists independently of its knowledge—but which can only be defined by its knowledge. In this second, theoretical, relation, the real is identical to the means of knowing it, the real is its known or to-be-known structure, it is the very object of Marxist theory, the object marked out by the great theoretical discoveries of Marx and Lenin, the immense, living, constantly developing

field, in which the events of human history can from now on be mastered by men's practice, because they will be within their conceptual grasp, their knowledge.[56]

The names Arius and Asterius could be substituted for those of Marx and Lenin in this passage with little loss of historical or philosophical accuracy. The Marxist has already answered all the questions posed by the Arian controversy in the Arian way. Since Marxism's premises exclude any consciousness higher than human consciousness and deny to language any validity higher than what can be established in what Asterius called "the intellectual world," the Marxist method cannot find any sense in the argument of Athanasius and the orthodox Church party. The Marxist's conclusion about Arianism is assumed in his premises and his whole analysis is a mere tautology.

So Newman and Athanasius may have been right, or at least they are not refuted by the best efforts of Arius's liberal descendants. Belief may be the preeminent category of human life, and the struggle that defines history may be, not the struggle of class against class, but the conflict of heresy and dogma. The feudalism of the middle ages may have arisen from the Christology of Athanasius, and the modern world may be the realization of the Arian heresy. Newman never doubted that the history of mankind could be read in the development of its beliefs, and, following the Arian thread, he unraveled the mystery of contemporary civilization.

## Arius Redivivus

For Newman, the councils of Nicaea and Constantinople had only scotched the snake of heresy, not killed it. After a thousand years, Arianism returned like a dormant infection to plague Western culture anew. The great heresy of the modern world was liberalism, and liberalism was only a more virulent strain of Arianism.

---

[56] Louis Althusser, *For Marx* (London, 1969), p. 246. The parallel between Marxist criticism and Arian theology is perserved in their similar verbal quibbles. The Arians tried to explain how the Son was *like* the Father without being identical with him; the Marxists try to explain how ideological events are *like* economic events without being identical with them. The Arians called the Son *homoisios*; the Marxists call events *homologous*. Both terminologies have generated charges of heresy. See Jameson, *The Political Unconscious*, pp. 43–45.

What had Bentham to do with Arius or Lord Melbourne with Eusebius of Caesarea? The connection between Alexandrian theology and English liberalism seems improbable to the modern world, Newman would say, precisely because the modern world is liberal. Like the Marxists, the modern world is accustomed to seek material connections between events. But for Newman belief has a life prior to the material conditions in which it manifests itself. Men are free at all times and places to choose the false beliefs of Arianism over the dogmatic truths of Catholicism. The modern West has made that bad choice.

The liberal will remain skeptical. What debt can his theories of enlightened progress owe to the benighted wrangles of the Byzantine Church? And how can he be influenced by dogmas of which he has never heard?

Newman is prepared to answer him on both points. The liberal is merely ignorant of the laws by which belief operates. "All heresies seem connected together," Newman wrote, "and to run into each other. When the mind has embraced one, it is almost certain to run into others. . . . Heresies run into each other, (one may even say,) logically."[57] The Arian doctrine furnished the logical premises from which modern civilization draws its seemingly paradoxical conclusions, and on these conclusions liberalism has raised its edifice of technology, pluralism, and doubt. Newman would also argue that Arianism has immunized us to the knowledge of our own depravity. From their resurgence in the seventeenth century, the errors of Arianism have spawned a theological ignorance so profound that people no longer recognize that their opinions are only variations of ancient unbelief. "Socinians, Sabellians, Nestorians, and the like, abound in these days, without their even knowing it themselves," Newman wrote.[58] The ancient heresies furnish the key to modern behavior even where their exponents are ignorant of their errors' antecedents. Here as elsewhere Newman owed a debt to scholasticism. For him history possesses an unseen substance in which its material manifestations inhere and this substance is best understood as belief. At bottom, history is a concatenation of beliefs that guide and shape human action individually and collectively.

Newman's record of modern culture would pay scant attention to the rise of the bourgeoisie, the invention of the printing press, or the

[57] *Ath.*, 2: 143–44.
[58] *Dev.*, p. 134.

expansion of international trade. Not that Newman denied that these would have occurred without the presence of the West's characteristic heresy. But he would have argued that in the absence of Arianism, their character would have been so altered as to make them virtually different events.

For Newman, the decline of the West and the rise of liberalism are interchangeable ideas. The process of the West's corruption can be traced to the Reformation attack on Catholic dogma, an attack engineered by three heresiarchs. "Luther did but a part of the work, Calvin another portion, Socinus finished it."[59] In Newman's view, these three heretics may have begun with conflicting doctrines, but by the rule that "heresies run into each other," they ended in a common Arianism. Beginning from different theological speculations, the leaders of the Reformation had converged on a single mastering premise—that belief can never be stated dogmatically. The extravagant and erring spirit of Arius returned to furnish the epistemological foundation of modern liberalism.

Socinus is now the least familiar of Newman's three modern heresiarchs, but he was the most important of them for Newman and his circle. The dark significance the Oxford Movement attached to the term Socinian may be gauged from Tract 36, where Newman's high-church ally Arthur Perceval listed Socinians first among those English dissenters "who reject the Truth," giving them pride of place over Jews, deists, and atheists.[60] Newman would have added that Socinianism logically involved these other errors.

---

[59] *Dev.*, p. 89. Newman can hardly mention the founders of Protestantism without linking them to their fourth-century forebears in heresy and underlining the fact that one heresy runs into all others:

> Lutheranism has by this time become in most places almost simple heresy or infidelity; it has terminated, if it has even yet reached its limit, in a denial both of the Canon and the Creed, nay, of many principles of morals. Accordingly the question arises, whether these conclusions are in fairness to be connected with its original teaching or are a corruption. And it is no little aid towards its resolution to find that Luther himself at one time rejected the Apocalypse, called the Epistle of St. James 'straminea,' condemned the word 'Trinity,' fell into a kind of Eutychianism in his view of the Holy Eucharist, and in a particular case sanctioned bigamy. Calvinism, again, in various distinct countries, has become Socinianism, and Calvin himself seems to have denied our Lord's Eternal Sonship and ridiculed the Nicene Creed. (*Dev.*, p. 184)

"Straminea" is "so much straw."
[60] *Tracts*, 1, Tract 36, p. 2.

The dissident theology of the Sienese reformer Fausto Sozzini (1539–1604), known as Socinus, was closer in spirit to the doctrines of Arius than either Lutheranism or Calvinism, and it was natural, at least in Newman's mind, that Socinus's more primal error should subsume these less developed forms of heresy. In his own day, Socinus found a following among Polish Anabaptists. Later, his doctrine was prominent in the ferment of ideas that constituted seventeenth-century English Protestantism. Today, he is claimed by the Unitarians as a founding father of their strict monotheism. But in Newman's mind the influence of Socinus was more extensive than his contribution to dissent. Socinus had revived the anti-dogmatic principle.

Socinus's Christology was more radical than Arius's—where Arius's Christ was a divine creator, the Socinian Jesus was a mortal man whom God had adopted as the messenger of his word. Technically, the Socinian heretic was a bolder apostate than the Arian, and exact theologians were careful to distinguish the one from the other.[61] But when Newman used the term Socinian, it is not only Socinus's unitarian Christology that he referred to but the general liberalism of his doctrine. Like the Arians, Socinus taught the ineffable unity of God. Like the Arians, he relied strictly on God's revelation as recorded in the New Testament, which could only be read by the individual exercising his reason on the text. His principles, like Arius's, logically led to toleration and humanism. Socinus had introduced the thin wedge of Arian thought which opened the way to the liberal apostasy.

When in 1834 Newman wrote Hampden to protest the opinions advanced in his *Observations on Religious Dissent,* he summarized his objection by noting that Hampden's principles would lead to "formal Socinianism."[62] "Formal Socinianism" encompassed for Newman the whole ideological program of Arianism. By this single charge, Newman meant to implicate Hampden in the entire system of false belief that had directed the course of Western history since the Renaissance.

Newman's use of the term Socinian preserved all the horror that orthodox Englishmen felt when they first encountered Socinus's heresy. In his study of the moderate Anglicanism that guided seventeenth-century English leaders like Falkland, Chillingworth, and Clarendon, Hugh Trevor-Roper examines the distinction made in the revolutionary

---

[61] See James Hay Colligan, *The Arian Movement in England* (Manchester, 1913), pp. 2–4, for a discussion of the differences between Socinians and Arians.

[62] *L.D.,* 4: 371.

era between Socinianism as mere denial of Christ's divine substance and Socinianism as an assertion of "the liberty to doubt." For Trevor-Roper Erasmus was "the father of Socinianism in both the wide and the narrow sense."[63] In the broad sense preserved by Newman, Socinianism was identical with humanism. Newman would only have added that humanism, like Socinianism, is a mutation of the Arian heresy. The Arian premises inherent in Socinianism led on the one hand to a denial of the Trinity and on the other to the rise of liberalism. The two faces of Socinianism were only aspects of a single heretical disposition, and in Newman's mind modern history was only intelligible as Arianism in action.

In fact, the Socinians themselves were happy to accept Newman's view of Western history, disagreeing with him only in his conclusion that Arianism is evil. Fresh from his efforts to isolate the element oxygen, the Socinian scientist Joseph Priestley in 1782 next isolated the religious traditions that made enlightened progress possible. His *History of the Corruptions of Christianity* (1782) and *Early Opinions Concerning Jesus* (1786) paint a picture of Western civilization very like Newman's. History had been a contest for right belief about the nature of Christ. The first round of this contest ended with the suppression of the Arian controversy and the second began with the rise of Socinianism. This second age is not yet finished. Priestley looked for the victory of reason, science, and Unitarianism. He supported the French Revolution in its attack on orthodoxy. He was the disciple of Socinus as Newman was of Athanasius, but the two shared the conviction that belief is the substance of history.

Those like Priestley or Newman or Trevor-Roper who regard history as a drama of belief are bound sooner or later to turn to the example of seventeenth-century England. Here was a century that began in dogma and ended in deism. Anyone who, like Newman, asserts the preeminence

---

[63] "The Great Tew Circle," in *Catholics, Anglicans, and Puritans* (Chicago, 1988), pp. 188–89. No one has written more amusingly of the Oxford Movement's intellectual deficiencies than Lord Dacre—see, for instance, *Archbishop Laud* (London, 1940), pp. 432–33, where Newman is described as "wasting time in the innocent but uninformative pursuits of hagiography and martyrology." But at heart there is an affinity between the historian and the hagiographer who both see history as a contest of beliefs. The distinction between Socinianism as denial of the Trinity and Socinianism as humanistic doubt was noted a century ago by S. R. Gardiner in the *DNB* entry for Falkland.

of ideas among the forces that shape human life will find in this development of ideas the pattern of the West's metamorphosis from ancient to modern. The liberal regards the transformation as the source of progress; Newman regarded it as the prologue to damnation.

What will a view of English history as the contest of heresy and belief look like? Once England had been dogmatic: men recognized the truth and punished error. As late as 1612, Church and state collaborated in the execution of two Arian heretics. Edmund Wightman was an Anabaptist who denied the divinity of Christ and proclaimed himself to be the Paraclete. The heresy of Bartholomew Legate was less ostentatious. He had imbibed Socinianism while traveling among the Mennonites and Anabaptists of northern Europe, and returned to England to preach that Christ was but "a meere man." James I took a personal interest in exterminating both heretics. Wightman was charged on information from the king himself, and in the course of his incarceration, Legate was several times interrogated by his monarch. "Finding that Legate no longer prayed to Christ, 'the king in choler spurn'd at him with his foot; Away, base fellow (saith he), it shall never be said that one stayeth in my presence that hath never prayed to our Saviour for seven years together.'"[64] The young William Laud sat on the consistory court that condemned Wightman, the venerable Lancelot Andrewes on the tribunal that denounced Legate. In those days monarchs and divines took it for granted that belief was a subject for civil and ecclesiastical scrutiny. Sharing this view, Newman looked back on the Stuarts as the last orthodox kings and revered the memory of Wightman's inquisitor, Laud. At the start of the seventeenth century, the dogmatic principle had been alive and well in England.

But the executions of Wightman and Legate marked the last occasions on which Englishmen died for crimes purely against dogma. After 1612, the anti-dogmatic principle was ascendant.

The last burning of Arians had coincided with the publication of the Authorized Version of the English Bible. Newman's critic and contem-

---

[64] See the entry for Legate in the *DNB*, which quotes Thomas Fuller's *Church History of Britain*. Legate and Wightman contend for the honor of being the last heretic executed under the provisions of the ancient writ *De haeretico comburendo*. Legate was burned on March 18, 1612, at West Smithfield. Wightman had almost been executed several days earlier, but recanted just as the flames touched him. Later, he recanted his recantation and "blasphemed more audaciously than before." He was finally consigned to the flames in April.

porary, James Martineau, claimed that the Authorized Version of 1611 had created English Unitarianism.[65] The Socinian doctrine that no single interpretation of the Bible could claim the sanction of absolute truth followed where everyone could read Scripture for himself, and so an officially sanctioned vernacular Bible prepared the way for the separation of belief and action. Whether by applying unaided reason, by reading the seditious treatises of Socinus, or by studying the ancient heresies of Arius, in the era of the English Revolution Arianism and Socinianism were powerful forces in English thought. Like the epithet communist in the 1950s, the expression Socinian came to mean any form of liberal dissent. There was the exact Socinianism of Puritans like John Bidle, who denied the divinity of Christ; the closet Arianism of revolutionaries like Milton, who avowed his heterodoxy only in the clandestine pages of his *De Doctrina Christiana;* and the still more intangible Socinianism of royalists like Falkland and Chillingworth, who professed the Trinity but also embraced the freethinking spirit of rationalism. So loosely defined—and Newman was always the advocate of loose definitions—the English seventeenth century was the age of Socinianism.

Nor did the Socinian upheaval end with the restoration of Charles II. By 1660, Socinianism had infected the whole apparatus of English belief, and its disruptive influence was apparent in science, religion, politics, and philosophy.

In science, Socinianism was the handmaiden to Newton's *Principia.* Newton was a thorough Arian in his religious opinions and a Socinian in the broad sense. His scientific view of a universe governed by physical law and ruled by a remote and ineffable divinity developed in tandem with a well-concealed Arianism in which Christ the subordinate Logos was the demiurge, while Jehovah remained an unutterable mystery behind the veil of absolute space and time.[66] In the dogmatic view of history advocated by Newman, it would be useless to inquire whether Newton's Arianism was the cause or the effect of his physics. Like the

[65] In Herbert McLachlan, *The Unitarian Movement in the Religious Life of England* (London, 1934), 1: 13.

[66] "He identified himself with Arius, both intellectually and emotionally. He relived the terrible struggles of the fourth century, when doctrine counted for more than charity, came to see Athanasius as his personal nemesis, and learned to hate him fiercely." A portrait of Newton in the 1670s, between writing "De gravitatione et equipondio fluidorum" and the *Principia.* Richard Westfall, *Never at Rest: A Biography of Isaac Newton* (Cambridge, 1980), p. 318. Chapter Eight of this book gives a résumé of Newton's Arian opinions.

Father and Son of orthodoxy, the two are consubstantial, indissolubly one even while appearing in the different personalities of science and theology.[67]

Nor was Newton's Arianism an ideological freak. It was shared explicitly by William Whiston, Newton's hand-picked successor in the Lucasian professorship of mathematics at Cambridge, and implicitly by a whole school of scientific thought from Newton's day to our own. When Stephen Hawkings, Newton's twentieth-century successor in the Lucasian professorship, asks of the universe, "What place, then, for a creator?" he continues both the science and the theology of his predecessors.[68] A historian of Newman's persuasion would argue that in the era of liberalism scientific thought and Socinian belief have proceeded hand in hand. Priestley, a Socinian chemist as well as a Unitarian ideologue, noted with pride that the first Arians had been men of science who had endeavored to show that a God in three persons was "more Gods than one. Such geometry as this, I doubt not, gave great offense."[69] The Socinians themselves believed the scientific spirit to be inherent in Arianism. Newman agreed.

A similar unity of belief and activity is apparent in statecraft, religion, and philosophy. The Socinian denied to the creeds of Christianity any transcendant truth, and so rejected the possibility of absolute truth. The political expression of this denial was religious toleration—hence the open or covert Socinianism of Whigs and radicals in the revolutionary era. Was not the very idea of toleration a Socinian innovation? Seventeenth-century contemporaries on either side of the issue thought so. When in 1676 Andrew Marvell defended the principle of toleration, he felt obliged to denounce the errors of the fathers of Nicaea in order to vindicate the liberties of Restoration Englishmen; "As to the whole matter of the Council of Nice, I must crave liberty to say, that from one end to the other, though the best of the kind, it seems to me to have been a

[67] Margaret C. Jacob, *The Radical Enlightenment: Pantheists, Freemasons, and Republicans* (London, 1981), and "The Anglican Origins of Modern Science," *Isis* 71 (1980): 251–67, survey the connections among science, heresy, and liberal ideology.

[68] Hawking, *A Brief History of Time* (New York, 1988), p. 141.

[69] *The History of the Corruptions of Christianity* (London, 1782), p. 73. Priestley took his information from the Lutheran historian Mosheim, who had pointed out the scientific bent of the first Arians. The seventeenth century had already noted the connection. "Francis Osborne in 1656 said that the Socinians were 'looked upon as the most chemical and rational part of our many divisions.'" See Christopher Hill, *The World Turned Upside Down* (New York, 1972), p. 234.

pityful humane business." Marvell excoriates the dogmatism of the fathers of Nicaea and their latter-day successors for "imposition of a new article or Creed upon the Christian world not being contained in express words of Scripture." Marvell's is the habitual Arian or Socinian principle of toleration, rooted in respect for the individual's freedom to exercise his reason: "No, a good Christian will not, cannot atturn and indenture his conscience ever, to be represented by others."[70] For Marvell as for Socinus, the cause of liberty demanded the rehabilitation of Arius.

The connection between Athanasian dogma and modern absolutism was evident to men like Marvell and Milton, and their readers shared the habit of discussing politics in the language of theology. Even without the evidence of *De Doctrina Christiana*, Milton's early critics sniffed out the heresy in his work. "Tainted with Socinianism," was John Dennis's judgment in 1704.[71] Traditionalists were quick to implicate reformers in the full horrors of ancient heresy. When, for instance, the orthodox looked for some way to impugn the liberal principles of Locke's *Treatises on Civil Government* (1690), they found it in the Arianism of his epistemology.

Locke's accuser was Edward Stillingfleet, bishop of Worcester and champion of what Newman would later call the *via media*. Stillingfleet's middle way sought to preserve all that was fundamental in Catholic dogma while embracing the virtues of rationalism. Stillingfleet the rationalist produced a *Rational Account of the Grounds of the Protestant Religion* (1664), but Stillingfleet the Anglo-Catholic could not countenance the assault on orthodoxy contained in Locke's philosophy. Had not Locke in his *Essay on Human Understanding* virtually argued away the existence of substance? And if substance were removed, what remained of the dogmatic formula whereby God and Christ were consubstantial? Locke had therefore implicitly rejected the Trinity, and with it the creeds and truthfulness of Christianity.

Locke protested in vain that he had not denied the reality of substance—he had in fact proclaimed its existence to be as probable as his own. Stillingfleet replied, "It is not Probability, but Certainty, that we are promised in this way of Ideas; and that the Foundation of our Knowledge and real Certainty lies in them; and is it dwindled into a

[70] Marvell, *Mr. Smirke; or, the Divine Mode* (London, 1676), pp. 122–23, 126–27.
[71] In Michael Bauman, *Milton's Arianism* (New York, 1987), p. 280.

Probability at last?''[72] The covert Arianism of Locke's philosophy reduced dogmas to probabilities and belief to illusion. No polity or religion built on these principles could survive.

Stillingfleet's quibble about Locke's epistemology is in fact a challenge to the foundations of liberal thought. At bottom, the program of toleration, balance, and civil liberties of which Locke was the most illustrious exponent rested on a denial not only of the Trinity, but of Christian truth itself. The latent Arianism of seventeenth-century liberal thought compelled traditionalists like Stillingfleet to defend fourth-century dogma in order to preserve the institutions of English society. The implicit denial of the Nicene concept of substance threatened to bring down both Church and state.

In the philosophy erected by scholasticism to justify Catholic dogma, substance is the genuine core of a thing. Perceptions and attributes of a thing are not the thing itself. The thing itself subsists in its substance, from which its attributes and our perceptions arise. But according to Locke, this thing in itself which is substance cannot be experienced directly, nor is knowledge of it innately present in the mind. The claim that substance exists, is, says Locke, ''only an uncertain supposition.''[73] But the orthodox ideas of God and truth are predicated on substance. God is not, after all, his attributes and manifestations, but some substance in which these adhere. The Father and Son cannot be one unless they are ''one in substance,'' and truth is not merely a list of dogmas, but some eternal substance which dogma expresses. Take away substance and God becomes merely a collection of all-too-human adjectives and truth merely a compilation of abstract nouns. Stillingfleet saw that a political theory constituted on this dangerous premise must end in the conclusion that God might be probable but was certainly irrelevant. For him as for Newman, the future of Christian civilization depended on a theological term, and it is no surprise to find Newman in his *Grammar of Assent*

---

[72] *The Bishop of Worcester's Answer to Mr. Locke's Letter* (London, 1697), pp. 67–68. The objectionable passages in the *Essay on Human Understanding* can be found at 1.4.19 and 2.23.1. Newman read Stillingfleet's *Origines Sacrae* (1666) in preparation for his *Essay on Miracles* (1827), in which he cites the bishop's work with approbation. The question raised by Stillingfleet against Locke, with minor revisions, is the question raised by Newman against Peel in ''The Tamworth Reading Room'': ''Life is not long enough for a religion of inferences; we shall never have done beginning, if we determine to begin with proof'' (*D.A.*, p. 295).

[73] *Human Understanding*, 1.4.19.

picking up the defense of dogma where the bishop of Worcester had left it almost two centuries earlier.

In the *Grammer of Assent,* Newman followed his usual method of arguing. He accomplished the resurrection of substance by adopting Locke's own argument and turning it against him. Locke had said the existence of substance was probable. Newman then devised a grammar of assent that converts probabilities into certainties. Thus the substance of truth is preserved to underwrite the objective validity of dogma, and the substance of God is saved to guarantee the truth of the Nicene Creed. The logic of Newman's argument in the *Grammar of Assent* was borrowed from Locke, but its spirit was Stillingfleet's. For Newman as for Stillingfleet, Arianism must be uncovered and defeated in whatever cunning disguises it is found lurking.

The churchmen of the seventeenth century met the Socinian challenge as Newman would in the nineteenth—by a defense of fourth-century orthodoxy. Faced with the onslaught of liberalism, Newman composed his *History of the Arians,* just as George Bull, bishop of St. David's and defender of the *via media* had in the 1680s replied to earlier Socinians in his *Defensio Fidei Nicaenae.*[74] But while this learned apology for the orthodoxy of Athanasius' theology commanded the admiration of Bossuet, it failed to stem the erosion of orthodox belief without or even within the English Church. Two years after Bull finished his defense of the Trinity, Dryden surveyed the challenge offered to civilization by "the bold Socinian" and wondered, "Must all tradition then be set aside?"[75] The forces of liberalism seemed to reply with a resounding yes, and in 1685 Dryden abandoned the precarious *via media* of English theology for the certain authority of the Roman communion.

By the time of the Settlement of 1688, Socinianism was entrenched in Whig politics, empirical philosophy, and Miltonic poetry. Next it infiltrated the English Church itself. The first two decades of the eighteenth century witnessed bitter theological warfare within the Anglican communion over the Arian questions revived by Socinus. Newton's protégé

---

[74] Bull finished the *Defensio* in 1680 but did not find a publisher till 1685. Modern scholars of dogmatic development are too quick to dismiss Bull's work as a reply to the errors of the Catholic Petavius, who held that before Nicaea many good Catholics had not believed in the consubstantial Father and Son. Petavius's was only one of many errors refuted by Bull. The opening chapters of the *Defensio* make clear that his target is Arianism in all its forms, ancient and modern, Protestant and Catholic.

[75] *Religio Laici,* 305, 312.

William Whiston, a priest as well as a professor, openly avowed himself a "Eusebian" in 1708, and thereafter denounced the Nicene Creed and Saint Athanasius. The Church repelled this assault on orthodoxy by depriving Whiston of his professorship and exiling him from Cambridge. Outside the establishment, he became a formidable champion of heresy, organizing in 1715 a society for the promotion of "primitive Christianity"—that is, Arianism—and relentlessly attacking the dogmatic foundations of the doctrine of the Trinity. Confronted with open clerical apostasy such as Whiston's, the Convocation of the English Church increasingly found itself sitting as a court of heresy. Whiston's *Primitive Christianity Revived* was condemned by Convocation in 1711. Then in 1712, Whiston's friend Samuel Clarke, another priest-scientist of the Newtonian circle, published his *Scripture Doctrine of the Trinity*. At its next meeting, the lower house of Convocation impeached him for Arianism.[76]

Worse was yet to come, next from within Convocation itself. In March of 1717, Benjamin Hoadly, bishop of Bangor and friend of Clarke, preached the most volatile doctrines of Socinianism from the pulpit of the royal chapel at St. James's. His sermon explicitly rejected the divine authority of the Church and implicitly embraced the Socinian principle that humans cannot with certainty state truth. Christ has left the world "no visible human authority; no viceregents who can be said properly to supply his place; no interpreters upon whom his subjects are absolutely to depend; no judges over the conscience or religion of his people."[77] Hoadly's defense of toleration and pluralism provoked the furor that came to be called the Bangorian Controversy in his honor. In the fourth century, Arianism so stirred the world that the shopkeepers of Byzantium interrogated the faith of their customers. Hoadlyism briefly achieved a similar notoriety in July of 1717 when commerce in the City of London came to a halt while men debated whether the Church of England was or was not dogmatic.[78]

[76] The lower house of Convocation consisted of deans, archdeacons, and other priests. The upper house was composed wholly of bishops and archbishops. In Clarke's case, the bishops refused to take up the indictment of the lower house.

[77] Hoadly, *Works* (London, 1773), 2: 404.

[78] Hoadly, *Works*, 2: 429. Leslie Stephen called Hoadly "the best-hated clergyman of the century amongst his own order. . . . His style is the style of a bore. . . . We owe, however, a vast debt of gratitude to bores who have defended good causes" (*History of English Thought in the Eighteenth Century,* 3d ed. [New York, 1949], pp. 152–53). So nineteenth-century agnosticism acknowledged its debts to eighteenth-century Socinianism.

When Convocation took up the errors of Hoadly, its debates became so fractious that George I prorogued it. The bishops and presbyters were dismissed not knowing whether their Church preached truth or not, and the cancer of Socinianism was left to fester in the bosom of orthodoxy. The Crown did not allow Convocation to transact any serious business for another 140 years, and clergymen like Keble and Newman complained in the nineteenth century that the Church had no voice with which to censure the new Hoadlyism espoused by Hampden and his ilk.

The fear of Arianism persisted among the orthodox for years after the king dismissed Convocation. In 1721 the poet-physician Richard Blackmore wrote several pamphlets to warn that society was already compromised by "multitudes of secret and clandestine Arians" who would stop at nothing to inflict the atheistical tenets of Zeno and Hobbes on the world. "Numberless are the wiles and double appearances of this protean race . . . these wild boars of the forest."[79] Blackmore was a hysteric, but there was enough truth in his portrait of an Arian conspiracy that a learned divine like Daniel Waterland, master of Magdalene College, Cambridge, might devote the last half of a distinguished career to the defense of the Nicene faith. In four volumes over fourteen years he fought the Arians in the knowledge that the same arguments used to dismantle the Trinity would bring down God, truth, and priesthood as well. Waterland rightly saw that the chief Arian tenet was not the created nature of Christ but the inexpressible nature of God. He conceded that God was ineffable, but denied that this concession made dogma unknowable:

> It is a property of the divine Being to be unsearchable: and if he were not so, he would not be divine. Must we therefore reject the most certain truths concerning the Deity, only because they are incomprehensible, when everything almost belonging to him must be so of course? If so, there is an end, not only of all revealed Religion, but of natural Religion too, and we must take our last Refuge in downright Atheism.[80]

---

For the support his theories lent the Whig cause, Hoadly was in 1721 translated from Bangor to Hereford, a see which seems destined to be the reward of heresy. Croft had it before him and Hampden after. Hoadly later ascended to the better-remunerated Salisbury and thence to the lucrative Winchester.

[79] Blackmore, *Modern Arians Unmask'd* (London, 1721), pp. 41, 3, 54.

[80] Waterland, *The Importance of the Doctrine of the Trinity Asserted* (London, 1734), p. 18. Even in his own day, Waterland would have found those who argue that incom-

Waterland wrote this defense of dogma in 1734. Convocation had been prorogued seventeen years earlier. It would not meet again for a century. Arianism flourished unchecked within the Church and furnished the intellectual principles of a great political party. Socinian sects abounded and flourished. In the century between Waterland's *Doctrine of the Trinity* and Newman's *Arians,* the Unitarians established themselves as a distinct denomination and anti-trinitarians like Priestley waged a campaign to establish Socinianism as a populist philosophy to replace Christian orthodoxy. In America their efforts eventuated in the sermons of William Ellery Channing and the essays of Emerson. In Britain, too, Socinianism became respectable. In 1812, two hundred years after Wightman and Legate were burned for their Arian opinions, Parliament passed without debate an act to remove all civil penalties imposed on those who denied the Trinity.[81] Some redoubtable churchmen could still be found to defend the orthodoxy of Bull, Stillingfleet, and Waterland. Between 1814 and 1816, Richard Mant, chaplain to Archbishop Manners-Sutton, preached a series of sermons at Oxford against "the Unitarian, or, more properly speaking, the modern Socinian heresy."[82] But Socinianism was by now so ubiquituous as to seem uncontroversial except to the most fastidious theologians. True, as late as 1831 a contingent of orthodox Anglicans defected from the non-denominational Bible Society because it refused to exclude Unitarians, and in 1833 Thomas Arnold acknowledged that "many good men draw a broad line of distinction between errors respecting the Trinity, and errors on any other point. They cannot unite, they say, with those who are not Trinitarians." Yet the zeal with which earlier generations had guarded belief and the words that expressed belief seemed to have departed from the English Church. "We are by no means bound to inquire," Arnold wrote in his plea for a broad Church,

> whether all who pray to Christ entertain exactly the same ideas of his nature. I believe that Arianism involves in it some very erroneous notions as to the

---

prehensibility is a good reason to reject an asserted truth. The names Waterland, Stillingfleet, and Bull are prominent in the notes to Newman's earliest writings. They were his first intellectual guides to Socinianism. "The standard divines are magnificent fellows . . . Bull, Waterland, Petavius, Baronius and the rest," Newman wrote in 1831 (*L.D.,* 2: 371).

[81] Overton, *The English Church in the Nineteenth Century* (London, 1894), p. 302.

[82] *Sermons Preached Before the University of Oxford at St. Mary's* (Oxford, 1816), p. 5.

object of religious worship; but if an Arian will join in our worship of Christ, and will call him Lord and God, there is neither wisdom nor charity in insisting that he shall explain what he means by these terms.[83]

Here was the blasphemy of Sirmium all over again! Not only did Arnold extend the hand of fellowship to the Church's Arian foes, but he adopted the central tenet of their heresy—that belief is after all only a form of words, and words are incapable of expressing divine truths. Churchmen steeped in Socinianism, like Arnold and Hampden, reflexively rejected the premises on which dogma reposes.

In this atmosphere of dogmatic decadence, even the most orthodox theologian might be forgiven for stumbling into heresy. Newman himself seemed to embrace Arianism in a sermon in May of 1827, or so his mentor Whately thought.[84] By this date, truth and dogma were not merely neglected, they were ridiculed. In 1817, the radical William Hone had constructed a political parody on the model of the Apostles' Creed. The Tory government haled him before Chief Justice Ellenborough on a charge of "impious, profane, and scandelous libel." When Hone's parody ("I believe in George, the Regent Almighty") was read by the attorney-general, the court erupted in laughter. Though the reactionary Ellenborough summed up against the defendant, the jury took only fifteen minutes to acquit him.[85]

Dogma was now fair game for public as well as private satire, as

---

[83] Arnold, "Principles of Church Reform" (1833), in *Miscellaneous Works* (London, 1845), pp. 284–85. "It is false that there exists in the Church any power or office endowed with the gift of infallible wisdom; and therefore it is impossible to prevent differences of opinion," says Arnold in the same pamphlet, p. 272. The provenance of this thought is Arius by way of Socinus, Locke, and Hoadly.

[84] "In a sermon 'On the Mediatorial Kingdom of Christ' in Oriel chapel in May 1827 he considered the terms of the Athanasian Creed 'unnecessarily scientific,' compared with the Nicene Creed. He later recognized that he had been indulging the freedom of language, afterwards declared heretical, about the Son's subordination as if he was inferior to the Father, which had been common in the early Christian centuries before the Council of Nicaea" (Sheridan Gilley, *Newman and His Age* [London, 1990], p. 63). Gilley's is the best of the studies of Newman to appear during the centenary of his death and provides a wealth of detail with style and authority. Of this sermon, Newman later said that he "took, without knowing it, Bull's doctrine of the 'Subordinatio Filii.'" *A.W.*, p. 211. Still stung by their reproach fifty years later, Newman anathematized his erstwhile accusers with a *tu quoque*: "Whately, Hawkins, and Blanco White were all verging then toward Sabellianism themselves."

[85] Hone, *The Three Trials of William Hone* (London, 1876), pp. 4, 70.

Newman learned within the bosom of his own family. After the publication of his *Arians,* his whimsical brother Frank tweaked the dogmatic nose of his older sibling by declaring in his presence that Jesus was not Jehovah, and then sat back to relish the absurd spectacle of John Henry discoursing on Arianism and the subordination of the Son.[86]

This was the legacy of Socinian contempt and dogmatic dereliction that Newman believed he had inherited from the English Revolution. What matter if the Church of England built new churches, educated the young, or sent missions to Senegal, so long as it neglected the dogmatic principle? To concede this to liberalism was to concede everything.

Newman's was the last good mind in which the dogmatic principle still excited all the ideological excitement of seventeenth-century controversy. As a result, he denominated ancient theological errors and modern social theories indifferently by the interchangeable names Arianism, Socinianism, Hoadlyism, and liberalism. Newman is the missing link between the belief of the old world and the ideology of the new. As he seemed absurd to his brother, so must he seem to us; his absurdity is inseparable from his message, which is that those things that the worldly mind of the modern era considers ridiculous—namely the orthodox assertion that belief has a real object, that truth is abiding, and that words can dogmatically state truth—are in fact sublime realities.

[86]*Contributions Chiefly to the Early History of Cardinal Newman* (London, 1891), pp. 52–53.

# 4

# What Is Truth?
# Newman's Theory of Belief

Newman devoted his life to a failed crusade against Arians, Socinians, and liberals. The demolition of his enemies' principles so consumed him that bystanders easily forgot that he had any of his own. Reviewing Newman's career in 1862, Walter Bagehot concluded that "he was much better skilled in finding out the difficulties of other men's creeds than in discovering and stating a distinct basis for his own. In most of his characteristic works he does not even attempt it. His argument is essentially an argument *ad hominem;* an argument addressed to the present creed of the person with whom he is reasoning."[1] Bagehot wrote eight years before the *Essay in Aid of a Grammar of Assent* appeared, but its mystical empiricism would have done little to alter his opinion. Newman's thought is obscured by the destructive power of his vituperative intellect, the systematic ambiguity of his language, and the willful obscurity of his leading ideas. But beneath these self-inflicted liabilities there is a philosophy all Newman's own. Newman never stated this

[1] Bagehot, *Collected Works* (London, 1965), 2: 249.

philosophy concisely. He believed that verbal precision insulted truth, and his philosophy has to be extricated from the curious amalgam of piety and invective that makes up his response to liberalism.

What was the error of liberalism? The liberals had rejected the dogmatic principle, and with that rejection they had denied the truth. Liberals like Hampden were so many jesting Pilates, and Newman's indefatigable assault on their sacrilege compelled him to answer the skeptic's question, "What is truth?"

The mind, says Newman, is made for truth. The combination of correct belief and right action is truth. The goal of life, then, is first to attain correct beliefs and second to act on them. Man finds truth when he acts believingly.

The search for truth begins in the instincts and the experiences of the mind itself. The mind is a conglomeration of ideas. Many or most of these ideas are false—that is, they do not correspond to anything outside the mind. But a few ideas do correspond to material or spiritual archetypes outside the mind. Because the mind is made for truth, it instinctively tries to distinguish these true ideas from the false.

The first step in this process is the choice of a view of life by which to judge ideas. Once the mind has adopted a view, it measures its ideas against this view according to the laws of reason. The conclusions the mind reaches when this process is complete are its beliefs. Each person constructs his world, both spiritual and physical, from belief, and each person is free to make his life what he will because he is free to choose his beliefs.

The beliefs which the mind constructs from its ideas and views necessarily result in action. Speaking, writing, and thinking are as much forms of action as doing. When belief is true and action conforms to belief, action is an expression of truth. So too with language. Words that conform to true beliefs are expressions of truth, and language can express divine ideas. This expression is Catholic dogma.

For Newman, views of life fall into one of five classes. A right view of life pursued according to right reason leads to Catholicism. A right view pursued by faulty reason produces confusion. A wrong view prosecuted by right reason leads to heresy or atheism. A wrong view pursued by wrong reason generates paganism. A refusal to take a view or, having taken one, to reason from it, constitutes barbarism. Of these five states, one leads to salvation, the others to damnation. The modern world has rejected the Catholic way and is embarked on four different roads to hell.

Ideas, views, reason, dogma, instinct, action—Newman strewed these key terms through his work like landmines, unobtrusive but lethal. Each of them has to be defused before it is possible to navigate with any security through Newman's thought.

## Ideas

For Newman, right action and right belief are two aspects of a single reality, which is truth. But truth is the goal, not the starting point, of human endeavor. Nothing can be said about truth at the outset of human thinking any more than mathematical solutions can be stated in advance of their problems. The search for truth must begin where the mind itself begins, with a jumble of ideas in space and time.

Although Newman's philosophy turns on the word idea, he meant no more by it than Locke had meant a hundred years earlier: ideas are the stuff of which mind is composed. There are simple ideas like the mental image of a dog or the mental residue of a rose, and complex ideas, like the concept of gravity or the doctrine of the Immaculate Conception. Ideas are not necessarily verbal. A child has valid ideas about its mother long before it can speak, and a person may have valid ideas about gravity without being able to articulate them. So far Newman's use of the word idea is uncontroversial.

The controversy comes from his assertion that some ideas are validly correlated with absolute realities and that ideas so correlated are correct. The ideas of dog, rose, and mother are connected with sensible realities; just so, the ideas gravity and Immaculate Conception are connected with equally real but insensible facts. The claim that certain insensible mental abstractions are correlated with objective realities was the scholastic fallacy that Hampden and the liberals condemned. Newman went to great lengths to defend it.

As usual in the combats between Newman and the liberals, their fundamental difference over ideas had its roots in the seventeenth century—in this case, in a philosophical difficulty both Hampden and Newman inherited from Locke. Hampden criticized Locke for perpetuating the scholastic error according to which ideas, "when we come to refer them to anything, as to their patterns and archetypes, . . . are capable of being wrong, as far as they disagree with such archetypes."[2] Hampden wanted to abandon Locke's archetypes as an unreal residue of medieval superstition; Newman had to perserve them as guarantors of dogmatic truth. For Newman, true ideas must have an objective reality outside of the minds that think them, and Locke's concept of archetypes supplies the need. A true idea, Newman wrote, has a "heavenly archetype, such, that that idea belongs to the archetype, in a sense in which no other earthly idea belongs to it."[3] False ideas, on the other hand, have no archetypes and are merely subjective. By rejecting the existence of archetypes, Hampden had reduced all ideas to false ideas, thereby denying what Newman called truth. Both Newman and Hampden were disciples of Locke, the one determined to finish the work of the seventeenth-century revolution in philosophy, the other to restore the damaged legacy of scholastic theology.

Locke had said that all ideas arise from experience. Newman and Hampden both agreed. Locke had said that there are two sorts of experience, sensation and reflection: we experience the outer world through the senses and the inner world through various faculties such as willing, doubting, thinking, and believing. Hampden admitted only sensation as a valid source of experience. He acknowledged the existence of ideas produced by reflection but denied that they have any valid relation to anything outside the mind. Reflection, said Hampden, is not necessary to preserve religion. Newman on the other hand had to admit both sensation and reflection as valid forms of experience because for him, Christianity arises as an idea inside the mind, the product of what Locke called "the perception of the operation of our own minds within us."[4] According to Newman, humans have access to a source of objective and factual ideas—their own reflections—which for Hampden

[2] Locke, *Essay Concerning Human Understanding*, 2.32.26. Hampden objected that in setting up archetypes to which individual ideas were to be compared, Locke is "closely following the worst part of the Scholastic Logic which he rejected. . . . To inquire into the *nature* of ideas, is an arbitrary speculation which has no existence but in the nomenclature of science" (*M.P.*, p. 264).

[3] *U.S.*, p. 340. Dean Inge, whose essay is still an excellent short introduction to Newman's thought, is uncharacteristically imprecise when he says, "Newman adopts the sensationalist (Lockian) theory of knowledge" ("Cardinal Newman," in *Outspoken Essays* [London, 1920], p. 189). This is a half-truth. Newman also accepts Locke's reflection theory of knowledge—a crucial addition.

[4] *Human Understanding*, 2.1.4.

and the liberals is purely subjective and delusionary. Newman agreed that ideas produced by reflection might be false but claimed that some of them did in fact have external archetypes that made them as legitimate as other real ideas produced by sensation. Our idea of a stone corresponds roughly to some hard, rough, heavy material object. The idea of the stone is imperfect and incomplete but based on a real relationship between archetype and mind. Just so, said Newman, the idea of an omnipotent deity answers to the reflection of the conscience that its operations would always be deficient without the complement of some external guide, namely God. The idea of God so formed is imperfect and incomplete but also based on a real relationship between archetype and mind.

Big, complex ideas were Newman's preoccupation. The *idea* of Christianity and the *idea* of a university were for him mental abstractions that have objective correlatives that we must inquire after.[5] Hampden attacked scholasticism to refute just this kind of reasoning.

Hampden accused the scholastics and their modern descendants of trying to make theology an exact science like mathematics, "established by necessary links of dependence on primary truths concerning God."[6] For him, no "necessary links" connected the reflections of the mind with the outer world. Hampden was a true disciple of the Arian Asterius, who had said that mankind's knowledge is confined to "the intellectual world" of its own mentality. The truth of mathematics was for Hampden purely mental, entirely relative to the intellect that invents the symbolic logic of scientific demonstration. Newman instinctively rebelled against this suggestion. Long before he heard Hampden lecture, he had defended the scholastic analogy between theological and mathematical truth. In his first foray into print, a letter to the *Christian Observer* written in 1821 when he was twenty years old, he asserted that "no science perhaps is more adopted to confirm our belief in the truth of Christianity than that of mathematics, when cultivated with a proper disposition of mind."[7]

Newman's fondness for mathematical analogies demonstrates not only the scholasticism but also the consistency of his opinions. His *Apologia* has misled some to believe that Newman underwent a turbulent evolution

[5] Owen Chadwick unnecessarily accused Newman of "inconsistent usages of the word *idea*" (*From Bossuet to Newman: The Idea of Doctrinal Development* [Cambridge, 1957], p. 149). In this one instance, Newman was faithful to Locke's terminology, in so far as Locke was faithful to scholasticism.

[6] *S.P.*, p. 355.

[7] *L.D.*, 1: 102.

of opinions. In fact, few nineteenth-century minds were as constant in their principles as Newman's. From his first appearance in print, he defended the scholastic line of thought assailed by liberalism. His alleged intellectual development is only the refinement of a fixed and unyielding predisposition. Late in life, when Newman prepared his collected works for a uniform edition, he found many occasions to clarify his youthful views but few to retract them. "I *stand by* my University Discourses," the Catholic Newman wrote of the University Sermons, "and am almost a zealot for their substantial truth."[8] To the end of his life he lavished the same approbation on all his earlier works, and the mathematical analogies that occupy his first publication are pressed with undiminished vigor fifty years later in the *Grammar of Assent,* where calculus is called upon to support Catholic theology. From the first, he contended for the primacy of truth, the archetypal reality of ideas, and the scientific demonstration of doctrine. The philosopher closest to him was Duns Scotus, whose similar views, recondite terminology, and scholastic metaphysics were a constant inspiration in Newman's later works.[9]

## Views

How can the mind know which of its ideas is connected with real archetypes, and therefore true? Hampden had a simple answer: it cannot. No idea is absolutely right, and all are merely human products relative to the mind that thinks them. Newman's philosophy developed as an attempt to salvage truth from this liberal skepticism.

He argued that there exists a single "grammar of assent" by which minds organize their ideas into beliefs, just as there exists a grammar of language by which minds organize words into sentences. Newman's theory of belief rested on a transformational grammar of ideas. At the deepest level, he maintained, the beliefs of all men are generated by a

[8]*L.D.,* 15: 381. After his conversion, Newman was quick to renounce anything in his Anglican writings that offended Roman Catholic doctrine, but he had been so Catholic while in the Church of England that these recantations were few and none of them crucial to his thought.

[9] At the very mention of Scotus, Newman was liable to break into schoolman's Latin. See his exchange with F. W. Faber on the Incarnation: "I certainly wish to take the Scotist view on that point"; "Ita Scotus, Suarez etc" (*L.D.,* 13: 335, 341–42). Examples of his devotion to Scotus might be multiplied.

common process. Newman thought that it was a persuasive argument in favor of God and truth that all men arrive at belief by this common process. A single, universal process implies a single, universal truth behind this process. Thus the very existence of "a grammar of assent" is proof of the dogmatic principle.[10]

How does the grammar of assent work? All people begin with ideas, and all people must choose an organizing principle for evaluating the ideas that come before their minds. Newman called this organizing principle a "view." A view precedes all reasoning. It is the first premise by which the mind organizes life. To hold a right belief, the mind must first have a right view. Typically, Newman returned to the Trinitarian question for an example to illustrate his conception of how a view operates. The Athanasian Creed is supposed to be a statement of right ideas. How do we know these are true?

> The Athanasian Creed professes to lay down the right faith, which we must hold on its most sacred subjects, in order to be saved. This must mean that there is one view concerning the Holy Trinity, or concerning the Incarnation, which is true, and distinct from all others; one definite, consistent, entire view, which cannot be mistaken, not contained in any certain number of propositions, but held as a view by the believing mind, and not held, but denied by Arians, Sabellians, Tritheists, Nestorians, Monophysites, Socinians, and other heretics. That idea is not enlarged, if propositions are added, nor impaired if they are withdrawn: if they are added, this is with a view of conveying that one integral view, not of amplifying it. That view does not depend on such propositions: it does not consist in them; they are but specimens and indications of it. And they may be multiplied without limit.[11]

For Newman, a view is what in medieval philosophy might have been called the essence of mentality, the unique and defining characteristic of each mind. Newman called the faculty that selects this controlling view of life "the illative sense." The term "illative sense" is Newman's improvement on the recondite expression "illation," denoting the process of inference. But for Newman the workings of the illative sense were

---

[10] "It is a grievous error to take a test of the reality of a belief as a test of its truth"—Leslie Stephen refuting the metaphysical implications of Newman's grammar of assent ("Newman's Theory of Belief," in *An Agnostic's Apology* [London, 1893], p. 225—the best book for those who would like to see Newman's arguments reduced to their logical impossibilities).

[11] *U.S.*, pp. 335–36. A. Dwight Culler, *The Imperial Intellect* (New Haven, 1955), pp. 193–95, gives an excellent account of Newman's use of the word "view."

anything but recondite. He called it "a grand name for a common thing." It lies at the heart of all judgment and action. The illative sense is "a rule to itself" that "appeals to no judgment beyond its own; and attends upon the whole course of thought from antecedents to consequents." It is that "action of the mind" that determines "those first elements of thought which in all reasoning are assumptions, the principles, tastes, and opinions, very often of a personal character, which are half the battle in the inference with which the reasoning is to terminate." The illative sense is unique in each individual. It is "a personal gift."[12] Each person is free to use or not to use his illative sense in his own way, and therefore the illative sense is the source of individuality and freedom.

Once the illative sense adopts a view, everything else in human thought follows from it. The illative sense may choose a view that believes everything or nothing: "Of the two, I would rather have to maintain that we ought to begin with believing everything that is offered to our acceptance, than that it is our duty to doubt of everything. The former, indeed, seems the way of true learning."[13] The mind that begins with a view that believes everything is embarked on the way of faith; the view that doubts everything leads down the road of skepticism.

## Reason

From these two different views, or from any of the infinite number of views that lie between them, all minds proceed by a similar process— reason. Using the same processes of reason, Hampden arrived at liberal apostasy, while Newman arrived at Catholic faith. Newman would have said the difference between him and Hampden lay not in the reasoning process but in the first premises from which reason proceeded.

Reason was a word that had been appropriated by the anti-dogmatists, and Newman used the term with conscious ambiguity as a retort to his liberal tormentors. By his own admission, he employed the term in at least four different and contradictory senses. He then claimed to mean by the word just what both Samuel Johnson and Pius IX did.[14] This way madness lies, and not surprisingly, many attempts to comprehend New-

[12]*L.D.*, 24: 275; *G.A.*, p. 233.
[13]*G.A.*, pp. 232–33, 243.
[14]*U.S.*, p. xiv; *T.P.*, 1: 141, 152.

man's thought have come to grief on the shoals of his mischievous terminology. As usual, what Newman meant by his abstract terminology becomes clear only by examining his very concrete hatred of liberalism.

"Reason is the faculty by which we arrive from things known to things unknown," he wrote in rebuttal to Mill's *System of Logic*.[15] Reason is a method of extrapolating from first principles, or views, which in turn are known by virtue of the illative sense. Reason is entirely neutral. It is the tool by which the mind, under the supervision of its view, converts the ore of ideas into the coin of belief. All valid beliefs must be reasonable, since they must represent valid deductions reached from correct views, but "great faculty as reasoning certainly is, it is from its nature in all subjects dependent upon other faculties. It receives from them the antecedent with which its action starts; and when this antecedent is true, there is no longer in religious matters room for any accusation against it of skepticism." But even heresy may be reasonable when it is the logical deduction reached from a false view. The Arians had practically worshiped reason, which had not saved them from error, and when the first Protestants invested the Bible with an exclusive authority, this was an example of "the illative sense, acting on mistaken elements of thought."[16] The Protestants had been wrong not in their reason but in their view.

When in an appendix to the *Apologia* Newman enumerated the heretical doctrines of liberalism, his first specification anathematized the proposition, "No religious tenet is important unless reason shows it to be so."[17] Newman did not disagree with the liberal premise that religious tenets must be reasonable. He objected to the assertion that reason alone validated belief. This he considered an absurdity that ignored the role of the illative sense in shaping a view of life.

## Dogma

Every individual's view of life is unique, but the reasoning process is everywhere the same. When applied to the chaotic assortment of views and ideas that constitute human life, reason guarantees some uniformity

[15] *T.P.*, 1: 47.
[16] *T.P.*, 1: 153; *G.A.*, p. 245.
[17] *Apo.*, p. 260.

in the finished product of articulated belief. In fact, individuals usually arrive at beliefs shared by many others and defended by institutions such as the Church or the state. Socinians like Hampden or Marx point to these shared beliefs as evidence that belief is a social phenomenon. Is it credible that citizens of a single civilization should freely and independently arrive at common beliefs in the Virgin Birth or in political equality, or is it more reasonable to assume that some historical necessity compels them to adopt a shared view? Newman did not dispute the liberals' contention that beliefs have material and historical causes. He quarreled with them because they had said not too much but too little, "it being almost a definition of heresy, that it fastens on some one statement as if the whole truth, to the denial of all others, and as a basis of faith, erring rather in what it rejects, than in what it maintains." [18] Newman denounced liberalism for maintaining that "no theological doctrine is any thing more than an opinion which happens to be held by bodies of men." [19] The key words here are "any thing more than." He admits that doctrines and dogmas are opinions held by bodies of men. Where they are formed at all, they have material and historical explanations, but these explanations are not exhaustive. Because dogmas are historical and material does not mean they may not also be eternal and spiritual. Belief is human, and its human elements constitute what the Marxist would call ideology, but belief has an object, and when that object is real and divine, belief merges into dogma.

Blanco White called Newman "my Oxford Plato"—a grotesque misreading of his thought, as Newman's attitude toward ideology demonstrates. [20] His assertion that doctrines are eternal and spiritual as well as historical and material was a translation of Aristotelian physics into the language of Anglican theology. For Newman, every doctrine, like every physical event, has four causes: material, formal, efficient, and final. The dogma of original sin, for instance, has always existed, Newman said, but before Pelagius, it existed like matter in chaos, undefined and inchoate. The advent of Christianity and the decline of the West were the efficient causes that compelled the doctrine of original sin to assume formal expression in the theological language of Saint Augustine. The challenge of Pelagius forced the Church to clarify what had before been a shapeless substratum of ideas.

[18] *U.S.*, p. 337.
[19] *Apo.*, p. 260.
[20] *L.D.*, 2: 105.

The material, formal, and efficient causes of the doctrine serve a fourth and final cause. The final cause of the dogma of original sin is the salvation of mankind and the extirpation of idolatry.[21] For Newman, every true doctrine has these four dimensions: an irreducible substratum of idea that exists apart from human minds and human words; a historical or efficient impetus that drives its development; a formal expression in language; and a final goal that justifies its existence. A doctrine lacking any of these four causes is either error or heresy. Pelagius's theory of free will, for instance, has no legitimate final cause and is therefore invalid.

Newman was particularly fond of demonstrating the validity of Christian belief from its final causes. Miracles, he says, really do happen, because a religious man expects just such a confirmation of his belief and therefore the miracle serves "to enlighten him and cleanse his heart."[22] Elsewhere Newman called this appeal to final causes an argument from "antecedent probability." For example, as we set out to discover the truth, it is more reasonable to reject the antecedent probability that the world is a random chaos and adopt the antecedent probability that it moves with ordered purpose. Newman's shifting terminology of final causes and antecedent probabilities merely disguises his consistent application of Aristotelian physics as the model for a science of truth.

Newman admitted that opinion or belief often develops only to rationalize the material facts of history: "And so, again, in Parliamentary

[21] I have already remarked upon the historical fact, that the recognition of Original Sin, considered as the consequence of Adam's fall, was, both as regards general acceptance and accurate understanding, a gradual process, not completed till the time of Augustine and Pelagius. St. Chrysostom lived close up to that date but there are passages in his work, often quoted, which we should not expect to find worded as they stand, if they had been written fifty years later. It is commonly, and reasonably, said in explanation, that the fatalism, so prevalent in various shapes pagan and heretical, in the first centuries, was an obstacle to an accurate apprehension of the consequences of the fall, as the presence of the existing idolatry was to the use of images. If this be so, we have here an instance of a doctrine held back for a time by circumstances, yet in the event forcing its way into its normal shape, and at length authoritatively fixed in it, that is, of a doctrine held implicitly, then asserting itself, and at length fully developed. (*Dev.*, p. 117)

Aristotle's four causes furnish the structure for this passage, as they do for the whole of the *Essay on Development*.

[22] *G.A.*, p. 274. "Now the Miracles of the Jewish and Christian Religions must be considered as immediate effects of Divine Power beyond the action of nature, for an important moral end; and are in consequence accounted for by producing, not a physical,

conflicts, men first come to their conclusions by the external pressure of events or the force of principles, they do not know how; then they have to speak, and they look about for some arguments."[23] There are also societies that forego the niceties of ideology and rationalization altogether. "The barbarians," said Newman of Turks in particular and Asians in general, "live without principle and without aim." They live like brutes, and like brutes, they feel no compulsion to explain themselves before or after they act.[24] In these concessions, Newman seems to have surrendered to the liberals—belief is only a by-product of material events or plays no significant role in human affairs. Newman would reply that while belief may sometime develop in response to events, or else not develop at all, the fact that some men abdicate their responsibility to act on belief does not mean that they cannot act on belief. They can: the false belief of Arius was the cause, not the effect, of the fourth century's woes, just as "Locke's philosophy was a real guide, not a mere defence of the Revolution era, operating forcibly upon Church and Government in and after his day. Such too were the theories which preceded the overthrow of the old regime in France and other countries at the end of the last century."[25] The English and the French revolutions, like most of the evil effects of Western history, had been caused by a few men's false beliefs. Belief is individual and freely chosen. The fact that men share ideologies does nothing to lessen their individual responsibility for those ideas, and the fact that most men concur that there is a God or that murder is a crime only helps to prove that individual belief can converge on universal truths.

Each person freely wills his beliefs or freely abdicates his ability to believe. By this free choice he defines himself and his world. For Newman, freedom is nothing but the freedom to believe. The individual

---

but a final cause" ("The Miracles of Scripture" [1826], *Mir.*, p. 18). This is a version of the argument from design, once thought to have been demolished by Kant. No part of Newman's system galled his contemporaries more than his belief in miracles. Edwin Abbott, for instance, called Newman's *Essay on Ecclesiastical Miracles* (1843) "that Abomination of Intellectual Desolation" (*Philomythus: An Antidote Against Credulity* [London, 1891], p. lxvii).

[23] *Dev.*, p. 42.

[24] "The Turks in their Relations to Europe," *H.S.*, 1: 183. "Again, perhaps there are politics founded on no ideas at all, but on mere custom, as among the Asiatics" (*Dev.*, p. 42). Newman's contempt for the East was boundless.

[25] *Dev.*, p. 42.

soul is characterized by the view of the world it adopts and the beliefs it deduces from this view. And just as surely as the individual shapes his personality out of his beliefs, he projects his beliefs on the world of matter and time, shaping these into the image of his opinions. Newman was careful to avoid the idealism of Berkeley, which made time and space wholly dependent on mind. Matter is for him "a real substance." But "we cannot rely on the senses for giving us any kind of idea of what matter is in itself or absolutely."[26] The senses tell us about time and space, but the senses may be wrong, or only partially correct, and finally our ideas about matter depend not so much on sense-data as on the view we adopt about sense-data. In this case the physical world itself is a function of our belief.

It is tempting to try to discern some parallel between Newman's thought and Hegel's. Both seem to trace the history of mankind in the evolution of belief. But in Hegel's pantheism, man is both the believer and the object of belief, and Hegel's highest revelation is that man is himself the absolute. Hegel's philosophy is only another variety of the solipsistic and materialistic liberalism Newman saw all around him in England. The liberals, like the Arians before them, erred in making belief the creature of self or of material forces outside the mind, when in fact the self and the material world are defined by belief.

## Imagination

Hampden and the liberals erred in stopping at efficient and material explanations, as if these exhausted what could be known about beliefs. In Newman's eyes, they were failed Aristotelians who missed at least half the reality of any doctrine they studied. It is tempting to say that Newman accused the liberals of a failure of imagination, but the temptation must be resisted. In fact, Newman's charge was that the liberals used only "imagination," and hence could not get beyond the world of their senses. His use of the word imagination not only illuminates his charge against liberalism, but also illustrates a curiosity of his philosophical method.

A few weeks after the Bampton lectures of 1832, Newman delivered

[26]*T.P.*, 1: 163–64.

his seventh University Sermon as a riposte to the heresy loosed on Oxford by the apostate Hampden. He admonished impressionable Oxonians against "trusting the world, because it speaks boldly"—as Hampden had just spoken. As was usual in cases where Newman despised an opponent, he refused to mention him by name. Hampden appeared in this sermon along with an equally nameless Gibbon ("an historian of the last century" of "cold heart, impure mind, and scoffing spirit") as a member of "a new school of error, which seems not yet to have accomplished its destinies, and is framed more exactly after the received type of the author of evil, than the other chief anti-Christs who have, in these last times, occupied the scene of the world." Newman's specific charge against these devils was that of "imposing on our imagination."[27] For Newman, the imagination is the faculty of the mind that coordinates thinking with sense-data. Imagination "is the great enemy to faith" because left to its own devices, imagination will reject as untrue any idea that cannot be reduced to material and efficient causes. "What is *strange,* is to the imagination *false,*" he said.[28] The liberals flattered themselves that they were the apostles of reason. But what they called reason Newman called imagination.

Here as everywhere, Newman sedulously avoided the liberal sense of words—imagination is not what Coleridge and the Romantics would make it, an esemplastic power reaching out to mysterious truths; it is the very opposite, an earth-bound faculty that rejects any idea that cannot be reconciled with the evidence of the senses. Newman's use of the word

---

[27] *U.S.*, pp. 122, 126. Forty-seven years later the phrases of this sermon echo through the Biglietto speech: "a new school of error . . . framed more exactly after the received type of the author of evil" (1832); "a device of the Enemy so cleverly framed and with such promise of success" (1879): Newman's amazing consistency of thought extended down to words and phrases. Newman was also consistent in suppressing the names of his enemies. Twenty years after his battles with Hampden, the heretic appears in the *Apologia* (pp. 66–67) as "a memorable appointment" of Lord Melbourne. To name a heretic was to give him undeserved notoriety.

[28] *T.P.*, 1: 47. Newman occasionally lapsed into the ordinary usage of imagination as "inventive power," but when he took his time, he carefully restricted the term to the sense of "the power which attends upon memory . . . making present the absent." See John Coulson, *Religion and Imagination in Aid of a Grammar of Assent* (Oxford, 1981), pp. 82–83, where this passage from Newman's notes is mysteriously offered as proof of what it explicitly refutes, that Newman held Coleridge's theory of imagination. Coulson is not alone in coming to grief on Newman's terminology. See for instance Stephen Prickett, *Romanticism and Religion* (Cambridge, 1976), where a similarity of language among Newman and the Romantics is confused with a similarity of meaning.

exemplifies the difficulty of making sense out of his thought. He refused to use modern terminology because the liberals had tainted that terminology. He was purposely equivocal, not to deceive but to preserve. The liberals had coopted the most basic terms of philosophical discourse for their own twisted purposes. To rebuke them, Newman continued to use words like imagination and reason in their medieval senses. His use of the word imagination makes no sense when read in the context of Blake and Coleridge; it makes perfect sense when read in the tradition of scholastic philosophy, where it preserves that meaning Newman wanted to maintain against Hampden and the reformers.[29]

## Language

Newman departed from scholasticism in one particular. The schoolmen had devised a highly technical language in which to state the dogmatic truths discovered by reason—the "symbolic language" excoriated by Hampden. Newman was much more circumspect about the connections between truth, reason, and language. He believed with the schoolmen that human language can express divine truth, but he differed from them about the precision with which it does so.

All belief must be reasonable, but reason need not be verbal. Newman was fond of demonstrating this point from the life of his disciple, the Dominican nun, Mother Margaret Hallahan. In the *Grammar of Assent* he quotes her biographer's observation that her faith "was almost like an intuition of the entire prospect of revealed truth. Let an error against faith be concealed under expressions however abstruse, and her sure instinct found it out. I have tried the experiment repeatedly. She might not be able to separate the heresy by analysis, but she saw, and felt, and suffered from its presence."[30] Truth can be known but the method of its ap-

---

[29] For the scholastic, "imagination was the power of fixing the fluctuating impressions of the senses in a lasting and definitive form as a preparation for the processes of reason" (R. W. Southern, *Robert Grosseteste* [Oxford, 1986], p. 40). Newman would have agreed with every syllable of this definition.

[30] *G.A.*, p. 217. The key words in this description of Mother Margaret's intuitive dogmatism are her biographer's: "I have tried the experiment repeatedly." Like Clever Hans, Mother Margaret gave her interlocutor the answers he wanted. Privately, Newman had his doubts about Mother Margaret's infallible intuitions. "Mother Margaret said on Whit Sunday, 'I am so fond of the Holy Ghost.' Did she not mean to speak of the Feast, the Devotion, or the thought of it?" (*L.D.*, 24: 263).

prehension may be inexpressible. So Newman seemed to hover on the brink of mysticism. But if Mother Margaret had reasoned her way to truth without the intermediacy of words, most minds must reach truth by reflecting in language, even if faith "is complete without this reflective faculty."[31]

At moments, Newman seemed as skeptical as Hampden about the possibility of stating truths in language. Verbal reasoning "cannot, like mathematical proof, be passively followed with an attention confined to what is stated, and with the admission of nothing but what is urged." Words that claim to describe truth are only "earthly images, which are infinitely below the reality." The mysteries of the spiritual world form a "vast and intricate scene of things" that "cannot be generalized or represented through or to the mind of man."[32] As usual, however, Newman conceded everything his liberal opponents could demand except the major premise. The liberals had said that language was not merely inadequate to describe reality, which Newman suavely conceded, but that it was totally divorced from that reality, which Newman hotly denied. To separate language from reality because it is inadequate is the same as divorcing action from belief because action is imperfect. No human utterance can ever encompass the truth, any more than any human action can duplicate the perfect behavior of Christ, but both can approximate to their ideals. Verbal explanations "do but approximate to a representation of the general character of the proof which the writer wishes to convey." Similarly, "God has condescended to speak to us so far as human thought and language will admit, by approximations."[33] Words represent ideas, and ideas may be true. Words, then, can have a real object—the truth. Even if they can never be congruous with their object, they can converge on it with increasing accuracy.

Characteristically, Newman used a mathematical analogy to explain his point. Language has the certainty not of geometry but of calculus. "The principle of concrete reasoning" that gives birth to language, opinions, and doctrines

> is parallel to the method of proof which is the foundation of modern mathematical science, as contained in the celebrated lemma with which Newton opens his "Principia." We know that a regular polygon, inscribed in

[31] *U.S.*, p. 277.
[32] *U.S.*, pp. 268–69.
[33] *G.A.*, pp. 275, 269.

a circle, its sides being continually diminished, tends to become that circle, as its limit; but it vanishes before it has coincided with the circle, so that its tendency to be the circle, though ever nearer fulfillment, never in fact gets beyond a tendency. In like manner, the conclusion in a real or concrete question is foreseen and predicted rather than actually attained.

The truth is a circle "in a narrow compass." Around this "circle of truths that make up that great thought" of God, language builds a square, and by successive refinements describes ever more exact models of its object.[34] The dogmas uttered by the general councils of the Church and perfected by Catholic theology are linguistic statements tending toward truth as their limit.

Some such account of language was necessary if Newman was to preserve the indefectibility of Christian dogma. Otherwise, the councils and creeds of the Church would be what Arius or Marvell or Hampden had said they were—social expedients unconnected with any higher reality. For Newman, they remained approximations, but approximations tangent to a real if narrow circle of truth.

Newman, Hampden, and the liberals all worked within the tradition of Anglican thought, but Newman's belief that language conveys truth in some real and mathematical way separates him utterly from the main line of development in English philosophy that finally issues in logical positivism. Newman enthusiasts sometimes try to salvage his reputation as a modern thinker by drawing the parallel between his thought and Wittgenstein's, but it is no surprise to find that Wittgenstein had a low opinion of Newman. Wittgenstein's and Newman's thoughts on language have exactly the similarity that Hampden's and Newman's thoughts do: they share everything but what is most essential. Newman believed that language is connected with truth, Wittgenstein that language and truth are irreconcilably separate.[35]

Newman's theory of language as approximation converging on truth came to him intuitively, and it is manifested in his prose style, just as

[34] *G.A.,* pp. 207–8, 71. *L.D.,* 5: 45.

[35] William R. Fey, *Faith and Doubt: The Unfolding of Newman's Thought on Certainty* (Shepherdson, WV, 1976), and M. Jamie Ferreira, *Doubt and Religious Commitment: The Role of the Will in Newman's Thought* (Oxford, 1980), are two attempts to make Newman's thought relevant by association with the thoughts of Wittgenstein. Both concede that Newman did not in fact agree with Wittgenstein's position, but neither sees that these two minds were in total opposition on basic points. For Wittgenstein's opinion of Newman, see Norman Malcolm, *A Memoir* (London, 1958), p. 71.

Hampden's liberalism is incarnate in his uncouth lucubrations. Hampden treated his prose with all the disdain he held for dogmatic formulations. His words were a means to an end, and he deployed them with a savage pragmatism. Newman, on the other hand, was always conscious that his words touched on some great mystery. When Ruskin went up to Oxford, his mother warned him against Newman's seductive ambiguities. "Any time I have heard Mr. Newman preach," she wrote, "he seemed to me like Oliver Cromwell to talk that he might not be understood."[36] Newman would have argued that if he was less than lucid, that was because he was reverential in the presence of the truth behind language. He was careful never to assert the identity of any approximate word with the absolute reality behind it, and the result is ambiguity and confusion in his terminology. Precision in language would have been an act of Arian insolence. Newman's much-admired style, caustic and ironic in refutation of error, pious and lyrical in affirmation of orthodoxy, is the reflection of his view of truth.

## Interpretation

If words can state truths, how can we overcome the difficulty that the same words may have completely incompatible meanings to various people? In the fourth century some Arians had acquiesced in the Nicene formula that declared the Son to be consubstantial with the Father and then had interpreted consubstantiality in a way that mocked orthodoxy. The Socinian bishop Hoadly had proclaimed in his heretical sermon of 1717 that "whoever hath an absolute authority to interpret any written, or spoken laws; it is he, who is truly the lawgiver, to all intents and purposes: and not the person who first wrote, or spoke them."[37] If language might be construed to mean anything the interpreter desired, surely words meant both everything and nothing. Dogma, then, would be pointless, and truth an illusion.

Once again, Newman accepted his enemies' premises about interpretation and drove them home to orthodox conclusions. Words do mean what the interpreter says they do. But some interpreters approximate to truth and therefore some interpreters are accurate, while others have no

[36] E. T. Cook. *The Life of John Ruskin* (London, 1911), 1: 72.

[37] Hoadly, *Works* (London, 1773), 2: 404.

truth in them and are false. Scriptural study illustrates the true method of interpretation. "Every passage of Scripture has some one definite and sufficient sense," said Newman. "It is this true meaning of the text, which it is the business of the expositor to unfold."[38] Though words may have various meanings to us, they have only one connection with their archetypes, and the interpreter's business is to enunciate this one connection.

An accurate interpreter may develop the doctrines he explicates, but he cannot contradict himself without violating the laws of reason and therefore truth. Contradiction is a sure sign of erroneous interpretation. It is unthinkable that God would give us words to speak the truth and then deny us some institution to guarantee the consistency and the validity of our interpretations. Only one institution has never contradicted but only developed its beliefs: the Catholic Church. Therefore, the Catholic Church is that single infallible interpreter of language which Arian scoffers like Hoadly thought to be an absurdity.

In his *Essay on the Development of Christian Doctrine* Newman set forth the rules by which a valid interpretation can be distinguished from a false one. True interpretations of true beliefs will have continuity of principle, power of assimilation, logical sequence, and chronic vigor. For a century or more, his admirers and detractors have mistaken this digression into the mechanics of dogma for the gist of Newman's theory of belief.[39] But the important point for Newman was not so much the method of distinguishing true from false interpretations as the assurance that true interpretations exist in the first place.

Monsignor Talbot was rightly suspicious of Newman's Catholicism.

---

[38] *Ari.,* p. 60. Newman almost falls into the trap prepared for orthodox churchmen by Bentham, who reasoned that if priests only proclaim the one definite sense of the Christian religion as established in written formularies, they ought to be replaced by less well-paid lay readers and the saving passed along to a grateful public. See *Church-of-Englandism* (London, 1818), pt. 2, pp. 107–9.

[39] The rules by which a valid interpretation can be distinguished from a false one are set forth in *Dev.,* pp. 159–91. Admirers of Newman's rules for the development of doctrine include Ker, which gives a good summary of the theory, pp. 302–15; J. M. Cameron, *The Night Battle* (London, 1967), pp. 203–18; and most intelligently, Owen Chadwick, *From Bossuet to Newman* (Cambridge, 1957). In what G. M. Young called "a cruel little essay," Dean Milman dismantled Newman's rules while reviewing the *Essay* for the *Quarterly Review.* See *Savanarola, Erasumus, and Other Essays* (London, 1870), pp. 296–373. The most balanced view of Newman's theory of development—in fact, of Newman's whole career—is probably still to be found in Charles Frederick Harrold, *John Henry Newman* (London, 1945).

Newman's conversion to Rome was an act of submission not so much to the Holy See as to the logical necessities of his own philosophy. His theory of belief demanded that the world contain a single imperishable oracle of truth, and only Rome supplied this need. When in 1870 the Vatican council prepared to declare the pope infallible, Newman wrote Bishop William Bernard Ullathorne of Birmingham to lament "the prospect of having to defend decisions which may not be difficult to my private judgment but may be most difficult to maintain logically in the face of historical facts."[40] The egoism which made the authority of the Church depend on the invincibility of Newman's logic infuriated his less intellectual coreligionists. Talbot wrote to Manning that Newman had never "acquired the Catholic instincts" and opined that "his spirit must be crushed."[41]

If Ultramontanes were appalled by the egoism of Newman's views on interpretation, Protestants were flabbergasted. "And has Mr. Newman lived in such utter seclusion," asked the dean of Saint Paul's, "as to suppose that any power on earth can wring this great principle of the plain literal interpretation from the practical good sense of the English religious mind?" Newman's theory denied the cherished right of private judgment, the Protestant theory of interpretation according to which the individual's reason understands the literal sense of a text with the aid of divine illumination. Private judgment, Newman wrote, "leads different minds in such different directions." If, as the Arians held, truth was a relative matter, then the various opinions concocted by private judgment would be a matter of no importance, since "where there is nothing to find, there can be no rules for seeking."[42] But on the orthodox supposition that truth does exist, private judgment is an obvious absurdity, since it leaves us no way to distinguish truth from error. The right of private judgment is only another Socinian error.

These wrangles over exegesis serve as a humbling reminder that the fashionable intellectual puzzles of our secular age often have been constructed from the ruins of arcane religious controversies. New criticism, semiotics, structuralism, deconstruction—the current theories of interpretation that revel in their modernity have only deconsecrated the antique Protestant doctrine of private judgment and pursued it to its

[40] E. C. Butler, *Life of Bishop Ullathorne* (London, 1926), 2: 58.

[41] Purcell, *Manning* (London, 1896), 2: 323.

[42] Henry Milman, *Savanarola, Erasmus, and Other Essays*, p. 314. "Private Judgment," *Ess.*, 2: 336.

logical limits. All texts are now said to be rewritten in the reader's mind and to have those variable meanings that time, place, and mores endow them with. A text's possible interpretations are limited only by its possible number of interpreters. Here is private judgment with a vengeance. As usual, Newman stands in total isolation from these developments of liberal thought. His theory that words, scriptural or otherwise, have "one definite and sufficient sense" now seems risibly out of date. "How can anyone know that his interpretation is the true one?" the liberal scoffer asks of Newman. "Because it conforms to the interpretation of the infallible Church? But how do you know the words of your interpretation conform with the words of the Church's interpretation? Is not a further interpretation necessary to validate the first interpretation, and so forth into an endless regress? And therefore we are left with infinite interpretations and no truth." Newman replied that the infinite regress of human interpretation was halted by the unappealable decision of the instincts.

## Instinct

By restricting themselves to deductions about "facts," the liberals ignored the existence of their own instincts. Liberals have views, too, said Newman. "After all, the Theist needs Faith as well as the Christian," Newman chuckled in his notebooks.[43] A liberal like John Stuart Mill hoped to escape the despotism of faith by resting his system on sense-data. Newman reminded him that belief in sense-data is an act of faith in itself, since "it should be considered whether our senses can be proved to suggest any real idea of matter."[44] Skeptics like Hampden or Nietzsche reject the assumptions of rationalism. "If nothing is to be assumed," asked Newman, "what is our very method of reasoning but an assumption?"[45] The anti-dogmatic principle was itself a dogma.

Hampden had tried to escape from the tyranny of dogma by admitting that no philosophy, his own included, could ever validate itself by an

[43] *T.P.*, 1: 148.
[44] *U.S.*, p. 339.
[45] *G.A.*, p. 243.

appeal to the empty words of "symbolic language." In Hampden's world, the human will confronts the facts of matter. So situated, it can only rely on "the instincts of right which exist in the heart."[46]

Newman answered this attempt to escape from the necessity of dogma by an appeal to Hampden's own assumptions. He pointed out that a belief in the supremacy of the instincts is itself an organizing view of life, and one that if treated fairly, justifies Newman's scholastic theology.

Newman admitted "instinct as a force which spontaneously compels us, not only to bodily movements, but to mental acts." One of our instincts is the will to truth: "The mind without any doubt is made for truth," he said.[47] The proof of this is that men instinctively search for truth. Newman's premise here was that every instinct has a real object; therefore the instinctive will to truth must have a real object, namely truth.[48] The instinct for truth tells us that truth really exists. Reason is the faculty that enables the mind to pursue its instinct for truth until it obtains its object, and therefore reason has a valid and definable relationship with absolutes outside of itself. Starting from Hampden's own principles, Newman compelled instinct to defend reason, and Hampden's liberalism was made to support Newman's scholasticism.

This argument demonstrates Newman's habitual mode of argument. His thought emerged from an attack on the enemy's position. His tactic was to adopt his opponent's most cherished premise and turn it against him. The audacity of his method confounded the opposition but obscured Newman's own principles. In this case, the point he was making is central to his philosophy. Instincts or reflections in the mind have real correlates in the universe at large. This presumption borrows from Aristotle's theory of final causes—instincts move toward real goals—and marries it to Locke's belief that the internal faculties are a genuine source

[46]*M.P.*, p. 13.

[47]*G.A.*, p. 47; *T.P.*, 1: 152.

[48] "Unless this is truth, there is no truth; but as I cannot do without truth, this must be true" (James Fitzjames Stephen's parody of Newman's argument from instincts to truth, *Saturday Review* 2 [1856]: 734). The Stephen brothers learned to ridicule Newman in the family circle. When Leslie was sixteen and James nineteen, they would have read their father's droll account of the "unmasculine terror of everything vulgar in belief or sentiment" that characterized the piety of Keble and Newman and learned of Newman's contempt for "all who have been weak enough to be dazzled and misled by the glare of his sophistry" (James Stephen, "The Evangelical Succession," in *Essays in Ecclesiastical Biography* [London, 1879], 2: 174, 194).

of experience—the goals toward which instincts move are real and objective, not imaginary and subjective.[49]

This marriage gave birth to Newman's central article of faith. Everything Newman held true depends on the unprovable assumption that subjective human instincts have objective metaphysical correlatives. Is there a God? Yes, because he complements the lonely soul. Is he a just God? Yes, because justice alone answers the perplexity of "the moral sense." Is there original sin? Yes, because only universal depravity can explain the heart's limitless guilt. So instinct guides the illative sense, which chooses a view, which reason shapes into belief, which is expressed as dogma, which is interpreted by the Church, which can state truth.[50]

Newman's whole philosophy would come down in ruins if the cry of *In Memoriam* were correct:

What find I in the highest place,
    But mine own phantom chanting hymns?
    And on the depths of death there swims
The reflex of a human face.

Newman was haunted by a nihilism similar to that conjured up by Tennyson. In the *Apologia,* he speaks of how the world seems "to give the lie to that great truth" of God's existence, and he echoes the language of *In Memoriam* when he says, "If I looked into a mirror, and did not see my face, I should have the sort of feeling which actually comes upon me, when I look into this living busy world, and see no reflexion of its Creator."

[49] Or, in the language of contemporary philosophy, "Newman is basing normative judgments on empirical judgment in the sense of claiming both that non–*a priori* normative inquiry is the only sort possible, and that such an inquiry reveals objective norms" (Jamie Ferreira, *Doubt and Religious Commitment: The Role of the Will in Newman's Thought* [Oxford, 1980], p. 70).

[50] "Each of the affirmations of his conscience is, if I may say so, charged with dogmas" is Henri Brémond's felicitous distillation of Newman's theory of belief (*The Mystery of Newman,* trans. H. C. Corrance [London, 1907], p. 335). Harold Weatherby says that Newman's reliance on instinct leads to "the tyranny of the idea or of the subjective experience" (*Cardinal Newman in His Age* [Nashville, TN, 1973], p. 226). Weatherby regrets that Newman's philosophy is not more like Thomas Aquinas's. He is perhaps the first critic since Monsignor Talbot and the Ultramontanes who has accused Newman of being too modern.

This vision is for Newman the nightmare of liberalism. Liberalism maintains that the instincts have no correlates other than their own phantoms "chanting hymns." "The difficulty is to realize the groundlessness of our belief," said the twentieth-century heretic Wittgenstein.[51] Newman could not comprehend or accept the groundlessness of belief. He recognized that his own thought was built on a subjective if devout premise: my instincts confirm my beliefs, and my beliefs confirm my instincts. His way around the logical deadend of this circular argument was to support his faith by a rhetorical appeal to empirical evidence.

## Faith and Empirical Evidence

Newman used the abusive term "rationalistic" to describe liberals who would not admit that their philosophy was built on faith. He freely admitted that his own thought rested on faith, and he found more empirical evidence to corroborate his view than existed to support the liberal position.

In marshaling this evidence, Newman argued with the skill of a great attorney. Although Newman confessed to "much suspicion of legal proceedings and legal arguments, when used in questions whether of history or of philosophy,"[52] he wrote from first to last as if he were a special pleader addressing a jury of skeptical Englishmen. Not everyone was impressed. Edwin Abbott, the compiler of the *Shakespearian Grammar,* surveyed Newman's rhetoric and found only "oscillation, lubrication, and assimilation."[53] Newman would have answered that like any lawyer, he was entitled to address the instincts as well as the pure reason of the jury.

Newman's clients were God and the Church, whom liberalism had arraigned for fraud and deceit. The prosecution was led by Hoadly,

[51] *In Memoriam,* cviii; *Apo.,* p. 216; Wittgenstein, *On Certainty* (Oxford, 1969), p. 24e.

[52] *G.A.,* p. 273. An excellent legal text on the use of circumstantial evidence could be compiled from Newman's work: for example, "It is obvious that we should be induced to distrust the most natural and plausible statement when made by a person whom we suspected of a wish to deceive, or of relating facts which he had no sufficient means of knowing. Or if we credited his narrative, we should do so, not from dependence on the reporter, but from its intrinsic likelihood, or from circumstantial evidence" (*Mir.,* p. 72).

[53] Abbott, *Philomythus,* p. xxxvii.

Hume, Gibbon, Hampden, Mill—the whole bar of liberalism. How, Newman asked the jury, was the case to be decided? "In all matters of human life, presumption verified by instances, is our ordinary instrument of proof, and, if the antecedent probability is great, it almost supercedes instances."[54] Begin with the presumption that God exists, and that the dogmas of Catholicism express his truth. The presumption satisfies our deepest needs and makes sense out of an otherwise meaningless universe. Common sense tells us to expect order in the universe, and the doctrines of Catholicism constitute the only presumption that satisfies this expectation. Therefore the antecedent probability is all on the side of Newman's clients. But if evidence is demanded to substantiate the claims of instinct, the evidence too is on Newman's side. Consider the character of the defendants, and compare it with that of the prosecutors. On the one side we find the honest Augustine, the long-suffering Athanasius, the angelic Aquinas, the brave Loyola. Their character is reflected in enduring beliefs and imperishable institutions. On the other side we have the shallow Pelagius, the dishonest Arius, the self-centered Luther, the cynical Gibbon, the depraved Byron. Their ideas have produced sorrow, and their legacy is confusion. They have argued among themselves and soon will be no more. Evidences could be multiplied, and all to the same effect. On the very grounds of common sense to which the liberals would have recourse, the jury must deliver a verdict in favor of God and dogma.

## Kant and German Philosophy

Thus buttressed by the circumstantial evidence of history, character, and probability, the most amorphous and inarticulate cravings of the mind are made to support the dogmatic formulas of Catholic theology. A professional philosopher might reply to this mixture of logic, instinct, and rhetoric with a single dismissive syllable: Kant. "How different the fortunes of the Church of England might have been if Newman had been able to read German," Arthur Stanley sighed.[55] Newman often seems to be giving pious answers to questions that Kant and the German philosophers had demonstrated ought not to be asked.

Newman's philosophy clings to three propositions: the objective exis-

[54]*Dev.*, p. 105.
[55]Mark Pattison, *Memoirs* (London, 1885), p. 211.

tence of truth, the possibility of its dogmatic exposition, and the empirical demonstration of both from the experiences of the mind. Before Newman was born Kant had disposed of all three. "It is quite impossible, and indeed absurd, to ask for a general test of the truth," Kant wrote, "for although our knowledge may be in complete accordance with logical demands, that is, may not contradict itself, it is still possible that it may be in contradiction with its object." The whole edifice of Newman's Catholicism seems to come down in ruins in Kant's refutation of dogmatic truth, and Newman's attempt to resurrect the dogmatic principle by an empirical appeal to the order or method of nature, the mind, or the instincts, is forestalled by Kant's destruction of the argument from design: "To advance to absolute totality by the empirical road is utterly impossible."[56]

Stanley supposed that Newman would have been enlightened by the withering logic of Kant's anti-dogmatism. But Stanley was mistaken, first, because Newman grappled with Kant's logic even if he was unaware of doing so; second, because a close reading of German philosophy would have changed none of Newman's opinions; and third, because Newman's own interests were not really those of Kant, despite a superficial similarity.

Whether through a historical coincidence of ideas or through chance, nineteenth-century Anglicanism independently asked and answered the same questions that German philosophy had confronted half a century earlier. What issue was raised by Kant that was not addressed in Hampden's own critique of pure reason, the Bampton lectures of 1832? (Hampden, not Newman, was the Anglican who might have profited from a familiarity with the rigor of German philosophy.) Newman did not need to read Kant when he had Hampden and the liberals.

Would a reading of Kant have made a difference to Newman's development? In fact, Newman eventually read the German philosophers—or at least he read about them in H. M. Chalybaus's survey, *The Historical Development of Speculative Philosophy from Kant to Hegel,* translated from the German and published in Edinburgh in 1854. The German philosophers hardly caused a ripple on the surface of Newman's piety. "I do not think I am bound to read them in spite of what Chalybaus says, for notoriously they have come to no conclusion." A cursory glance at the thought of the German philosophers persuaded Newman that they were

[56] *Critique of Pure Reason* (New York, 1965), pp. 98, 523 (1.2.3 and 2.3.6).

only latitudinarians with an "obstinate assumption that all things must be reduced to *one* principle."[57] At least English liberals were unsystematic and ambiguous, qualities Newman admired. The Germans compounded their heresies with a mechanical precision of thought that got them no further than Hampden.

Somewhere Newman acquired a copy of Kant's *Critique of Pure Reason;* its pages remained uncut at his death.[58] What little he learned of Kant's philosophy from Chalybaus's survey provoked only the same response he had made to liberal Anglicanism:

> Kant . . . would say as to consciousness, "Yes, it bears witness to internal facts of the mind, but it is impossible to connect them, whatever they are, with any thing external to it. The *experience* is only of ourselves." Well, then, I say this:—You can indeed reduce me to a state of absolute skepticism about everything external to consciousness—but this is a reductio ad absurdum of all knowledge external to us whatever, of *senses* as well as (I shd say *much more* than) supersenuous knowledge—but if you do not go *this extreme length,* which makes it hopeless even to reason or investigate at all, you must allow *something*—& all I ask you to allow me is *this*—that it is *true* that *I am*—or that my consciousness that I am represents the fact external to my consciousness (viz) of my existence. Now see what is involved in this one assumption, viz: My consciousness that I am not *immediate,* but indirect—"Sentio, ergo sum." . . . But if one external unexperienced fact may be known by *reasoning upon* experience, perhaps another may. Therefore the idea is not absurd that as from "sentio" I infer the existence of myself, so from "conscientiam habeo," I infer the existence of God.[59]

This passage presents the philosophical rationale for Newman's statement in the *Apologia* that from an early age his mind had come to rest "in the thought of two and two only absolute and luminously self-evident beings, myself and my Creator."[60] Newman's response to Kant was simply to restate his own philosophy as it had first been revealed in his youth and had later developed in response to Arius, Locke, and Hampden. Here in the short compass of an entry to Newman's notebooks is his whole theory of belief. Grant my instinct that I exist is valid, and you

[57] *Phil. N.,* 1: 228–29. Apparently Newman did not look at Chalybaus's book until 1859, when he made several notes on it.

[58] *Phil. N.,* 1: 229.

[59] *Phil. N.,* 2: 78.

[60] *Apo.,* p. 18.

have already admitted that feeling or instinct has an objective archetype. The archetype of my reflection that I exist is me. If there is one such archetype in the universe, why not more? For instance, the archetype of my reflection that I have a conscience is a just God. I have as much reason to believe in the truth of his existence as I do in the truth of my own. So instinct supported by reason narrows the polygon of language around the circle of truth. Newman's reply to Kant was his habitual scholastic reply to Socinianism.

## Action

But Newman was not really interested in the subtleties of German metaphysics. The Germans bored him. That a theologian who spent his life ruminating on ideas, views, instincts, and dogmas should condemn German philosophy for its bloodless abstractions will seem at first to suggest a paradox. The paradox disappears on close inspection of Newman's theory of belief. Arians, liberals, and Germans had made belief purely intellectual, while for Newman, belief was inseparable from action. He would happily have endorsed Marx's critique of liberal German philosophy: "Man must prove the truth, i.e. the reality and power, the this-sidedness of his thinking in practice. The dispute over the reality or non-reality of thinking that is isolated from practice is a purely scholastic question."[61]

Belief is for humans what knowledge is for God. God's knowledge is always realized; so is man's belief. For God to know light is for light to exist. God's truth is a perfect union of knowledge and action. Human truth is constructed after the divine model, but our truth is an imperfect pairing of belief and action. Human action can only be understood in light of the belief, or the lack of belief, from which it proceeds. Belief thus conceived is the standard against which every thought and every deed is to be judged.

Newman treated this theory of belief in exhaustive theological detail in his *Lectures on Justification,* composed in 1837 in the months following Hampden's ascendency to the regius professorship, while the horrors of

[61] "Theses on Feuerbach," *Selected Writings,* ed. David McLellan (Oxford, 1977), p. 156.

liberalism weighed heavily on Newman. Newman's subject was huge and his treatment of it technical, but his conclusion is briefly stated. What justifies a man in the eyes of God? "A mind that acts, believingly," he replied.[62] Action is essential to justification, but action divorced from belief is either error or vice. By separating action from belief, the Protestants followed Cicero and Arius in paving the way for every form of personal immorality and social anarchy.

In the *Lectures on Justification,* Newman took for his object of abuse not Hampden or any living representative of the liberal school, but Thomas Haweis, an obscure Methodist of the eighteenth century in whom liberalism's roots in Evangelicalism were fully exposed and reduced to self-parody. The liberalism of Hampden or Mill was only a more refined version of Haweis's sentimental Protestantism.

"If you know not experimentally what is meant by 'fellowship with the Father and His Son Jesus Christ,'" Haweis had preached, "your book, not your heart, hath spoken: instead of the fervent effectual prayer of the righteous man, your babblings have been no better than the sounding brass and tinkling cymbal." The Evangelicals had created an "experimental" morality that reduced belief to "babbling" and elevated contemplation of feelings to the eminence of a guiding principle, so that, according to Newman, "religion is made to consist in contemplating ourselves instead of Christ." Like the Arians before him, Haweis emasculated belief by rendering it merely intellectual. The Evangelicals and the liberals who came after Haweis were content to enumerate what they knew about their engines or their souls, and to call this enumeration belief. Like Cicero, they amused themselves in the contemplation of mere sensations. In the *Lectures on Justification* Newman rose to a rapture of sarcasm to rebut their ignorance:

> Poor miserable captives to whom such doctrine is preached as the Gospel! What! is *this* the liberty wherewith Christ has made us free, and wherein we stand, the home of our own thoughts, the prison of our own sensations, the province of self, a monotonous confession of what we are by nature, not what Christ is in us, and a resting at best not on His love toward us, but in our faith towards Him! This is nothing but a specious idolatry; a man thus minded does not simply think of God when he prays to Him, but is observing whether he feels properly or not; does not believe and obey, but considers it enough to be conscious that he is what he calls warm and spiritual; does not contemplate the

grace of the Blessed Eucharist, the Body and Blood of His Saviour Christ, except—O shameful and fearful error!—except as a quality of his own mind.[63]

Properly speaking, Protestants and liberals of Haweis's sort do not believe at all. Belief demands a view of life along with intellectual and rational assent to realities outside of self, but all the Protestant knows is the nebulous concatenation of his visceral responses. Belief requires an object and results in action, but the Protestant calculus of emotions has no object outside of self and leads to no action beyond "the prison of the sensations."

Newman's denunciation of Evangelical heresy contains the gist of his criticism of the modern world. The sins of modernism are first-order sins, mistaken views about the most basic elements of life. The modern world is damned because it does not believe, and therefore cannot "act believingly." The necessary conjunction of right thought and right action is a doctrine that Newman worked to apocalyptic conclusions.

Newman added a long and illuminating note to his condemnation of Haweis and liberalism. In it, he contrasted traditional Catholic with modern Protestant modes of treating the deathbed. His texts were the ancient order for the visitation of the sick from the Book of Common Prayer and the contemporary Evangelical fable, *The Dairyman's Daughter*. In the Evangelical story, the pastor asks the dying dairymaid, "Do you not feel that you are supported? . . . Do you experience any doubts or temptations on the subject of your eternal safety?" Newman allows that these ministrations may be "not only innocent, but natural and beautiful," but they do not move beyond the enumeration of sensations, and therefore they do not address the central issue on which justification rests—belief. The ancient Catholic ritual, on the other hand, requires the pastor to say to the dying penitent, "I shall rehearse to you the Articles of our Faith, that you may know whether you do believe as a Christian."[64] The priest's proper function is to address the dying man's ideas, views, and reason, not his feelings. Newman's God might have mercy on our

[63] *Jfc.*, pp. 330–31. G. M. Young noted the comprehensive indictment latent in Newman's apparently narrow theology: "The Lectures on Justification . . . translated out of the technical terms of theology, is applicable to the whole age. Introspection within a closed circle of experiences was the trouble" (*Portrait of an Age* [Oxford, 1977], p. 67n).

[64] *Jfc.*, p. 330. *The Dairyman's Daughter*, by the Reverend Legh Richmond, had appeared in 1824. It enjoyed a mild popularity; a second edition sold 10,000 copies.

passions, but he demands a strict accounting of our beliefs. And for Newman, the injunction to believe is not reserved for the intelligentsia. Right belief is the highest Christian obligation, as binding on milkmaids as on theologians.

Newman began with a philosophy that subordinated reason to the guiding instinct of the illative sense, but following his theory of belief to its logical conclusion, he ended in a doctrine that supported the absolute authority of reason in human affairs. Peasants and professors are all equally compelled to obey their reason. The instincts intimate to us that God and truth exist, but only reason can reduce these intimations to intelligible precepts for action. Belief is not just the acknowledgment of some vague sensation, but the organization of that sensation into practicable dispositions that eventuate in doing. Belief is what right reason makes out of pious instincts. For Newman, the primacy of belief implied that "when the subject is too young to have reason, he is too young to have faith." Although Newman's belief was built on instinct, it was held together by reason as surely as the scholasticism denounced by Hampden. "In religion the imagination and affections should always be under the control of reason," Newman says.[65]

The ascendency of reason out of the philosophy of instincts is not as paradoxical as it may seem. "The fundamental tenet of rationalism," A. J. Ayer wrote, "is that thought is an independent source of knowledge."[66] Newman's only quibble with this tenet was that thought is but one among many instincts in the mind—what Locke had called reflections. All the reflections and instincts are independent sources of knowledge. On this premise he constructed his own brand of rationalism, in which Duns Scotus could have asked for no fuller subordination of will to reason. Hampden was right to treat Newman and the schoolmen as fellow spirits.

Newman's imperative enjoins that our actions ought to be governed by right beliefs. This is not the platitude that it at first appears to be. It is not a parody to say that Newman suggests the thief and the drunkard should begin their reformations by reflecting on the union of Persons in the Trinity. In practice, such a theory would do much to reduce the cost of rehabilitation programs. It is not, however, a position that most people in the twentieth century in or out of the churches will find easy to accept.

---

[65] T.P., 1: 27; G.A., p. 83.
[66] Language, Truth, and Logic (1946; New York, 1964), p. 72.

According to Newman, our actions ought to be governed by right beliefs. By action Newman did not mean reflex movements like breathing or blinking. Action is synonymous with conduct, the area of behavior over which the mind is thought to exercise conscious control. By belief Newman did not mean mere rational acknowledgment of some proposition, but reasoning so passionately connected with feeling and instinct that it is "intimately connected with what is individual and personal." Teenagers may infer from the laws of physics that a Camaro hitting a phone pole at one hundred miles an hour is liable to pulverize its driver, and they may assent to the statement that anyone motoring at this speed violates the law. In spite of these acknowledgments, teenagers continue to behave as if they were immortal. They do not believe what they pretend to know. Here reason acknowledges but conduct does not reflect the validity of an idea. Newman calls such acknowledgments "inference" or "notional assent" and dismisses them as unworthy of the name of belief. "Acts of notional assent, and of inference, do not affect our conduct, and acts of belief, that is, of real assent, do (not necessarily but do) affect it." Belief results when divine grace and human faith cooperate to rescue an idea "from being a mere notion, and bring it home with power to the mind." This faithful belief "exists only in its results."[67] If teenagers really believed in the hazards of fast driving, they would try to drive slowly, although they might on occasion break the speed limit.

Belief is always correlated with conduct, and for conduct to be even potentially good, the belief from which it proceeds must be right. Because Arius and the French revolutionaries acted on false belief, they were damned. Right action is informed by true belief, which in turn proceeds from pious instincts instructed by right reason. If belief is false, if the instincts are perverse, or if reason is corrupt, the action that results will be bad, no matter how noble in appearance. Good deeds must come from correct beliefs.

This "must" is not mere moralizing. Newman's injunction to believe is enforced by an "or else." Action that is not correlated with right belief is punished either here or hereafter. An act that is based on false belief or on no belief at all is as invalid as the view of life from which it proceeds. It is punished by God as an offense against truth. "Truth always avenges itself" was a watchword with Newman.[68]

[67] *G.A.*, p. 64; *Jfc.*, p. 327, 293.
[68] *Jfc.*, p. 189.

History is usually competent to avenge truth. Marat, Danton, and Robespierre have had their reward. But where the ordinary course of events is insufficient to accomplish the vengeance of truth, God may interpose a miracle. For instance, when ten years after Nicaea orthodox churchmen at Constantinople had failed in their efforts to prevent the readmission of the apostate Arius to Christian communion, they "conjured Christ . . . to deliver the Church." Within hours, the heretic, who until that moment had been robust in victory, was seized in the public square with violent abdominal pains. Removed to a public latrine, the blasphemer's intestines exploded, and within minutes the heretic was no more. So God killed Arius to vindicate the truth.[69]

If truth is right action proceeding from right belief, and if we are free to choose right beliefs and so potentially to perform nothing but right actions, are we not able to make ourselves perfect by our own exertions? To escape the Pelagian implications of this theory, Newman fell back on the ingenious arguments of the Counter-Reformation to demonstrate that his belief in the saving efficacy of works does not detract from his groveling submission to God's omnipotent will.[70] This flirtation with heresy was necessitated by Newman's insistence that each person has the freedom to choose his beliefs. At the final judgment, God would hold each individual accountable for his beliefs and the actions dictated by

[69] *Mir.*, p. 331. Gibbon says that Arius's "bowels suddenly burst out in a privy"—according to Newman, a replication of Judas's fate. Gibbon invited disinterested readers to choose between "poison and miracle" in deciding the cause of Arius's demise. Newman opted for miracle: "When a Bishop with his flock prays night and day against a heretic, and at length begs of God to take him away, and when he is suddenly taken away almost at the moment of his triumph, and that by a death awfully significant, from its likeness to one recorded in Scripture, is it not trifling to ask whether such an occurrence comes up to the definition of a miracle?" (*Mir.*, pp. 330–31). This was written by a forty-one-year-old man supposedly in full possession of his senses.

[70] In working out the implications of belief, Newman adopted the so-called semi-Pelagian view of grace and free will approved by the Council of Trent. Forty years after their delivery, Newman still felt compelled to defend the orthodoxy of his lectures on justification against charges of heretical Pelagianism. "Though, then, there be but one *formal cause*" that justifies the soul, "we are at liberty to hold that it is, not the renewed state of the soul, but the divine gift which renews it." In other words, while justification may be achieved by "a mind that acts believingly," this apparent freedom to will our own justification is in fact a gift of divine grace ("Advertisement to the Third Edition" [1874], *Jfc.*, p. xi). Thomas Sheridan, *Newman on Justification* (New York, 1967), is also at pains to defend Newman from the charge of Pelagianism: "True, the unjust can obey, but this obedience is not pleasing to God because of original sin" (p. 258).

those beliefs. How could a just God legitimately hold men responsible for what necessity compelled them to believe? Newman's theory of belief could only survive where individuals were invested with an unfettered freedom.

## The Tamworth Reading Room

Five years after he delivered his *Lectures on Justification,* Newman's recondite theology of belief became the basis of his most public indictment of modern civilization. In 1841 Sir Robert Peel spoke at the dedication of a public library in his constituency at Tamworth. Melbourne's Whig government was then tottering toward its dissolution, and at the dedication Sir Robert addressed not only his Tamworth constituents but also the new generation of Englishmen, whose votes would make him prime minister in the coming election. His remarks drew heavily on the truisms of modern politics. "In becoming wiser a man will become better," the prime minister opined. Science is the means of progress, and when a man studies it, "he will feel the moral dignity of his nature exalted." Sir Robert thought the Tamworth library had been wise to exclude from its shelves controversial works of divinity in favor of practical texts full of egalitarian knowledge. Practical knowledge dissipates party feeling and defuses religious conflict. "We are harmonizing the gradations of society, and binding men together by a new bond."[71] These ennobling sentiments were designed to appeal to the new men of industrial England, many of them recently enfranchised by the Reform Bill. As he listened from Oxford, Newman did not miss the parallel between Peel and the archetypal *novus homo,* Cicero.

In seven wilting letters to the *Times,* which collectively came to be known as *The Tamworth Reading Room,* Peel's truisms were weighed against Newman's exacting standard of belief and found wanting. Newman's autopsy on Cicero's skepticism and his anatomy of Arian heterodoxy had prepared him for the vivisection of Peel's apostasy. What was the provenance of Sir Robert's truisms? "Cicero handed the recipe to Brougham, and Brougham has passed it on to Peel."[72] Sir Robert was in

[71] *The Tamworth Reading Room, D.A.,* pp. 261, 283, 285.

[72] *D.A.,* pp. 261, 264, 285. As an Edinburgh Reviewer and sponsor of the Reform Bill, Lord Brougham was the last man in England to whom a conservative candidate would wish to be compared.

league with both the pagan and the contemporary schools of liberalism. The knowledge they offered the world is "not a victory of mind over itself," but "a philosophy of expedients." Sir Robert was only Cicero in a frock coat.

Like Cicero, Peel offered mere speculation in the guise of enlightenment, and he eschewed any system of belief by which these speculations could be turned into good actions. He ignored "the higher instincts" that strive after truth and assumed that man was merely a calculating machine operating by unaided reason. Newman was a rationalist, but like all rationalists, his philosophy rested on an instinctual commitment beyond reason, and for Newman, objective reason was never more in danger than when left to fend for itself without the pious support of subjective reflection: "After all, man is *not* a reasoning animal; he is a seeing, feeling, contemplating, acting animal," he said in reply to Peel's scientism. As always, Newman insisted that man's instincts for God and truth must be addressed before his reason is engaged. "First comes Knowledge, then a view, then reasoning, and then belief." Peel, like Cicero, would exclude faith and begin with the playthings of reason. "I want faith to come first, and utility and amusement to follow," said Newman.[73] If faith would disturb the apathy of Peel's empire of reason, so much the better: "The badge of Christian saintliness is conflict." The Christian is ineluctibly driven to conflict by the logic of belief: "Christianity is faith, faith implies a doctrine; a doctrine propositions; propositions yes or no, yes or no differences. Differences, then, are the natural attendants on Christianity, and you cannot have Christianity, and not have differences."[74] True action is impossible in the humanistic school, where the belief on which true action depends is stifled by the sacrilegious principle of toleration. All that remains for liberals is the sterile "knowledge of premisses and inferences upon them." "This is not to *live*," said Newman.

> Life is not long enough for a religion of inferences; we shall never have done beginning, if we determine to begin with proof. We shall ever be laying our foundations; we shall turn theology into evidences, and divines into textuaries. We shall never get at our first principles. Resolve to believe nothing, and you must prove your proofs and analyze your elements, sinking further and further, and finding "in the lowest depth a lower deep," till you come to

[73] *D.A.*, pp. 294, 293, 381.
[74] *D.A.*, pp. 287, 284.

the broad bosom of skepticism. I would rather be bound to defend the reasonableness of assuming that Christianity is true, than to demonstrate a moral governance from the physical world. Life is for action. If we insist on proofs for everything, we shall never come to action: to act you must assume, and that assumption is faith.[75]

This remarkable passage is as much prophecy as polemic. The modern world constructed by liberalism is as Newman foresaw a network of inferences without a beginning. The modern believes everything and nothing. He adopts a new philosophy monthly or yearly. He builds his inner and outer worlds new again daily and is as quick to discard his first principles and adopt their contraries as he is to rear cities and demolish forests. Divines have in fact disappeared as spiritual leaders, to be replaced by textuaries whose interpretations are limited only by the self-imposed restriction that no words mean anything beyond their variable human significations. Feeling has become the measure of morality and technology the measure of the human spirit. Newman saw where the relativism of Hampden or Peel would lead. The liberal position, which seems to promise the ceaseless activity of material evolution, in fact guarantees only the stutifying inertia of skepticism masquerading as progress.

The modern world is likely to regard Newman's theology as ineffectual, exactly the charge he brought against the modern world. Newman claimed not only that men *ought* to live by belief, but that all life worthy of the name *is* lived by belief. Because it does not believe, the modern world lives in a state of paralysis. "Many a man will live and die upon a dogma; no man will be a martyr for a conclusion. . . . No one, I say, will die for his own calculations; he dies for realities."[76] Liberalism tolerates everything because it believes nothing. It is always weakness, because its deepest tenets are only opinions riddled with pusillanimous doubts. Toleration produces the worst of sins against truth: the sin of inanition, by which action becomes meaningless because divorced from the dogmas of belief. Newman put his own convictions into action when he shunned the company of men like Whately and Hampden. How could he profess to believe in the narrow compass of truth and at the same time embrace the enemies of truth? That was the characteristic policy of liberals.

[75] *D.A.*, p. 295.
[76] *D.A.*, p. 293.

The obvious reply to Newman's diatribe against Cicero and Peel is to point to the achievements of their liberalism. Cicero's humanism bequeathed to the world Roman law and Latin culture, while the practical sciences that Peel recommended to his constituents had in a lifetime transformed Western society into a dynamo of social progress. These accomplishments seem more like action than the contemplation of the Trinity that occupied the ages of faith revered by Newman. In his *Idea of a University* Newman dismissed this objection peremptorily: "In the province of physiology and moral philosophy, our race's progress and perfectibility is a dream, because Revelation contradicts it, whatever may be plausibly argued in its behalf by scientific inquiries."[77] Without moral progress, material progress is empty or wicked, and moral progress comes only through action rooted in Catholic belief.

## Politics

Humans define themselves by their beliefs. In Marxist terminology, it was Newman's contention that belief is the base of human life, and economic, political, and social institutions the superstructure. A culture built on false belief is destined to ruin because false belief is always subject to decay. Only a culture built on true belief can aspire to permanence. There is only one true system of belief, which is Catholicism. Therefore, only a Catholic society can endure the vicissitudes of time.

Some cultures exist without any beliefs. These Newman called barbarous. Sparta and Ottoman Turkey are examples of barbarian cultures. Barbarians have the ideas from which belief might be constructed, but they do nothing with their ideas: "They have a principle of union congenial to the state of their intellect, and they have not the ratiocinative habit to scrutinize and invalidate it."[78] Having no beliefs, barbarians are not really human. Theirs is "the terrible fury of wild beasts," Newman wrote of the Turkish infidels in his *History of the Turks*, a work of racial hatred written in 1853 as England prepared to ally herself with the Ottoman empire in the Crimean conflict. Newman would have preferred an alliance with Orthodox Russia to sweep the animal Turks out of the

---

[77] *Idea*, p. 73.
[78] "The History of the Turks," *H.S.*, 1: 171–72.

way. Barbarian cultures like the Turkish have "the life of a slave." They can only be "destroyed from without." Destroying them raises no serious problem of human rights because they are not human.[79]

Cultures that do believe were in Newman's vocabulary civilized. Civilization is above barbarism as humans are above animals. But though civilizations believe, they almost invariably believe wrongly. They are destroyed from within by the poisons of error and heresy. "Their distinguishing badge is progress," said Newman, and progress is only at first the increase of knowledge and power. Inevitably, progress necessitates decline. "Where thought is encouraged, too many will think, and will think too much." Then "selfishness takes the place of loyalty, patriotism, and faith," he said,

> parties grow and strengthen themselves; classes and ranks withdraw from each other more and more; the national energy becomes but a self-consuming fever, and but enables the constituent parts to be their own mutual destruction; and at length such union as is necessary for political life is found to be impossible. Meanwhile corruption of morals, which is common to all prosperous countries, completes the internal ruin, and, whether an external enemy appears or not, the nation can hardly be considered any more a state. It is but like some old arch, which, when its supports are crumbled away, stands by the force of cohesion, no one knows how. It dies a natural death.[80]

For Newman, history obeys the law of belief. He was an advocate of the cyclical theory of history variously proposed by Vico and Spengler, but in Newman's view the theory only applies to civilizations that hold false beliefs. True belief permits a civilization to escape the cycle. A culture for which "supernatural truth is its sovereign law" will not decline but develop. Such a civilization is "synonymous with Christianity."[81] Such a civilization will not "think too much." It will conform its beliefs and actions to Catholic dogma.

The implications of Newman's theory of belief for Western civilization are not benign. The West of Newman's day and our own is committed to the Socinian errors of toleration, pluralism, and relativism.

---

[79]*H.S.*, 1: 158, 220, 162. "The Turks are simply in the way" (1: 222). Newman envisioned diaspora rather than genocide as the solution to the Turkish problem. After their defeat, "the fiercer spirits, I suppose, would of their free will return into the desert. . . . Those, however, who remained, would lead the easiest life under the protection of Russia" (*H.S.*, 1: 228).

[80]*H.S.*, 1: 167, 174.

[81]*H.S.*, 1: 165.

It has produced civilization, but "civilization is not necessarily Christianity," and the West is doomed to undergo the usual cycle of progress and decline that awaits whatever is not Catholic. When the inevitable process of self-destruction is complete, the only civilization left among the ruins will be Catholicism.

## Catholic Civilization

Like Augustine, Newman chose to be a citizen of the city of God, the one true civilization that develops and never decays. If it were realized here on earth, what would the institutions of this civilization be? Newman himself admired the models of pre-Socinian English history. The settlement of 1688 had made the attainment of Christian civilization difficult; the innovations of the nineteenth century had made it impossible. Better the Stuarts, better still the Plantagenets (when Newman wrote, the researches of Maitland had not yet shattered the pleasant illusion that in the happy past before the English Revolution bishop and king had collaborated to defend Christian civilization).

But Newman did not allow his nostalgia for an imaginary past to dictate his vision of what Christian civilization should be like. He was prepared to accept that Christian civilization might express itself in almost any political form. Much as he loathed democracy, the modern world was not for him corrupt merely because it was democratic. The Athenians' "profession of philosophical democracy" had been realized, he thought, in his own Catholic order of Oratorians.[82] Christian civilization might have any style of government so long as it held and enforced Christian beliefs.

A Christian civilization requires the hierarchy of the Church and such institutions as are necessary to enforce its dogmas. The hierarchy of the Church is necessary to proclaim dogmas, and dogmas are only effective where the means exist to make belief and action conform to dogma. A democratic government that supported the Catholic hierarchy and en-

---

[82]*H.S.,* 3: 86. And see Thomas Kenny, *The Political Thought of John Henry Newman* (London, 1957), pp. 181–85. This excellent study of Newman's political prejudices arrives at the bizarre conclusion that "there is a very real liberalism in Newman," p. 162. As is so often the case with Newman's liberal admirers, the wish has been father to the thought.

forced its dogmas would be as holy, as Christian, and as civilized as the monarchy of Charles I.

Newman's interest in the enforcement of dogma was evident as early as 1833. In the third of the *Tracts for the Times*, he lamented that excommunication was no longer employed as an inducement to right belief. Doctrine without power is weakness or hypocrisy. The parish priest should excommunicate and then refuse to bury "open sinners, blasphemers, and the like." "Why should they have Christian burial at all?"[83] A year later he reprinted "Bishop Wilson's Form of Excommunication" as Tract 37. Here the priest learns how "to secure the integrity of Apostolic doctrine" by administering the appropriate anathemas. In his letters to Froude, Newman was more insistent still that no civilization could endure which failed to enforce Christian dogma:

> The abandonment of State prosecutions for blasphemy etc. and the disordered state of the Christian Knowledge Society when books are taken cognizance of and condemned, render it *desirable* that there should be some (really working) court of heresy and false doctrine. . . . The effect of this upon the divinity of the Clergy would be great indeed. At present you hear Nestorianism preached in every other pulpit, etc. etc. (and the more I think of those questions, the more I feel, that they are questions of *things* not *words*.)[84]

If Lord Melbourne had empowered the Church to treat words as things in courts of heresy, then his Whig government would have adhered to the true belief of Christian civilization.

The England of Newman's childhood had retained the fundamental tenets of Christian civilization. "When I was young, the state had a conscience, and the Chief Justice of the day pronounced, not as a point of absolute law, but as an energetic, living truth, that Christianity was the law of the land." Up to the age of Peel,

> it was a first principle with England that there was one true religion, that it was inherited from earlier time, that it came of direct Revelation, that it was to be supported to the disadvantage, to say the least, of other religions, of private judgment, of personal conscience. The Puritans held these principles as firmly as the school of Laud.

Even Protestant England had been a Christian civilization so long as it enforced the dogmatic principle. Newman called the English state

[83] *Tracts,* 1, Tract 3, pp. 6–7.
[84] *L.D.,* 5: 10.

founded on the dogmatic principle Toryism. He mourned that it had "gone its way" in his lifetime, to be replaced by "the sham Toryism of Peel and Disraeli."[85]

What attitude should the orthodox Christian adopt toward this liberal and heretical state? In Rome, Pius IX attempted to stave off the encroachments of liberalism first by issuing the Syllabus of Errors of 1864 and then by convening the Vatican council of 1870 to proclaim him infallible, the better to combat the errors of modernism. Moderates in and out of the Church were stunned by the reactionary nature of the pope's policy. In Rome, Odo Russell read the Syllabus as a papal declaration of war on modern civilization, and in 1874, between bouts as prime minister, Gladstone found the time to write two pamphlets denouncing the menace of Rome's "Asian monarchy." The first of Gladstone's attacks on the Vatican sold 150,000 copies.[86] It also brought Newman back into the lists to defend not so much the papacy as the dogmatic principle he had first expounded forty years earlier.

The world was much changed since a younger Newman had hoped for the restoration of Christian civilization. In his reply to Gladstone, which took the form of an open letter to England's preeminent Catholic layman, the Duke of Norfolk, Newman no longer called for courts of heresy or rituals of excommunication. He accepted the realities of the liberal society around him, in which political and dogmatic allegiances were separated. *The Letter to the Duke of Norfolk* persuaded readers then and afterward that Newman had mellowed. He appeared now as the apostle of an enlightened Catholicism adapted to the exigencies of modern culture. "I see no inconsistency in my being at once a good Catholic and a good Englishman," he wrote. Forty years later the socialist Harold Laski could still be seduced by the apparent liberalism of Newman's theory of dual allegiances. He ranked it with the works of Maine and Maitland as one of the profoundest statements of a new theory of sovereignty striving "towards a greater freedom."[87] Even now Newman is considered a

---

[85] *Letter to the Duke of Norfolk, D.A.,* 2: 262–64. The chief justice who enforced Christianity in Newman's youth was Lord Ellenborough, who had fought to retain the pillory and the lash as instruments of correction. He presided at the trial of the Socinians Hone and Eaton.

[86] Noel Blakiston, *The Roman Question: Extracts from the Despatches of Odo Russell from Rome, 1858–1870* (London, 1962), pp. 302–3; Philip Magnus, *Gladstone* (New York, 1954), pp. 235–36.

[87] Harold Laski, *Studies in the Problem of Sovereignty* (New Haven, 1917), pp. 202, 208.

political mentor to liberal Catholicism. "From disapproving condemna-
tions of national apostasy Newman develops to a positive acceptance of a
non-ideological, pluralist and open society," raves a contemporary
disciple.[88]

This testimony to Newman's powers of charm and persuasion obscures
the central point of *The Letter to the Duke of Norfolk*. If he now admitted
that modern civilization would not permit the enforcement of the dogmatic principle, he did not relinquish the conviction that it ought to:

> The Pope has denounced the sentiment that he ought to come to terms with
> "progress, liberalism, and the new civilization." I have no thought at all of
> disputing his words. I leave the great problem to the future. God will guide
> other Popes to act when Pius goes, as He has guided him. No one can dislike
> the democratic principle more than I do. No one mourns, for instance, more
> than I, over the state of Oxford, given up, alas! to "liberalism and progress,"
> to the forfeiture of her great medieval motto, "Dominus illminatio mea," and
> with a consequent call on her to go to Parliament or the Heralds' College for a
> new one; but what can we do? All I know is, that Toryism, that is, loyalty to
> persons, "springs immortal in the human breast"; that religion is a spiritual
> loyalty; and that Catholicity is the only divine form of religion. And thus, in
> centuries to come, there may be found out some way of uniting what is free in
> the new structure of society with what is authoritative in the old, without any
> base compromise with "Progress" and "Liberalism."[89]

An ideal civilization would be untainted by progress or liberalism. It
would restore "what is authoritative." It would be a civilization in which
Newman's theory of belief is the common practice of society enforced by
the institutions of law.

Newman was seventy-three when he wrote his *Letter to the Duke of
Norfolk*. Twenty-five years earlier he had been less reticent in describing
the difference in spirit between liberal and dogmatic civilization, which
he exemplified in the varying treatment of condemned criminals in
London and Rome. Liberal England and Catholic Italy both sent the
murderer to the gallows, but with very different motives. The English

---

[88] John Coulson, *Newman and the Common Tradition* (Oxford, 1970), p. 239. The
evidence for this complete misreading of Newman is his "refusal to condemn Bradlaugh's
wish to affirm his allegiance on taking his seat in Parliament." Does this mean that in 1880
Newman had learned to tolerate atheists like Bradlaugh—or what is more intelligible, that
he saw no reason to exclude them once Jews and Unitarians had been enfranchised? Dean
Inge rightly cautioned religious modernists that Newman "would gladly have sent some of
them to the stake" (*Outspoken Essays*, p. 146).

[89] *Diff.*, 2: 268.

state, conceiving no higher power than itself, punishes the felon for insulting its supremacy, and its condemned are sacrificed to the vanity of liberalism. "Amid the jests and blasphemies of myriads, they pass from a world which they hate into a world which they deny." But the Catholic executioner "infuses the ministry of life into the ministry of death." In Rome, no effort is spared in reconciling the sinner to the God he is about to meet, and when he dies, the Roman mob utters an "instantaneous shout of joy" that the miscreant has died in the true faith. "We come to poor human nature as the Angels of God, and you as policemen."[90] Belief is everything. The civilization that executes believingly is the model of Christian civilization.

So liberalism was rejected in thought, word, and deed, and defined in such a way as to include the whole of Western civilization, dogmatic Catholicism excepted. No reading of Newman can be faithful to its original that fails to emphasize the universal scope of his anathemas, the self-willed totality of his isolation from all things modern. In his lifetime he found the taint of Arianism, Socinianism, or liberalism in every idea or institution which we would consider constitutive of the nineteenth century. Whigs, radicals, Protestants, atheists, Shelley, Bentham, Mill, Macaulay, Melbourne—these were self-confessed heretics. But their opponents were no better. Conservatives, Anglicans, Evangelicals, Wordsworth, Disraeli, Peel—these were a twaddling lot masking error with moderation—as if apostasy could be done by halves. Liberalism was everywhere, and finally Newman meant by liberalism what Nietzsche means by nihilism: "The view that *every* belief, every considering-something-true, is necessarily false because there simply is no *true world*."[91] For both Nietzsche and Newman, this view was the key to understanding the modern world.

The liberal heresy of the West was not in Newman's mind a merely venial episode in history. It foreshadowed, he guessed, the Apocalypse. Newman's fullest description of liberalism is found not in the *Apologia* or the *Letter to the Duke of Norfolk,* but in the sermons he delivered in 1835 on "The Patristical Idea of Antichrist." Liberalism, he thought, was in all likelihood the great apostasy prophesied in the book of Revelation. It was the world's penultimate contest with Satan himself:

[90] "Twelve Lectures Addressed in 1850 to the Party of the Religious Movement of 1833," *Diff.,* 1: 253–58.

[91] *The Will to Power,* trans. Walter Kaufman (New York, 1968), p. 14.

Whether this very Apostasy is to give birth to Antichrist, or whether he is still to be delayed, as he has already been delayed so long, we cannot know; but at any rate this Apostasy, and all its tokens and instruments, are of the Evil One, and savour of death. Far be it from any of us to be of those simple ones who are taken in that snare which is circling around us!

Forty-four years later Newman repeated these sentiments and even these phrases without regrets and without modification in his Biglietto speech. No Victorian was as consistent, as resolute in his belief as Newman: liberalism was the instrument of Antichrist. Newman had learned his lesson from Arius and Hampden and never altered his opinion:

Far be it from us to be seduced with the fair promises in which Satan is sure to hide his poison! Do you think he is so unskillful in his craft, as to ask you openly and plainly to join him in his warfare against the Truth? No; he offers you baits to tempt you. He promises you civil liberty; he promises you equality; he promises you trade and wealth; he promises you a remission of taxes; he promises you reform. This is the way in which he conceals from you the kind of work to which he is putting you; he tempts you to rail against your rulers and superiors; he does so himself, and induces you to imitate him; or he promises you illumination,—he offers you knowledge, science, philosophy, enlargement of mind. He scoffs at times gone by; he scoffs at every institution which reveres them. He prompts you what to say, and then listens to you and praises you, and encourages you. He bids you mount aloft. He shows you how to become as gods. Then he laughs and jokes with you, and gets intimate with you; he takes your hand, and gets his fingers between yours, and grasps them, and then you are his.

Shall we Christians allow ourselves to have lot or part in this matter? Shall we, even with our little finger, help on the Mystery of Iniquity, which is travailing for birth, and convulsing the earth with its pangs?[92]

This sermon on the Antichrist gives Newman's definitive portrait of liberalism. He accommodated himself to the liberal state because he believed that civilization would have to endure its tribulation before it consummated its rapture.

[92] "The Patristical Idea of Antichrist," *D.A.*, pp. 60–61.

# 5

# Last Things:
# The Greatness of Newman

Is Newman still a great Victorian? His claim to be anything more than a religious curiosity must rest on his theory of belief and his dissent from liberalism. One is an abstruse series of philosophical speculations, the other a detailed indictment of the modern spirit. Do either of these arguments deserve our attention? Is either true? Is either useful?

## Victorian Truths

Newman asserted the existence of divine truth and undertook to explain human life as the relation of belief to this truth. It is notoriously problematic to establish the truth of claims about truth. "This is the true method of apprehending truth" is circular, just as "The truth is that there is no truth" is paradoxical. And the utility of Newman's theory seems almost as difficult to establish as its validity. Aside from its role as a stimulant to a dwindling number of devout intellectuals, it does not seem to serve any useful purpose. And yet the theory of belief deserves respect both for its potential utility and its possible validity. Why this is so emerges from an examination of its unique place in nineteenth-century thought.

It will at first seem bizarre to claim that because he venerated truth and defended belief, Newman was unique in his own century. After all, every Victorian was pious about truth. "My only desire," the young George Eliot wrote, "is to know the truth, my only fear to cling to error."[1] Her sentiment would have been endorsed by Spencer and Swinburne, Huxley and Hopkins. But the apparent solidarity of Victorian reverence for truth was in reality an illusion fostered by the ambiguous use of the word. The Victorians were not devotees of truth but of competing truths, no one of which was quite like the others. In a general way, however, most Victorians would have found the truth proclaimed by Hampden familiar and comfortable and the truth espoused by Newman alien and grotesque.

Newman's theory of truth and belief rested on four interlocking principles that few Victorians and fewer moderns could accept together: first, that some abstract ideas are correlated with objective realities; second, that the instincts and reflections of the mind offer sufficient evidence to distinguish these true ideas from false ones; third, that with the assistance of reason the mind can state truth; and fourth, that human life can and should be understood by examining ideas and beliefs.

Few Victorians could join him in any three, let alone all four of these propositions. Curiously, it was John Stuart Mill who came closest, a proximity that helps explain Newman's fascination with his work. But the similarity of Mill's to Newman's position only emphasizes the chasm that separated them.

Mill's *On Liberty* is a hymn to belief and one that agrees with Newman in three of his cardinal principles—the objectivity of truth, the intelligibility of belief, and the primacy of ideas. Mill spoke of truth as some definite, attainable objective toward which civilization moves. What is more, Mill's truth is not the relative and evanescent verbal construct of Hampden's philosophy. It is absolute and abiding. Truth is reached by the mind forming beliefs and testing them. "The well-being of mankind may almost be measured by the number and gravity of the truths which have reached the point of being uncontested," he wrote.[2] Truths come to

[1] George Eliot, *Letters* (New Haven, 1954–78), 1: 120–21; and see Noel Annan, *Leslie Stephen: The Godless Victorian*, 2d ed. (Chicago, 1986), p. 217. Chapter 7 of Annan's biography is an invaluable survey of the Victorians "Rhetoric of Truth."

[2] *On Liberty* (New York, 1975; Norton Critical ed.), p. 42.

be uncontested not simply because everyone agrees to them, but because they are objective, real, and fully known. And in Mill as in Newman, the battle for progress is primarily a contest of beliefs. To understand this contest is to know history. So Mill can be made to sound very much like Newman.

But Mill and Newman were worlds apart, because Mill excluded from his definition of truth the subjective or instinctive element so essential to Newman's thought. Mill's truths are the hypotheses of the sciences as proved by the method set forth in his *System of Logic*. All the rest is untruth: "If a person assents undoubtingly to what they think true, though he has no knowledge whatever of the grounds of the opinion . . . this is not knowing the truth. Truth thus held, is but one superstition more."[3] With modifications, Mill's version of truth leads to the positivist doctrine that "a sentence says nothing unless it is empirically verifiable."[4] Mill would not allow that Newman's subjective knowledge of his instincts provided valid grounds for an opinion, and so he would classify Newman's truth as credulity.

Mill's colleague and biographer Alexander Bain wrote "that belief has no meaning, except in reference to our actions." At first glance, this looks like another coincidence of opinion between Newman and his liberal adversaries. But again the similarity is an illusion. Bain claimed that no belief should be accepted "without good positive evidence," that belief is inherently unstable "due to the ascendancy of emotion," and that ultimately belief is nothing but an expedient of the will by which the mind protects itself from the terror of uncertainty.[5] Each of these arguments found fuller expression later in the liberal era in the philosophy of pragmatism, in the theory of cognitive dissonance, or in the psychol-

[3] *On Liberty*, p. 35.
[4] A. J. Ayer, *Language, Truth, and Logic*, 2d ed. (New York, 1952), p. 73. To turn Mill into a logical positivist it is necessary to discard his contention "that the propositions of logic and mathematics have the same status as empirical hypotheses." Mill had conceded too much to scholastic reasoning by this admission, Ayer alleged. "The truths of logic and mathematics are analytical propositions or tautologies," says Ayer. They are true "because we never allow them to be anything else" (p. 77). In his inelegant way Hampden had attempted to express the same thought.
[5] *The Emotions and the Will* (London, 1859), pp. 568, 47: "The temper of belief, confidence, or assurance in coming good is, in the first place, the total exclusion of all this misery; in so far the influence is simply preventive or remedial" (p. 575). Here is the beginning of a psychological theory that would treat Newman's Catholicism as an exercise in pathology.

ogy of the unconscious, and each of them contradicts some essential aspect of Newman's philosophy. Newman thought valid belief might do without "positive" or empirical evidence. He was convinced that belief might rise above emotion. And he would hardly have entertained the notion that his mind had invented the idea of God as a cerebral narcotic. How could that be true when, as he knew too well, right belief was so painful to hold?

If Newman's notions of truth and belief bore some tenuous similarities to Mill's or Bain's, they were more clearly rejected by other Victorians. Protestants of all descriptions raged against Newman precisely because they believed he had betrayed the truth. "Truth, for its own sake, had never been a virtue with the Roman clergy," was Kingsley's famous charge that provoked Newman's *Apologia*. "Father Newman informs us that it need not, and on the whole ought not to be."[6] The young James Anthony Froude, once a Tractarian disciple, cited Newman's equivocation as his reason for abandoning his Christian faith.[7] What did these Protestant champions have to offer in place of Newman's duplicitous Catholic truth? In his maturity, Froude decided that "a true religion, it cannot be too often repeated, is not a history, but a declaration of the present relation which exists at all times between God and man." This "present relation" is variable to an infinite extent and relative to historical conditions. "Truth is thus of more kinds than one," he said.[8] The truth of religion can never be reduced to formulas, because it is utterly unlike the truth of science. Religious truth is best understood as we understand the truth of a poem or a play—sentimentally and indefinitely. In the end, Froude came down about where Arius and Hampden had landed.

Newman's great critic Leslie Stephen combined the relativism of Froude with the rationalism of Mill in formulating the great Victorian definition of truth. Stephen admitted with Newman that creeds may dictate social events: "it is, however, as clear as it is more important, to

[6] See *Apo.*, p. 341.

[7] A sentence from the University Sermons shattered Froude's faith in Newman's capacity for truth: "Scripture, for instance, says that the sun moves and the earth is stationary; and science, that the earth moves, and the sun is comparatively at rest. How can we determine which of these opposite statements is the very truth, till we know what motion is?" (*U.S.*, p. 348). To Froude, this analysis meant that "Scripture tells us nothing except what may be a metaphysical unattainable truth"—a conclusion neither he nor any other serious Victorian could accept (*Nemesis of Faith,* 2d ed.[London, 1849], p. 158).

[8] "Origen and Celsus," *Short Studies: Fourth Series* (London, 1883), pp. 280–81.

remark that the social development reacts upon creeds." In time, the material facts of life compel all men to become empiricists:

> The ultimate victory of truth is a consoling, we may hope that it is a sound, doctrine. If the race gradually accommodates itself to its environment, it should follow that the beliefs of the race gravitate towards that form in which the mind becomes an accurate reflection of the external universe. The closer the correspondence between facts and our mental representation of facts, the more vigorous and permanent should be the creed which emerges.[9]

In this "accurate reflection" theory, material and historical forces guide the evolution of belief, and truth is an empirically verifiable correspondence between human terminology and "the external universe." Here truth is certainly not, as Newman insisted, something the mind obtains by inspecting its instincts, nor does it express itself in religious dogmas.

It is no surprise that liberals like Stephen, whose life exemplified the progression of Protestantism into unbelief, could not agree with Newman's interlocking theses on truth. But even Anglicans and Catholics who considered that they followed in Newman's footsteps found themselves restating Hampden's heresy and rejecting Newman's belief. Henry Mansel's Bampton lectures of 1858, *The Limits of Religious Thought,* were orthodox enough to be called "loathsome" by Mill, and the reviewer for the Catholic *Rambler* paid them the compliment of alleging that they had been lifted from the thoughts of Newman himself.[10] But if Mansel was borrowing from anyone, it was from Hampden, not Newman, since Mansel argued that human minds could never apprehend, nor human language express, the divine. He asked for "a recognition of the separable provinces of reason and faith,"[11] and by so doing, relegated belief to the realm of mystical abstractions, while for him morality became merely regulative. Mansel restated Hampden's opinion that theology can never state divine truths, though he did not have the intellectual courage that compelled Hampden to the conclusion that theology was therefore defunct. Mansel maintained a kind of mystical status for theology as the study "not of what is, but only of what is not."[12] When Hampden had expressed the same thoughts twenty-five

[9] *History of English Philosophy in the Eighteenth Century,* 3d ed. (1902; reprinted, New York, 1949), 1: 12, 17.

[10] See the introduction to Mansel's *Limits of Religious Thought,* 3d ed. (London, 1859), p. xxv.

[11] *Limits of Religious Thought,* p. 61.

[12] *Limits of Religious Thought,* p. xxi.

years earlier in language considerably more arcane, he was threatened with the stake. Mansel on the other hand became the choice of a conservative government to fill the deanery of Saint Paul's. In the quarter century between Hampden's and Mansel's Bampton lectures, Oxford opinion had evolved so far that Mansel's liberal effusions were treated as almost passé.

The one Victorian who seemed to have been faithful to the rigors of Newman's doctrine of belief was Lord Acton. If anything, Acton was more Newmanesque than Newman. He ranked himself with those who assert "that the world is governed ultimately by ideas." History "must be studied as the history of the mind."[13] Here, as in Newman, the abstractions of belief took precedence over the accidents of matter. As in Newman, the ideas that compose Acton's history are not relative. History is the struggle for the victory of true ideas, ideas that are absolutely and enduringly real. Like Newman, Acton admitted that the ideas that constitute civilization are likely to be erroneous, "for History is often made by energetic men, steadfastly following ideas, mostly wrong, that determine events."[14] However, the truth is eternal and ever available to those who make history, and Acton thought he recognized in the spirit of liberalism the evolution of the enduring truth behind Catholicism. Christianity had nurtured the ideas of individual freedom and social decency. The age of revolution had begun to convert these beliefs into realities. Newman had little sympathy with Acton's politics, but Acton's theory of truth and ideas seems a duplicate of Newman's own.

And yet even this most faithful of his followers fell far short of fidelity to Newman's principles. For Newman truth was real, absolute, present to the human mind, and determinative of all action worthy of the name. So far Acton could agree. But for Newman the truth was also verbal and personal, the standard of individual salvation, while for Acton truth was realized not in individual intuitions but in mass movements. Universal civilization, not individual justification, is its goal. Asked to exemplify truth in action, Acton would have pointed to the French or the American revolution, while Newman would have pointed to Athanasius alone in his desert exile.

Acton summed up his difference with Newman in a letter of 1890 memorializing the recently deceased cardinal. Newman was a man "who

---

[13]*Essays on Church and State* (London, 1952), pp. 465, 421.
[14]*Lectures on Modern History* (New York, 1961), p. 77.

was always looking for a view, for something tenable logically, whether tenable historically or not.''[15] Newman's truth was private, personal, logical. If it differed from the opinions of civilization and found no echo in society, Newman was content to dismiss civilization and society. But for Acton the truth was public and political. A belief that did not express itself in the great events of history or in the institutions of society was for him no truth at all. While Acton flattered himself that he agreed with none of his contemporaries,[16] his devotion to the liberal ideal of progressive civilization places him closer to Mill, Arnold, or Marx than to Newman.

And then there is Darwin. It was Mark Pattison who observed that Newman first "started the idea—and the word—Development" that found its scientific expression in the *Origin of Species*. Ever since, there have been those who have argued that Newman was not only in the mainstream of nineteenth-century thought but had in fact inaugurated the study of evolution.[17]

Newman himself was indifferent to Darwin's theory. He was willing either to "go the whole hog with Darwin, or, dispensing with time and history altogether, hold, not only the theory of distinct species, but that also of the creation of fossil-bearing rocks."[18] He may have been the only Victorian who could have accepted either the science of Darwin's *Origin* or the creationism of Philip Gosse's *Omphalos*. This lack of interest in the details of science is characteristic of Newman. He did not care if science proved that he was a monkey's uncle so long as he was a monkey's uncle who believed correctly. The discoveries of twentieth-century science would not have shaken his faith in the least. His interest was in the first principles of belief that govern scientific as well as all other human inquiry. So long as the sciences limited their inquiries to the facts of material existence and refrained from metaphysical speculations, he was prepared to accept their conclusions. But if the sciences should try to intrude on the world of metaphysical speculation, "they

---

[15] *Selections from the Correspondence of the First Lord Acton* (London, 1917), 1: 67.

[16] See Gertrude Himmelfarb, *Victorian Minds* (New York, 1968), p. 155.

[17] See Owen Chadwick, *From Bossuet to Newman* (Cambridge, 1957), p. x. Chadwick rightly notes that "Newman never believed in progress," and therefore is an unlikely candidate to be placed among the Darwinists (p. 97), but the notion that the *Essay on Development* is "the theological counterpart of the *Origin of Species*" still persists; see *Ker,* p. 300.

[18] *Phil. N.,* 2: 158.

exceed their proper bounds, and intrude where they have no right.''[19]

If Darwin had claimed metaphysical status for his biological theories, he would have met with a stiff rebuff from Newman. If, for instance, Darwin's theory of development were applied to intellectual history, Newman's idea of truth would collapse. If belief obeyed the same laws of evolution as Darwin described for species, today's dogma might be well adapted to the present intellectual climate, but any random fluctuation in the *Zeitgeist* might assure its extinction and promote some obscure heresy to the status of truth merely because it was better suited to the random circumstances of material life. Darwinism as applied to belief would hold that all doctrines are relative, that ''not one living species'' of belief—not even Catholicism—''will transmit its unaltered likeness to a distance futurity,'' and that even the terms law and nature contain no truth higher than the human mind that thinks them.[20] Hampden could have asked for no apter pupil than Darwin. The whole tenor of Newman's thought opposes any application of the Darwinian theory outside the narrow boundaries that Newman assigned the sciences. No Victorian shared Newman's idea of truth or belief.

But do Newman's opinions on truth and belief really exist in such splendid isolation? Does not every intellectual tacitly accept Newman's theory of belief? Surely every liberal who has not yet declined into imbecility or cynicism professes that belief can topple empires and that the truth shall make us free. Did not even the Bloomsbury atheists cling to the doctrine ''that belief could affect action, so that it was in the power of mankind to decide rationally to follow a certain course of action''?[21] The most hardened Marxist has to believe in his own belief and the most fickle pantheist in the truth of his relativism.

Yes, but—everything depends on what is meant by truth and belief. In the mouths of liberals, Newman would argue, these orthodox expressions invariably assume heretical meanings. The liberals' truth is merely relative to man's fallible reason, and the empirical facts of nature were for Newman merely ideas, not truths at all. The belief that can do no more than acknowledge its own subjugation to the forces of history or to the

[19] *Idea,* p. 74.

[20] ''I mean by Nature, only the aggregate action and product of many natural laws, and by laws the sequence of events as ascertained by us'' (*Origin of Species,* 6th ed. [1872; New York, 1958], p. 88 [ch. 4]).

[21] Paul Levi, describing the shared ideology of Bloomsbury intellectuals and Cambridge Apostles, in *G. E. Moore and the Cambridge Apostles* (New York, 1979), p. 62.

laws of nature is no belief, and the rational choice that only selects various relative and material options is no choice. Truth must be the handmaiden of God, not the daughter of time. Belief must have an enduring object above nature. Choice must be free to select between what is absolutely true and what is absolutely false. Whoever among modern intellectuals can agree with these definitions can agree with Newman, but the rigor of his system almost certainly leaves Newman undisturbed in his dogmatic isolation.

Newman's views stand out among those of his contemporaries as singular and antagonistic to the whole intellectual spirit of the time—a remarkable accomplishment in itself, supposing the liberal hypothesis according to which time and place ought to dictate a similarity of ideas to be correct. And it is precisely because of its intellectual isolation that Newman's philosophy is useful. It offers a point of departure not provided anywhere else for those who would question the pervasive orthodoxy of liberalism. In performing this service it does not matter whether Newman is correct so much as that he offers a perspective from which the received opinions of the modern era can be questioned. This is a necessary and valuable service.

## Belief among the Liberals

Until very recent times, liberal scholarship did not much concern itself with the question of belief, much less with the refutation of Newman's theories. The Socinian views of Hampden or of Alexander Bain held the field. Belief was an inner state inexplicable except by reference to its causes or its effects. It made sense to study the material forces that shaped belief, and it made sense to study the concrete behaviors that expressed belief, but it made no sense to study intangible belief as an independent force. "Belief itself has received surprisingly cursory treatment," Anthony Quinton wrote in the 1960s, and as late as 1982 the distinguished neurologist Peter Nathan could survey language, learning, behavior, and the other fundamental expressions of human life that arise in the nervous system without once alluding to belief.[22]

[22] See Quinton's article on knowledge and belief in *The Encyclopedia of Philosophy* (New York, 1967), 4: 345. H. H. Price, *Belief* (London, 1969), is one of a handful of books devoted to belief since Newman's day, but in the liberal spirit of the age, Price comes down

No longer. The further liberal scholarship has progressed on its anti-dogmatic assumptions, the more frequently it has run up against the question of belief. Under names like functionalism, identity theory, and homunctionalism, the cognitive sciences have revived Newman's interest in providing an anatomy of belief. Nor would Newman have objected that the scientists and philosophers now debate whether belief is localized in the left hemisphere of the brain or whether it can be modeled on a computer. He would have been as indifferent to these scientific details as he had been to the biological evidences of Darwinism. He cared only to establish that belief is a reality that defines human life, and in this the sciences have moved an inch or two toward his position.

For instance, Michael Gazzaniga, the neurosurgeon whose split-brain experiments have helped put the study of mentality on an empirical footing, takes belief very seriously. While he describes belief as a complex interaction between various modules of the brain, he is at least willing to admit that as a result of these interactions, "we are free, by having beliefs, to overide responses to immediate gains and losses offered up by the environment." "Our species must have belief," he argues.

> It guides, it controls, it dictates the rules of behavior. We all demonstrably develop one about ourselves. It is a short jump to imagine how we must also have one about extrapersonal events as well. Call it Christ, Muhammad, or quantum mechanics, these are all beliefs that allow for human action.[23]

This statement from the frontiers of neuroscience is a virtual paraphrase of Newman's sentiments in the *Tamworth Reading Room*. Here, as in Newman, "life is for action," and belief, apparently free and indepen-

---

in favor of "an empiricist view of religion" by which theistic belief can be scientifically verified (pp. 487–88). Nathan is an ardent exponent of the anti-dogmatic principle and excludes the study of belief as a remnant of medieval superstition: "When Christianity took over, human behaviour ceased to be based on a real thing, the brain, and was considered to arise from a wisp of nothingness, the soul" (*The Nervous System,* 2d ed. [Oxford, 1982], p. 168).

[23] Michael Gazzaniga, *The Social Brain* (New York, 1985), pp. 197, 180. Perhaps a liberal explanation can be found for the coincidence of Newman's and Gazzaniga's rhetoric. Gazzaniga was raised a devout Catholic for whom "absolution followed by receiving Holy Communion gave rise to the most intense feelings of worth," p. 203. Does this mean that Gazzaniga's science is suspect because it might be the product of his Catholic belief or is this a confirmation of Newman's thesis that correct belief is the foundation of valid science?

dent, guides action. Unfortunately, what neuroscience concedes with one hand it takes away with the other. Gazzaniga concludes that our perception of free belief is "largely illusionary." In fact, he says, beliefs are shaped "in response to a variety of social forces."[24]

But even such concessions as Gazzaniga does make moves science nearer to Newman's position than Mill or Leslie Stephen could have believed possible. Still, if the cognitive sciences have made the study of belief once again respectable, modern thought has yet to reach Newman's conclusion that belief takes precedence over action. The Marxist continues to maintain that mind limps after reality, the behaviorist that belief is indistinguishable from action, and the cognitive scientist at most admits that where action contradicts belief, belief yields to the overpowering logic of phenomena. The most idealistic modern commentator is liable to place belief somewhere below genetic traits, social compulsions, historical necessities, economic imperatives, and unconscious drives in the hierarchy of explanations offered for human behavior. In any of these views, belief seems rather trivial. Belief may exist for study, it may rationalize experience after the fact, it may even influence action, but finally it is determined by material and external events, and there is no sense in which my freedom to believe is anything more than a very limited choice within a narrow range of necessities.

Newman held not only that the mind *ought* to act believingly, but that it *does* act believingly. Action is only intelligible by reference to belief, and belief is ultimately free and superior to all other categories of explanation. On this proposition Newman's claim on the attention of the modern world rests. If Newman was right, then the edifice of modern thought is built upon a false premise. And how much grander the world would be if belief, the intellectual's stock-in-trade, determined the course of history! The priest and his successor, the professor, would, contrary to all appearances, be the masters of destiny. Some such conviction must have consoled Newman in his failure. But while Newman's opinions may be suspect because self-serving, they are not necessarily false, and the primacy Newman accorded belief in human affairs is not self-evidently wrong merely because it consoled him.

Newman's view that the modern world is a realization of Socinian beliefs makes as much sense as the liberal argument that Socinian beliefs are a rationalization of the modern world. If it is difficult to believe that

[24] *The Social Brain*, p. 7.

the complex of contemporary civilization originated in the distorted beliefs of Arius, it is also difficult to see how Newman can be honestly refuted. Shall we say that he is merely absurd? This is not argument. Shall we say with Wittgenstein that belief in metaphysical doctrines is inane because "*how* things are in the world is a matter of complete indifference for what is higher. God does not reveal himself in the world"?[25] This is only to adopt Arius's argument against Athanasius, not to prove its truth. Shall we say that the evidence points to material causes shaping ideological effects? This is contradicted by history itself, as in Newman's example of the Arians, in which belief preceded the social structures to which it corresponded. Shall we say that some individuals and cultures do not believe, or that, believing, they do not make action correspond to belief? This does not prove that they could not act believingly nor does it refute Newman's contention that their existence is determined by their very lack of belief. Newman's thought has continuing value as posing to his liberal opponents a fundamental question that they have not yet been able to answer. The assertion that human life is determined by its belief or lack of belief may be unfashionable, but it is at least a challenging hypothesis.

## The *Apologia*

Newman, of course, went beyond hypothesis. One set of beliefs was right, all others wrong. Catholicism alone was "destined to last unto the end."[26] In the *Apologia,* Newman offered himself as a proof of his ideas. The *Apologia* was called into being by Kingsley's slur on Newman's truthfulness, and Newman used the occasion to give the world a portrait of his theories about belief and truth as they operate in human life—and more precisely, in his life.

The *Apologia* is sometimes called Newman's autobiography, but to the modern sensibility it must seem a very odd example of the genre. Of his parents Newman has nothing to say—we learn that he was "brought up," but not by whom.[27] Of his family there is hardly a mention. Nor does Newman make any concession to the Romantic interest in nature and

---

[25] *Tractatus Logico-Philosophicus* (London, 1961), p. 73.
[26] *H.S.*, 2: 141.
[27] *Apo.*, p. 15

locality. Where Ruskin in his *Praeterita* devotes a chapter to the formative influence on him of the Herne Hill almond blossoms, Newman in the *Apologia* does not even bother to inform the reader where he was born, or if he had ever noticed a tree. The evolution of the sentiments, which since Rousseau's *Confessions* has been a staple subject of autobiography, is ruthlessly excluded from the *Apologia* so thoroughly that the death of Hurrell Froude, the most crushing personal loss of Newman's young manhood, is reduced to a bloodless sentence.[28] True, Newman records that when his friend Bowden died in 1844, he "sobbed bitterly over his coffin," but he is quick to absolve this moment of any hint of mere animal feeling—he wept because he had expected Bowden's illness to bring "light to my mind, as to what I ought to do" about leaving the Anglican Church. "It brought none," and so Newman wept over his own intellectual confusion.[29]

Gone, too, from Newman's narrative is the creative dialogue between imagination and memory that has inspired autobiographers from Chateaubriand to Nabokov. "I cannot rely on memory," says Newman, and, true to his word, he fills the pages of the *Apologia* with written documentation from his letters and diaries. The liberals and their Romantic allies had substituted the distortions of recollected sentiment for the precision of truth. Newman avoided their error. When he wrote at the start of his second chapter, "I have no romantic tale to tell," he was engaging in a profound form of understatement.[30] In defending his own reputation for truthfulness, Newman was defending the existence of truth itself against the skepticism indissoluably bound up with relative memory and egocentric sentimentality.

Since the *Apologia* refuses to conform to the modern idea of autobiography, it is tempting to classify it in some other way. Its title, after all, places it with Socrates' *Apology* and Athanasius' *Apologia pro fuga sua*. The *Apologia* is arguably not the history of Newman's life, but merely what is claimed in its subtitle, the history "of his Religious Opinions." And yet Newman himself calls it the "history of myself."[31] The *Apologia* truly is an autobiography—that is, a history of self as

---

[28] "Dying prematurely, as he did, and in the conflict and transition-state of opinion, his religious views never reached their ultimate conclusion, by the very reason of their multitude and their depth" (*Apo.*, p. 34).

[29] *Apo.*, p. 204.

[30] *Apo.*, pp. 137, 44.

[31] *Apo.*, p. 15.

Newman understood self. What makes it so peculiar is his very unmodern idea of selfhood.

For Newman, there was no distinction between "a history of his religious opinions" and the "history of myself." The self is not developed by parental or social nurture, not defined by place or nation; it is not an amalgam of feelings or events. These facts are accidental, in the same way that the physical properties of the consecrated communion bread are accidental to its spiritual essence. Underneath the accidents of selfhood is its real presence: belief. We are what we believe.

Like everything else Newman wrote, the *Apologia* is uniquely antagonistic to the whole current of modern thought. From its first page, it asks us to accept that the only important characteristic of selfhood is the believing mind in its search for absolute truth. What Newman tells us about his childhood is that he read the Bible, "but I had formed no religious conviction till I was fifteen." There is therefore no sense in dwelling on anything prior to this birthday. When he was fifteen, he had a great revelation, similar in intensity to the second births of Augustine or Bunyan—and yet utterly unlike them. When Augustine took up the book and read, "the light of confidence," he says, "flooded my heart." Newman's "great change," on the other hand, touched the mind, not the heart. He writes that he "received into my intellect impressions of dogma, which, through God's mercy, have never been effaced or obscured."[32] Here belief is not merely a part of life, but life itself, and the faculties that support belief—views, reason, logic, and the grammar of assent—are not merely adjuncts of the human personality, but the limbs and organs with which humans must fight for eternity. The *Apologia* is meant to demonstrate in the person of John Henry Newman the living reality of the theory of belief.

The modern world expects its autobiographies to move toward moments of oceanic self-revelation like Wordsworth's spots of time or Joyce's epiphanies. In these oceanic moments, individuals know themselves by experiencing some deep emotional or spiritual connection with the larger universe. Newman too has moments of revelation, but they are not like these. In fact they must strike the modern reader as absurd because they are so far removed from our Romantic expectations. Here is Newman in the summer of 1839, studying the history of the early Church as he tries to decide whether he can remain an Anglican: "It was during

[32] *Apo.*, pp. 15, 17; *Confessions*, 8.12.

this course of reading that for the first time a doubt came upon me of the tenableness of Anglicanism. . . . My stronghold was Antiquity; now here, in the middle of the fifth century, I found, as it seemed to me, Christendom of the sixteenth and the nineteenth centuries reflected. I saw my face in that mirror, and I was a Monophysite."[33] We expect our autobiographers to classify themselves according to some preference or some passion. For us, people are what they do or what they feel. Within these limits, we are even prepared to accept self-classification on religious grounds. But by modern definitions, Newman is not really classifying himself religiously here. What William James calls the "enthusiastic temper of espousal" that characterizes our modern idea of religious experience is willfully excluded from this passage, and in its place we are given the man as idea.[34] Because of our liberal indoctrination, we are torn between laughter and amazement when confronted by a human who defines himself in terms of doctrines, but Newman's hope was to make us see in his example that it is infinitely more important to believe rightly than to feel right.

The *Apologia* is a clinical demonstration of the primacy of belief. But Newman's narrative has another aim as well: to explain the proper object of belief. Belief is life, but only right belief is good life, and the *Apologia* means to show in Newman's example what the good life is. And here again, in its structure, the *Apologia* purposely confounds our modern expectations of what we should find in an autobiography. Modern autobiographies begin with their subjects' nebulous absorption in family, in class, in nation, or in their own undifferentiated ids. From this point of departure, the autobiography describes the process of self-realization and self-definition. For us, autobiography is nothing but the unfolding of individuality.

As usual, Newman took this procedure and reversed it. He began as an individual and ended by being absorbed into the body of Catholicism. So long as he was an Evangelical, or an Anglican, or a Monophysite, he was unique—a condition he regretted. The climax of his life came with the conversion of 1845, after which "of course I have no further history of my religious opinions to narrate," because those opinions were identical in all respects to Catholic teaching.[35] The goal of belief, and therefore of life, is to bring selfhood within the narrow compass of truth. After his

[33] *Apo.*, p. 108.
[34] James, *The Varieties of Religious Experience;* (1902; New York, 1982), p. 48.
[35] *Apo.*, p. 214.

conversion, Newman wrote another chapter, but now it was no longer the voice of Newman the distinct individual speaking, but Newman the Catholic, whose personal opinions have imperceptively merged into the larger truth of dogma.

Newman was well aware of what he was doing. He knew that his readers, brought up in the liberal sensibility, would equate his progress from individuality into Catholicism as a negation of freedom and of selfhood. He took pains in Chapter 5 to address what he considered to be their error. After announcing his absolute submission to Catholic teaching, he wrote,

> All this being considered as the profession which I make *ex animo*, as for myself, so also on the part of the Catholic body, as far as I know it, it will at first sight be said that the restless intellect of our common humanity is utterly weighed down to the repression of all independent effort and action whatever, so that, if this is to be the mode of bringing it into order, it is brought into order only to be destroyed. But this is far from the result, far from what I conceive to be the intention of that high Providence who has provided a great remedy for a great evil,—far from borne out by the history of the conflict between Infallibility and Reason in the past, and the prospect of it in the future. The energy of the human intellect "does from opposition grow"; it thrives and is joyous, with a tough elastic strength, under the terrible blows of the divinely-fashioned weapon, and is never so much itself as when it has lately been overthrown . . . ; as in a civil polity the State exists and endures by means of the rivalry and collision, the encroachments and defeats of its constituent parts, so in like manner Catholic Christendom is no simple exhibition of religious absolutism, but presents a continuous picture of Authority and Private Judgment alternately advancing and retreating as the ebb and flow of the tide;—it is a vast assemblage of human beings with wilful intellects and wild passions, brought together into one by the beauty and the Majesty of a Superhuman Power,—into what may be called a large reformatory or training-school, not as if into a hospital or into a prison, not in order to be sent to bed, not to be buried alive, but (if I may change my metaphor) brought together as if into some moral factory, for the melting, refining, and moulding by an incessant, noisy process, of the raw material of human nature, so excellent, so dangerous, so capable of divine purposes.[36]

In this passage belief and style, personality and dogma have all come together. Newman spoke for himself, but because he believed rightly, this self spoke "on behalf of the Catholic body," there having ceased to

[36]*Apo.*, pp. 225–26.

be a distinction between the two. Newman next considered whether one who submits to the Catholic body can be said to speak for himself, and here style as much as logic carried the message. The liberal's objection to Newman's view is phrased in the balanced syntax of eighteenth-century rationalism: "if this is to be the mode of bringing it into order, it is brought into order only to be destroyed." Newman moved away from this fearful symmetry by a soaring use of anaphora. The loss of freedom is "far from the result, far from what I conceive, . . . far from borne out." Inside the narrow compass of truth, individuality lives in dynamic tension with dogma, and now Newman's style demonstrated this tension through antithesis—not the symmetrical antitheses of Dr. Johnson's prose, but the erratic antitheses of Beethoven's music, antitheses that express individuality within the framework of a larger order. The energy of the human intellect "thrives and is joyous, with a tough elastic strength, under the terrible blows of the divinely-fashioned weapon." The purposeful failure to achieve parallelism between the verb forms "thrive" and "is joyous" and the jarring placement of the prepositional phrases heighten the sense of individual conflict, which is then resolved into the larger rhythm of a controlling paradox: individual energy "is never so much itself as when it has lately been overthrown."

The believer who subsists within Catholicism never loses his individuality, and Newman proved his own freedom by switching metaphors, calling the reader's attention to his eccentric independence even as he professes his absolute subordination. He himself had begun as "the raw material of human nature"—a distinct individual. Within the moral factory of the Church, he had been refashioned into something better—a believing Catholic. So Newman's inimitable style becomes not only the vehicle, but also the proof, of his contention that individuality, which is belief, can exist only within the framework of Catholic truth. The *Apologia* contains Newman's fundamental argument couched in the form of an anti-liberal autobiography.


## The Critique of Liberalism

What of Newman's other claim to greatness? Like the theory of belief, his critique of liberalism can lay claim to historical significance if for no other reason than its singularity.

Swinburne yoked Newman and Carlyle as twin Furies visiting primordial curses on an age that had struggled from darkness into light. Then as now, Newman sounded like only a more eloquent member of that guild of culture critics of whom Carlyle is the chief. With Carlyle and his progeny, Newman denounced the spiritual desolation, the political expediency, and the psychic vulgarity of modernism. But Newman's dissent from liberalism is different in kind from that of the usual culture critic, as a moment's reflection on Swinburne's comparison with Carlyle demonstrates.

Carlyle looked for human fulfillment in the social sphere. It is our destiny, it is God's will (there is for Carlyle no distinction) to recreate ourselves and our world. "The mandate of God to His creature man is: Work!" cried Carlyle,[37] and he admonished the world to obey the divine commands of time and civilization. If he had used Newman's sense of the word, Carlyle would have said that the modern world is not too liberal but not liberal enough. We must subordinate our wills to the energy of the liberal *Zeitgeist* that impels us to our greater fate.

Newman thought it more likely to be Satan's than God's voice that spoke through the spirit of the times. Arius and Socinus had been perfectly attuned to the temper of their ages, as Hampden and Mill were to the mood of Newman's society. "Each is, in his turn, the man of his age, the type of a generation, or the interpreter of a crisis," Newman said of the great thinkers who characterize their times. But being characteristic of their times in no way assures that great writers will produce a single thought worthy of belief. The literature they produce is "the exponent, not of truth, but of nature,"[38] and nature, far from being the model of belief, is a wilderness in which the believing mind finds itself lost. Carlyle thought that nature, time, and civilization were starry messengers fit to be obeyed. Newman rejected them all and looked for truth in eternity.

For Carlyle, the thought was in the work, for Newman, the work in the thought. Carlyle conjured up a prophetic vision of Captains of Industry who would lead the world into the new age of creativity. Newman summoned the shade of Athanasius to exorcise these troubling phantoms of liberalism. Newman and Carlyle's opposed views on contemporary culture only coincide in their disgust with the present state of affairs.

[37] Carlyle, *Past and Present* (Boston, 1965; Riverside ed.), pp. 271–72.
[38] *Idea*, pp. 256–57.

The only critic in the English-speaking world who approaches Newman's thorough rejection of the modern spirit is T. S. Eliot:

> The Universal Church is today, it seems to me, more definitely set against the
> World than at any time since pagan Rome. . . . The World is trying the
> experiment of attempting to form a civilized but non-Christian mentality. The
> experiment will fail; but we must be very patient in awaiting its collapse;
> meanwhile redeeming the time: so that the Faith may be preserved alive
> through the dark ages before us; to renew and rebuild civilization, and save the
> World from suicide.

This peroration from Eliot's essay on the Lambeth Conference of 1930
might have been lifted entire from the pages of Newman's sermons on the
Antichrist, just as Eliot's *Idea of a Christian Society* takes the substance
of its argument as well as the style of its title from Newman. And Eliot
was one of the few critics willing to accept the totalitarian implications of
Newman's Christian civilization. Would a return to Christian mentality
entail the restoration of ecclesiastical tribunals of censorship? Eliot was
ready to accede to this necessity as a means of "redeeming the time" in
the age of the Waste Land.[39] But severe as Eliot's appraisal of Western
civilization was, it fell short of Newman's pristine Christian dissent.
Eliot was seduced from the path of perfect fidelity to Newman's ideal by
the allures of culture, and he ended by making that compromise with
liberalism that Newman had anathematized.

Eliot is the twentieth-century's spokesman for the Anglican *via media*.
He would save Christian dogma, but he could not relinquish liberal
humanism. "Humanism," he wrote, "makes for breadth, tolerance,

---

[39] "Thoughts After Lambeth," *Selected Essays* (New York, 1964), p. 342. Eliot paid
Newman the compliment of citing him as the legitimate successor of the metaphysical
poets, whose legacy had been destroyed in the eighteenth century. He wrote to Richard
Aldington, "I am not sure that the greatest nineteenth-century *poets* (in your sense!) are not
Ruskin and Newman. Do you know them well?" (*Letters* [New York, 1988], 1: 470). Eliot
did know them well and shared Newman's fondness for ecclesiastical tribunals: "Some
time ago, during the consulship of Lord Brentford, I suggested that if we were to have a
Censorship at all, it ought to be at Lambeth Palace; but I suppose that the few persons who
read my work thought that I was trying to be witty" (*Selected Essays*, p. 323). Like
Newman, Eliot affected to believe in an ideal English past when Church and state had
collaborated in the defence of Christian civilization. Newman idolized the dogmatic
Stuarts. Eliot's nostalgia looked further back to the Plantagenets. He wore a white rose and
attended mass every August 22 to commemorate the death on Bosworth Field of England's
last rightful monarch, Richard III. See Peter Ackroyd, *T. S. Eliot* (New York, 1984),
p. 166.

equilibrium and sanity. . . . There is no opposition between the religious and the *pure* humanistic attitude."[40] Newman abandoned the Anglican communion precisely because he felt there was such an opposition. He accepted what Eliot could not—that believing in dogma, it is impossible to strike a deal with even the purest variety of humanism, whose breadth and tolerance threaten the exclusive rigor of the dogmatic principle. If being a good Christian meant giving up Donne, Milton, and Wordsworth, Newman was willing to make the sacrifice gladly, willingly, without a second thought. He did make it. Eliot could not, and Newman would have classed him with the weak-willed churchmen of the nineteenth century who allowed their love of civilization to subvert their duty to religion.

To whom then will we liken Newman? Among the laity, William F. Buckley seems a good candidate. Catholic, dogmatic, and conservative, he has tirelessly crusaded against the liberalism of the age. But even Buckley cannot measure up to the rigorous standards of Newmanism. His lingering affection for the American constitution and his wistful evocation of the principles of *On Liberty* expose his true nature. In modern parlance, Buckley is called a conservative, but his ideology is a species of nineteenth-century liberalism.

The connection between the modern thought of the right and the liberalism of Newman's age is clearer still in the case of Friedrich Hayek and his followers, whose notion of truth is adapted from the theories of Jefferson, Mill, and Stephen—the very thinkers whom Newman spent a lifetime refuting. Hayek's truth is "something to be found, with the individual conscience as the sole arbiter of whether in any particular instance the evidence (or the standing of those proclaiming it) warrants a belief."[41] Here, thinly veiled as twentieth-century political theory, is the dissolving spirit of Protestant relativism that scoffed at Newman's Catholic authority and Newman's Christian tradition. Newman is the devout opponent of the so-called conservatism of a Buckley or a Hayek.

Nor would Newman feel any kinship with the latest wave of critics who have come forward to denounce the prevailing liberalism of the modern world. He might applaud the insight of writers like Michael Oakeshott, Alasdair MacIntyre, or John Gray, who have exposed the fallacies on which the liberal thought of Mill and Hayek rests. But Newman would

---

[40] "Second Thoughts about Humanism," *Selected Essays,* pp. 436, 438.
[41] *The Road to Serfdom* (Chicago, 1944), p. 163.

find their alternative to liberalism only another species of the thing they purport to reject. They too are liberals in Newman's sense.

In his essays on liberalism, the political philosopher John Gray almost equals Newman in the vigor with which he attacks the intellectual and emotional bankruptcy of liberalism. Gray dismisses the claims of Mill and others to have discovered universal rights or to have measured human happiness. He looks forward to a post-liberal society that will abandon the rationalistic pretense to knowledge of absolutes and return instead to the study of customs rooted in the practical traditions of local history. Gray's sense of tradition might seem to place him in the orbit of Newman's thought—Newman the champion of the West's Christian legacy—and a similar intellectual debt seems owed by Alasdair MacIntyre, another advocate of tradition who within philosophy has analyzed and discarded the dominant liberalism of the modern era. MacIntyre venerates the memory of Newman and urges a return to the virtues of scholasticism. Here if nowhere else the heart of Newmanism seems to be preserved.

But if Newman's thought bears a superficial resemblance to anti-liberal philosophies like those of Gray or MacIntyre, his Catholicism is at bottom the opposite of their traditionalism. They love tradition because they can find no other ground for order and decency. Gray, for instance, proposes a "post-liberal form of theorizing" that "in abandoning the search for universal principles of justice or rights . . . also relinquishes the liberal illusion that theory can ever govern, or even substantially illuminate practice."[42] Following Oakeshott, Gray would abandon liberal ideology for traditional practice, not because tradition contains truth, but because there is no truth, and tradition alone provides a guide to experience in a world devoid of absolute values. MacIntyre's traditionalism likewise surrenders the central premise it seems to defend. "There are no tradition-independent standards of argument," he writes, a concession that leaves Newman's theory of belief in ruins.[43] For Newman, the instincts are separable from tradition, and the dogmatic principles of Catholicism, though expressed in the heritage of Western thought, are independent of it. Gray and MacIntyre say that we should preserve

---

[42]Gray, *Liberalisms* (New York, 1989), p. 236.

[43]*Whose Justice? Which Rationality?* (Notre Dame, IN, 1988), p. 403. MacIntyre concedes that his Newmanism is laden with so much "qualification and addition . . . that it seems better to proceed independently, having first acknowledged a massive debt" (p. 354).

tradition because we have nothing more serviceable to replace it. Newman would have recoiled from this argument from expediency. He insisted that Christianity be preserved not because it is useful as culture or inescapable as tradition, but because it is absolutely true. For Newman, theory can and does govern practice, and the post-liberalism of Oakeshott, Gray, or MacIntyre would seem to him only another liberal assault on truth.

Another school of critics, disciples of Leo Strauss, the favored philosopher of America's so-called neo-conservatives, has followed Newman in excoriating the crimes and follies of modernism. Newman would have dismissed them too as crypto-liberals. What does a Straussian diatribe like Allan Bloom's *Closing of the American Mind* have to do with Newman's dogmatic principle? Bloom and his fellow neo-conservatives sing the praises of humanistic education, the very evil Newman so passionately resisted. The tradition they would impose on culture is not that of Aristotle's logic and Athanasius' doctrine but of Plato's dialectic and Locke's empiricism—Plato who made semi-Arians and Locke who festered in Socinianism!

In his lifetime Newman exposed the impossible position of high churchmen who revered Catholicism but loved England more. Anglicans, he thought, would eventually have to abandon the *via media,* choosing between Rome's dogmatic truth and England's heretical civilization. Today, Newman continues to be a reproach to so-called conservatives of Eliot's or Buckley's or Bloom's stripe who believe in similarly irreconcilable ideals. He would scorn the refurbished *via media* of the contemporary traditionalist who wants to enjoy the fruits of pluralism while denouncing its excesses. Newman considered these posturings a low species of dishonesty. The honest conservative ought either to embrace the dogmatic principle with all its implications for hierarchy, censorship, and totalitarianism, or else avow his own self-centered liberalism. It was the essence of Newmanism that no compromise is possible between these positions. You cannot be a heretic by halves. You cannot be a little bit liberal. There is for him "no medium between Atheism and Catholicity."[44] That is why he left the Anglican communion. Those who are not for Newmanism are against it, and properly understood, Newman's is not a view of life that will win many friends among those who now pass for Western conservatives.

[44]*Apo.,* p. 179.

Among the clergy, perhaps Pope John Paul II has most fully adhered to Newman's Catholicism. He has fought to defend the ancient truths of the church in the face of incomprehension or even insubordination on the part of progressives within his own fold, and he, much more than the accommodating John XXIII, is the pope whom Newman would recognize as a worthy successor to Peter, Leo, and Gregory. And yet the pontificate of John Paul II has been a succession of struggles with a modernism that has rendered European and American Catholicism indistinguishable from anti-dogmatic Protestantism. The declining congregations of the Roman communion repeat the formulas of the schoolmen but perform the deeds of liberalism, espousing Socinian doctrine in practice if not in words. The nun who dreams of the ordination of women, the priest who campaigns for economic justice, the congregation that joins hands during the folk mass—what are these but manifestations of liberal pluralism, liberal politics, and liberal sentimentality, now ensconced within the Church itself? How many Western Catholics believe rightly about the Trinity—or care whether they believe rightly?

## The Virtues of Newman's Dissent

Is Newman's dissent from modernism anything more than a freak of intellectual history? Just because it is extreme and radical, Newman's indictment of liberalism commends itself to contemporary civilization both for its beauty and its utility.

Newman's scornful detachment from modern life provides two sorts of aesthetic satisfaction independent of its moral outrage. First, there is the pleasure evoked by any sweeping hypothesis that is simple, consistent, and comprehensive. Those of us inside the dynamo of liberalism see only accident, chaos, and confrontation. From his celestial perch Newman sees pattern, order, and cohesion. Newman is not usually given credit for his objectivity, but his pious invective should not prevent him from being recognized for the clinical grandeur of his vision. Newman's theory explains everything modern, and though its very comprehensiveness leaves it open to Karl Popper's objection that a "theory which is not refutable by any conceivable event is non-scientific,"[45] Newman would

---

[45] Karl Popper, *Conjectures and Refutations* (New York, 1965), p. 36.

have argued that he was not creating anything so ordinary as falsifiable scientific theory. He was advancing truths which he could only do by rising to a lofty eminence beyond the suspect protocols of the liberals' version of knowledge.

The difficulty of achieving this lucid detachment can be gauged by the small number of those who have attained it compared to the multitudes who have tried. Perhaps only Nietzsche stood so far away from the culture about which he wrote. Another aesthetic reward of Newman's great dissent is the lucid purity of its irony, a quality Newman's writing shares with Nietzsche's.

Both Newman and Nietzsche were sublime satirists whose comedy the world has been slow to appreciate. The ordinary satirist writes from within the system he ridicules. He is a reformer, chastising what he would improve and subscribing to the same principles his victims profess but do not practice. But the sublime satirist mocks the principles as well as the hypocrisy of his contemporaries. Instinctively his readers sense that he is not one of them, and they do not easily laugh with their enemy. Nietzsche knew this well enough and addressed his revolutionary comedies to "the Hyperboreans," his "predestined readers" of the future. The same readers who have learned to laugh with Nietzsche ought to derive a similar pleasure from the often hilarious pages of Newman's *Idea of a University* or the *Lectures on Justification,* and even a novice Hyperborean should howl with mirth when reading *The Tamworth Reading Room.* "One must be accustomed to living on mountains," Nietzsche said.[46] His mountain was located in a future beyond liberalism, while Newman's was situated in the past before liberalism. But both achieved a rare detachment that has in the highest measure whatever value we accord to the objective study of human belief. In Nietzsche's case this objectivity was paid for in madness and alienation. The price of Newman's detachment from modernism was personal failure and eclipsed reputation. The *Apologia* is a testament defending this detachment very much in the spirit of Nietzsche's *Ecce Homo.*

But Newman's critique has utilitarian as well as aesthetic value. It is arguably the most searching rebuke available to liberalism's cosmic pretensions, and it stands as an unanswered challenge to liberalism's most cherished principles.

Western culture presents itself in the guise of a fluid dialectic in which

[46]*The Anti-Christ* (New York, 1968), pp. 114–15.

opposed beliefs contend for mastery. It revels in its illusions of difference, distinction, and division. Socialism vies with capitalism, popular
with elite culture, the bourgeoisie with the proletariat. Left confronts
right, and the dynamic of political opposition appears so strong that
traditional parties collapse because there are as many ideologies as there
are voters. Catholics, Protestants, and Jews are divided by internal
contests between fundamentalists, moderates, and progressives, and all
sects contend with the ever-bolder challenge of atheism or infidelity.
Meanwhile, in the schools perpetual war seems to rage between myriad
competing and irreconcilable creeds of science and interpretation.

In Newman's view, these clashes are only squabbles within a larger
ideology that is universally shared and virtually unchallenged. For
Newman all the heat of modern civilization is generated by one dark star
of heresy. Newman invites us to examine our culture as a unified
phenomenon. He had nothing but contempt for this phenomenon, but we
can adopt his vantage without concurring in his prejudice. What we see
from Newman's perspective is not a dynamic civilization in dialectical
evolution but a static culture paralyzed by its universal acquiescence in a
single stultifying doctrine. Newman called this doctrine liberalism, the
anti-dogmatic principle.

"All heresies run together," Newman said. Newman's definition of
liberalism certainly embraces those who now go by the name liberal.
They are steeped in Socinianism. But so-called conservatives are also
liberals by Newman's definition. In our day, Newman's definition of
liberal would embrace both the deconstructionist critic and the television
evangelist, each of whom subscribes to the self-centered relativism of
private judgment. It would include the Marxist revolutionary and the
country-club Republican, who concur in a doctrine "made to consist in
contemplating ourselves instead of Christ." It would take in the abandoned hedonist and the Catholic modernist, the one seeking self-
gratification in material pleasures, the other titillating himself by the
manipulation of his religious feelings, and both believing in nothing
beyond "the prison of our own sensations, the province of self."[47] By
Newman's standards, the triumph of liberalism has been so complete that
the world looks in vain for somewhere to stand and assess its victory. For
a moment Leninism seemed to offer a dogmatic alternative to liberalism,

but now Leninism itself has succumbed to the pluralistic tendencies of *glasnost* and is vanishing into *perestroika*. The liberal philosopher Richard Rorty wants to believe that he belongs to a beleaguered minority of relativists.[48] Newman would have laughed at such self-aggrandizing delusion. Liberalism reigns supreme, he would say, and has invented the myth of its minority status as an excuse for the incessant republication of its now trite and aging slogans.

For fifteen hundred years and more what Newman described as liberalism was a heresy. The forces of virtue combined to suppress the opinions of Arius and Socinus, and as late as 1683 John Locke found it prudent to avoid the official censure of the English establishment by fleeing to Holland. Today, after a millennium and more in opposition, liberalism finds itself in uncontested command of the ideological field. Flush with a victory unparalleled except in the rise of Christendom, some liberals, in spite of Rorty's false modesty, have grown bolder in proclaiming liberalism's universal sovereignty. Forty years ago one group of liberals dared to speak of the death of ideology. More recently another school has triumphantly announced what the American policy-maker Francis Fukuyama calls "the end of history." The end of history, which we are said to have now reached, is described as an absolute Hegelian moment, "a moment in which a final, rational form of society and state became victorious." Newman would agree with Fukuyama's assessment once it was rephrased in theological terms: the end of history is the worldwide victory of Antichrist in the Arian and pantheistic rationalism of liberal philosophy. Over a hundred years ago, Newman saw liberalism as "an error overspreading, as a snare, the whole earth." Fukuyama has only translated Newman's observation into geopolitical language describing the collapse of communism and "the universalization of Western liberal democracy as the final form of human government."[49]

Newman considered the triumph of liberalism apocalyptic. Fukuyama finds it merely tedious:

> The end of history will be a very sad time. The struggle for recognition, the willingness to risk one's life for a purely abstract goal, the worldwide

[48] Rorty classes himself with the "ironist intellectuals" who do not believe in "an order beyond time and change which both determines the point of human existence and establishes a hierarchy of responsibilities." Supposedly, the ironists "are far outnumbered" (*Contingency, Irony, and Solidarity* [Cambridge, 1989], p. xv).

[49] Fukuyama, "The End of History?" *The National Interest* (Summer, 1989), pp. 4, 13.

ideological struggle that called forth daring, courage, imagination, and idealism, will be replaced by economic calculation, the endless solving of technical problems, environmental concerns, and the satisfaction of sophisticated consumer demands. In the post-historical period there will be neither art nor philosophy, just the perpetual caretaking of the museum of human history. . . . Perhaps this very prospect of centuries of boredom at the end of history will serve to get history started once again.[50]

This mournful elegy for the world we have lost to liberalism sounds like the invective of Newman's *Tamworth Reading Room* transposed into a minor key. But even though diagnosticians of the modern situation are unable to rise to his level of irony or anguish, Newman might find some solace in the fact that they have at least begun to glimpse what he understood so clearly—that liberalism promises individual freedom and social progress but delivers a new kind of ideological absolutism and cultural inertia. More and more, critics—even critics like Fukuyama or Gray, who are themselves what Newman would call liberals—are distressed that the victory of liberalism has been too complete.

For those who find the idea of post-historical liberalism terrifying or boring, Newman ought to be something of a prophet and martyr. Perhaps he will come to occupy in post-liberalism the place Thomas More occupied in liberalism itself. More, who died defending the dogmatic supremacy of the medieval papacy, was later hailed as a proto-liberal champion of toleration against the absolutism of the Tudor revolution.[51] By defending the medieval order, More kept alive the possibility of fundamental opposition to the principles on which the new regime had constructed itself. Newman is in a similar position as regards our future. He would have no more stomach for the post-liberal world to come than More would have had for the godless Enlightenment, and yet each in his own way made a different future thinkable.

[50] Fukuyama, p. 18.

[51] Where Cardinal Wolsey as chancellor assumed a benign and secular indifference in matters of heresy, More in the same office permitted the Church a much freer hand in dogmatic persecutions. "More's record in the matter is rather that of convinced and high-minded sixteenth-century believer that he was, than that of the nineteenth-century moderate liberal he is so often made out to be" (G. R. Elton, *England under the Tudors* [London, 1962], p. 111).

## The Master of Those Who Dissent

With the anti-dogmatic principle entrenched even in the Kremlin, the liberal can now crow, "I am large, I contain multitudes," but Newman is there to reply, "Still, you are not the universe. You do not contain me. I offer you a vantage from which you can examine yourself. I do not think you will like what you see."

In our day, a consistently anti-liberal critique, in the sense in which Newman meant liberal, can be found hardly anywhere but in the pages of Newman. The usual critic of contemporary society is an intellectual contortionist driven by bad faith. He is the product and the secret devotee of the narcissism and vulgarity he denounces. He would not for a minute consider surrendering the liberal privileges and indulgences he pretends to attack. How refreshing, then, to read in Newman's account of the modern world one of the few critiques of modernism that can claim to mean what it says. The great virtue of Newman's critique of liberalism is that it exists at all. That there should be one consistent view of the world opposed to liberalism root and branch, sharing none of its premises and despising all of its works is an inestimable benefit, for no one more than the liberal himself. Without some honest and unforgiving voice such as Newman's, the liberal would be lost in the labyrinth of his own ideology. He would smugly assume that the paradoxical tenets of his creed are what Jefferson assured him they were, self-evident truths.

Newman challenges this complacency. The poverty of feeling without belief, the politics that is expediency, and the humanism that denies truth all fall within the scope of Newman's invective and receive from him no quarter. He treats the ugliest manifestations of liberalism with the contempt they deserve but rarely provoke. Newman is the master of those who dissent.

Unfortunately, the price Newman would exact for acquiescence in his critique is submission to his theory of belief. There is no middle way for him, no *via media* that will preserve the holy truths of orthodoxy without sacrificing the benefits of liberal progress. Newman's logic is compelling. His argument that so-called moderates and conservatives are trapped in an indefensible paradox is persuasive, and he is entirely convincing when he contends that the modern world must choose between truth and heresy. He believed that an honest recognition of this stark choice would make the decision easy, and here too we may agree with him. As he presents them, heresy is in every way superior to truth.

Newman's great dissent is a timely reminder to liberalism that its vitality lies in its heterodoxy. As the twentieth century draws to a close, liberalism no longer seems much like a heresy or even an ideology. But for all its protestations, liberalism cannot escape the consequences of its own relativism. It can never take its first principles for granted but must always be proving their strength and their utility. And this relativity is the heretical virtue of liberalism. Without violating its own anti-dogmatism, it cannot assert the existence of its own absolute truth, and it remains humane only so long as it refrains from assuming the mantle of dogma and imposing those mental and social repressions implied by Newman's theory of belief. As long as liberalism remembers that it is a heresy and fights against the truth, the possibilities of relative decency and tolerant forbearance remain alive.

Newman hoped that liberalism would forget its heretical origins and be undone by its own success. "To denounce ideologies in general is to set up an ideology of one's own," is a law enunciated by E. H. Carr.[52] Newman thought that liberalism would forget this law. Once liberalism had mistaken itself for truth, he assumed that it would choke on its own doctrines. It would no longer be able to control its own excesses because it could not challenge the principles from which they arose. As a heresy believing in no truth, liberalism might still be able to question and alter its doctrines, since even its most cherished presuppositions would not be beyond the reproach of its Arian skepticism. But as a self-proclaimed truth, liberalism was sure to fail. It could no more renounce egoism and materialism than a Catholic could repudiate faith and reverence—both would be unimpeachable expressions of unquestioned doctrines, except that one was the expression of false beliefs fated to ruin and the other of imperishable truths destined to last forever.

True to half of Newman's prediction, liberalism seems determined to become what John Gray calls "an expression on intolerance."[53] It remains to be seen if it will fulfill the second part of Newman's prophecy and sink under the weight of its hypocritical dogmatism. Newman was sure that it would. He thought that the inevitable collapse of liberalism

[52] *The New Society* (Boston, 1957), p. 16. And see also the discussion of "the death of ideology" in Anthony Arblaster, *The Rise and Decline of Liberalism* (Oxford, 1984). Arblaster concludes that "the best of liberalism is too good to be left to the liberals" (p. 348), another way of saying what Newman prophesied, that in our age liberal values are the shared property of all creeds.

[53] *Liberalisms*, p. 239.

might be hastened by exploiting its internal inconsistencies. If, on the one hand, modern society was truly tolerant, then the Catholic could avail himself of this heretical forbearance to nurture his faith and plan for that "restoration in the moral world" which will be the second spring of true belief.[54] In due course, liberalism would destroy itself, and in the general disorder of ruined pluralism there would be time enough to restore the Inquisition, the hierarchy, and the other dogmatic institutions necesssary to crush liberalism forever. If, on the other hand, modern society sought to suppress the dogmatists, it would reveal its hypocrisy while simultaneously invigorating the cause of orthodoxy, as persecution is wont to do. This double bind is the implicit challenge that Newman offered liberal society in his *Letter to the Duke of Norfolk*. In our day, Leninism and Islam have articulated the logic of Newman's strategy in action, and if liberalism knew how to reply to Newman, it would also know how to deal with the true believers who continue to challenge its humanistic premises. Newman was among the first to demonstrate how terrorism might subvert liberal society.

Andrew Marvell said that the liberal principles that inspired the English Revolution of the 1640s constituted a cause "too good to have been fought for."[55] The virtues of a free and tolerant society are so self-evident to liberals like Marvell that they invest their principles with inevitability. But Newman reminds the liberal that his beliefs are not universally accepted, that his ideology is a frail coalition of heresies, that in the fourth century ascendant liberalism was crushed by an outnumbered orthodoxy, and that for a thousand years it struggled in dissent. In opposition, liberalism was precarious, and in victory it threatens to become the one good custom that corrupts the world. Anyone who believes in the principles of liberalism—that is, in the anti-dogmatic principle—must come away from the pages of Newman humbled by the knowledge that liberalism is not a truth but a heresy, and a heresy too good not to be fought for by being fought against.

54 "The Second Spring," *O.S.*, p. 169.
55 *The Rehearsal Transpros'd* (Oxford, 1971), p. 135.

# Index

Abbott, Edwin A., 167
Abelard, Peter, 83
Academy, of Athens, 97–100, 113n
Acton, Lord, 193–94
Aeschylus, 52, 64–65
Aetius, Arian heretic, 123, 124n
Alexander, bishop of Alexandria, 104–7,
  115, 118
Alexander Severus, emperor, 126
Allies, Thomas W., rector of Launton,
  17–18, 43
Allingham, William, 24n
Anabaptists, 131, 133
Andrewes, Lancelot, 133
Anglicanism. *See* Church of England
Anselm, Saint, 83
Antecedent probability, 154–55, 165–66,
  168
Antichrist: incarnated in R. D. Hampden,
  64; in Newman's thought, 81, 95, 186–
  87, 206, 213
Apocalypse, 186–87, 213–14
Apostles' Creed, 142
Aquinas, Saint Thomas, 77, 83, 166n
Arcesilas, philosopher, 98–99
Arches, Court of, 18, 73–74
Archetypes, 145–50
Arianism, 64n, 95, 127, 150, 156n, 186,
  199; and barbarism, 105–6; and deism,

111–12; essential doctrines and history
  of, 104–16; ideological origins of, 117–
  28; and interpretation, 161–62; and liberal skepticism, 101–2, 109–16, 148,
  152; Newman's interest in, 100–104;
  and politics, 106; revived in the Socinian heresy, 128–43; and seventeenth-
  century science, 134–35; social implications of, 118–28; and truth, 163. *See
  also* Arius
Aristotle: and the Arians, 112–13; Newman's use of, 99, 112–13, 153–54,
  165–66, 209; and Oxford curriculum,
  58–59, 63
Arius, heretic, 54, 101, 131, 160, 168,
  170, 187, 191, 213; damnation of,
  175–76; life and theology of, 104–17,
  118, 125–26, 128; recants, 108n. *See
  also* Arianism
Arnold, Matthew, 46, 53; *Literature
  and Dogma*, 92–93; on Newman, 25–
  26
Arnold, Thomas, 62, 92, 102n; exemplifies liberalism, 31, 141–42; Newman's sarcasm about, 59–60; supports
  Hampden, 69–70
Assize Sermon (1833), 9–11, 26
Association of the Friends of the Church,
  19, 22n

219

Danton, Georges, 10, 176
Darwin, Charles, 194–95, 197
Davies, Horton, 25
Deism, 132–33
Democracy, 182–83. *See also* Newman,
John Henry, political views of
Denman, Lord Thomas, chief justice, 74–
75
De Quincey, Thomas, 22
De Vere, Aubrey, 39
Digby, Kenelm, 36
Diocletian, emperor, 119
Disraeli, Benjamin, 27, 38, 184, 186
Dogma: and ancient skepticism, 98–100;
and Arianism, 101–4, 107–16; attacked
by R. D. Hampden, 75–76, 84–85, 87,
110; and Christian civilization, 182–87,
206–7, 216; and communism, 212–13;
contrasted with ideology, 117–28, 153;
decline of in early modern period, 140–
43, 207–10, 212; defended in Church
of England, 140–41; and language, 84–
87, 106–61; opposed by Socinianism,
131–48; and rationalism, 164–65; requires an indefectible interpreter, 161–
64; its role in Newman's thought, 54,
100–104, 145–46, 152–56, 161–69; in
scholasticism, 137; and science, 194–
95; its social formation, 129–30; transcends tradition, 208–9. *See also* Belief; Heresy
Dolben, Digby, poet, 39–40, 44
Dolling, Robert, slum priest, 29n
Donatists, 8
Donne, John, 207
Douglas, Lord Alfred, 40
Dryden, John, 138
Duns Scotus, 149, 174

Ecclesiastical Commission, 26
Ecumenicism, 46–51
*Edinburgh Review,* 25
Eliot, George, 45, 189
Ellenborough, Edward Law, chief justice,
142, 183–84
Eliot, T. S., 206–7, 209

Elton, Edward, vicar of Wheatley, 17,
23
Emerson, Ralph Waldo, 141
*Encyclopedia Metropolitana,* 77, 96–98,
100
English Church Union, 50
Erasmus, 132
*Essays and Reviews,* 19, 27–28
Eusebius of Caesarea, 117, 120, 122, 129
Eusebius of Nicomedia, 122
Eutychianism, 130n
Evangelicals, Evangelicism, 57–58, 172–
73, 202
Excommunication, 13, 183

Faber, Frederic William, Oratorian, 33,
37
Faith: Newman on, 167–68; and reason,
174, 192. *See also* Belief; Truth
Falkland, Lucius Cary, 131, 134
Fitzgerald, Edward, 26
Freedom: in contemporary thought, 197–
98, 214; as correct belief, 155–56,
176–77; and illative sense, 151; Newman on, 172–73, 175–77, 196; not ne-
gated by dogma, 203–4; and politics,
182–85
Free trade, 4, 31–32
French revolution, 10, 175–76
Froude, Hurrell, 35, 60n, 64, 66, 78,
183; in *Apologia,* 200; death of linked
to Oxford politics, 69–70, 78; and homosexuality, 46n; and politics, 11, 18,
62; on Romanticism, 41–42
Froude, James Anthony, 191
Fukuyama, Francis, 213–14

Gaisford, Thomas, 23
Gazzaniga, Michael, 197–98
George I, 140
George of Cappadocia, heretic bishop of
Alexandria, 122–23
Gibbon, Edward: on Arius and the Ar-
ians, 116n, 123, 176n; influence on
Newman, 48, 157, 168; on scholasti-
cism, 82n